MEDIATION IN POLITICAL CONFLICTS

This book provides a vivid reader on experiences of mediation throughout history and in many different regional, cultural and legal contexts. For experts in the field of mediation and legal anthropology it provides a series of fascinating case studies not previously reported on. For those not familiar with the field it provides a window on an alternative possibility for peacemaking in political conflicts. The book is held together by the editor's introduction, which defines political mediation, the research methodologies employed, the relationship of mediation to participatory democracy, and the growth of mediation in the past twenty years. The chapters which follow provide the anatomy of successful and unsuccessful mediations in contexts as widely diverse as the 30 Years War (1618–1648) which was ended following the intercession of the future Pope, Alexander VII. Three further chapters examine the role of the Catholic Church in other mediations—in the Basque conflict, in Burundi and in Chiapas, while a further group of chapters looks at conflicts in Ethiopia, Northern Ireland, Central America and Congo.

Oñati International Series in Law and Society

A SERIES PUBLISHED FOR THE OÑATI INSTITUTE
FOR THE SOCIOLOGY OF LAW

Recent titles in this series

Legal Institutions and Collective Memories
edited by Susanne Karstedt

Changing Contours of Domestic Life, Family and Law: Caring and Sharing
edited by Anne Bottomley and Simone Wong

Criminology and Archaeology: Studies in Looted Antiquities
edited by Simon Mackenzie and Penny Green

The Legal Tender of Gender: Welfare Law and the Regulation of
Women's Poverty edited by Shelley Gavigan and Dorothy Chunn

Human Rights at Workedited by Colin Fenwick and Tonia Novitz

Travels of the Criminal Question: Cultural Embeddedness and Diffusion
edited by Dario Melossi, Máximo Sozzo and Richard Sparks

Feminist Perspectives on Contemporary International Law: Between
Resistance and Compliance? edited by Sari Kouvo and Zoe Pearson

Challenging Gender Inequality in Tax Policy Making:
Comparative Perspectives edited by Kim Brooks, Åsa Gunnarson,
Lisa Philipps and Maria Wersig

Emotions, Crime and Justice
edited by Susanne Karstedt, Ian Loader and Heather Strang

**For the complete list of titles in this series, see
'Oñati International Series in Law and Society' link at
www.hartpub.co.uk/books/series.asp**

Mediation in Political Conflicts

Soft Power or Counter Culture?

Edited by
Jacques Faget

Oñati International Series in Law and Society

A SERIES PUBLISHED FOR THE OÑATI INSTITUTE
FOR THE SOCIOLOGY OF LAW

•HART•
PUBLISHING
OXFORD AND PORTLAND, OREGON
2011

Published in the United Kingdom by Hart Publishing Ltd
16C Worcester Place, Oxford, OX1 2JW
Telephone: +44 (0)1865 517530
Fax: +44 (0)1865 510710
E-mail: mail@hartpub.co.uk
Website: http://www.hartpub.co.uk

Published in North America (US and Canada) by
Hart Publishing
c/o International Specialized Book Services
920 NE 58th Avenue, Suite 300
Portland, OR 97213-3786
USA
Tel: +1 503 287 3093 or toll-free: (1) 800 944 6190
Fax: +1 503 280 8832
E-mail: orders@isbs.com
Website: http://www.isbs.com

British Library Cataloguing in Publication Data
Data Available

ISBN: HBK: 978-1-84946-078-1
PBK: 978-1-84946-069-9

Typeset by Compuscript Ltd, Shannon
Printed and bound in Great Britain by
Lightning Source UK Ltd

Acknowledgements

I owe special thanks to the Onati International Institute for the Sociology of Law, its director, Carlos Lista, and Malen Gordoa Mendizabal, Convener of Onati Workshops, who greatly contributed to the perfect organisation of the June 2008 conference which is at the origin of the present volume. Nothing would have been possible without the wholehearted dedication of the Institute's staff. Excellent conditions made our work both fruitful and rewarding in a very friendly atmosphere. All the participants who discovered the Institute and the city of Onati on this occasion were delighted by their stay in the Basque Country. I would also like to express my gratitude to Jonan Fernandes, director of the Batetik Centre for Peace in Arantzazu, who was a most perfect and generous host. Many thanks to Anne Lemonne, Marie Balas, Alberto Olalde and Fernando Espinos who took an active part in the workshops but did not wish—or have time—to send their papers in time.

Contents

List of Contributors

Pierre Anouilh is a PhD researcher in Political Science and International Relations at the Centre d'Etudes d'Afrique Noire (University of Bordeaux, France). His doctoral work focuses on the 'work for peace' of the Community of Sant'Egidio in Mozambique and in Burundi. His research interests include religious dynamics of mediation in violent political conflict, historical sociology. He is a specialist on Michel Foucault and Pierre Bourdieu in the field of international relations theory.

Viola Boelscher is a lawyer and a mediator. She co-founded Iber-Consult, and works mainly in the field of human rights in conflict or post-conflict countries, conflict transformation and gender. She is Associate Professor at the University of Barcelona (Spain) where she is in charge of courses on mediation.

Manel Canyameres is a lawyer and a mediator. He is a partner of 'Alter, Serveis Integrals de Mediacio, SL'. As a coordinator of the community mediation service in the city of Terrassa, he is currently collaborating in the preparation of the *White Book of Mediation* for the Generalitat de Catalunya (Spain).

Aurélien Colson is Associate Professor at *ESSEC* Business School Paris-Cergy (France). He is a lecturer at the *ENA* (Ecole Nationale de l'Administration—National School of Administration) and the Director of ESSEC IRÉNÉ (Institute for Research and Education on Negotiation in Europe). He is the co-author of *Méthode de Médiation* (Paris, Dunod, 2008).

Jacques Faget is a CNRS Research Director in Political Science, Criminology and Sociology of Law at the SPIRIT Research Centre, Sciences Po Bordeaux (University of Bordeaux, France). He has taught at a number of French and European universities (Padua, Barcelona, Brussels). He has widely published in the fields of sociology of law, penal policy and alternative dispute resolution. Recent publications include *Médiation et action publique. La dynamique du fluide* (ed) (Bordeaux, Presses universitaires de Bordeaux, 2005); *Sociologie de la délinquance et de la justice pénale* (Toulouse, Erès, 2007); 'Les métamorphoses du travail de paix. La médiation dans les conflits politiques violents' (2008) 58 (2) *Revue Française de Science Politique* 309–33.

Elise Féron is a Senior Lecturer in International Conflict Analysis at the Brussels School of International Studies (University of Kent) where she heads the International Conflict and Security Master Programme. She is a researcher at the Conflict Analysis Research Center (CARC, University of Kent). She is also associated researcher and invited professor at the Université Catholique de Louvain (Belgium), the Université Nationale du Burundi, and the Université Lumière de Bujumbura (Burundi). Her research focuses on conflict studies, with particular reference to Northern Ireland. She obtained her accreditation to supervise research in 2003, and received her PhD in Political Science at the University of Lille in 1999. Her most recent publications include 'Restaurer la confiance en Irlande du Nord? La négociation aux interfaces urbaines' (2008) 1 *Négociations* 41–54; 'Religions and Conflicts. Towards a Framework for Analysis' Arès no 59 Vol XXIII (1) April 2008, 37–55; 'Paths to Reconversion taken by Northern Irish Paramilitaries' (2007) 191 *International Social Science Journal* 225–39.

Xabier Itçaina is a CNRS Research Fellow in Political Science at the SPIRIT Research Centre, Sciences Po Bordeaux (University of Bordeaux, France). His current research work focuses on three main topics: religion and politics in Southern Europe; social economy and workers' cooperatives in France, Spain and Italy; identity politics in the Basque Country. He has several publications in these fields, including *Les virtuoses de l'identité. Religion et politique en Pays Basque* (Rennes, Presses universitaires de Rennes, 2007); with F Foret (ed), 'Dieu loin de Bruxelles. L'européanisation informelle du religieux' (2008) 24 *Politique européenne* (special issue); with J Palard and S Ségas (eds), *Régimes territoriaux et développement économique* (Rennes, Presses Universitaires de Rennes, 2007); 'The Roman Catholic Church and the Immigration Issue. The Relative Secularization of Political Life in Spain' (2006) 49(11) *American Behavioral Scientist Journal* 1471–88; 'Between Mediation and Commitment. The Catholic Church and the Basque conflict' in J Haynes (ed), *Religion and Politics in Europe, the Middle East and North Africa. Challenges to Citizenship, Secularisation and Democracy* (London, Routledge, 2009).

Alain Pekar Lempereur is a Negotiation and Mediation Chair Professor at ESSEC Business School, Paris-Cergy (France). He is the founder of ESSEC IRÉNÉ (Institute for Research and Education on Negotiation in Europe). He is also the co-author of *Méthode de Médiation*, (Paris, Dunod, 2008).

Anne Catherine Salberg is a lawyer and a professional mediator. She also works as a trainer in mediation (Switzerland). She took part in a research action programme on developing a restorative approach to handling racist violence. She is now participating as a trainer in a programme for the implementation of Restorative Justice in Ukraine, financed by the Swiss government and run by the NGO, the Ukrainian Centre for Common Ground, the Academy of Prosecution and the National Office of Prosecution.

Monika Sommer is a lawyer and a mediator. A doctoral candidate at the Department of Political Science, University of Hamburg (Germany), she is currently a Research Associate at the Department of Political Science and International Relations at Addis Ababa University (AAU, Ethiopia). She earned her European Masters in Mediation (EMA) at the Institut Universitaire Kurt Bösch in Sion (Switzerland). Her research interest is on conflict transformation and the inclusion of local capacity and potential in peacemaking processes.

Pilar Gil Tébar is a Professor in Anthropology at the University of Huelva (Spain). She received her PhD in Social Anthropology at the University of Seville. Her research focuses on religion, social movements and gender in Mesoamerica. She is currently working on a research project on 'the development policies of the indigenous women's NGO of Chiapas (Mexico)'.

1

The Metamorphosis of Peacemaking

JACQUES FAGET[1]

POLITICAL CONFLICT REGULATION has gone through a series of major changes over the last few years. The traditional role played by state diplomacy has increasingly been complemented or superseded by other modes among which mediation is probably the most remarkable. Mediation finds its origins in history, as illustrated notably by the publication of a volume entitled *The Ambassador and his Functions* written in 1680 by Dutch diplomat Abraham de Wicquefort (1606–82). The concept of mediation was indeed evoked by the author in the first chapter of his book (van Wicquefort, 1680–81) in which he proposed a surprisingly modern code of ethics for the benefit of ambassadors (Duss-von Werdt, 2005). However, it was not until the 1907 Hague Conference that mediation became a commonly used term in international political conflict resolution.[2] It somewhat fell into oblivion after the First World War broke out and only reappeared in the 1970s on issues strictly related to social, family and legal problems before progressively spreading to the field of politics.

In this matter, it is striking to note the increasing number of instances in which mediation efforts have been deployed since the end of the Second World War—20 per cent of political conflicts were mediated between 1945 and 1962 against 34 per cent between 1963 and 1989, and 64 per cent between 1990 and 1996.[3] One probable reason for this could be the incapacity of the United Nations and traditional diplomacy to ensure durable peaceful relations between states, not to mention the states' inability to maintain peace and harmony within their own frontiers. Mediation efforts have mostly been made with a view to regulating territorial or ethnic conflicts—or both as a matter of fact—opposing neighbouring countries or parties (Wilkenfeld et al, 2003). This is probably related to the fact that inter-state conflicts have significantly decreased and have been replaced by

[1] The author wishes to thank JF Allafort for the translation of this chapter.

[2] Convention for the Peaceful Resolution of International Conflicts (The Hague, 18 October 1907).

[3] International Crisis Behavior Project Data Archive: www.icbnet.org.

infra-state conflicts (Mack, 2005), thus calling for new solutions and exit strategies.

The objective of the present volume is to analyse this recent rise in mediation strategies and the emergence of new players in the peace building process—NGOs with various legal statuses, charismatic personalities, private groups, academics and religious networks. Their strategies may be apprehended through various paradigms which have marked international relations theories, notably the realist paradigm focusing on an institutional state-centred approach and the pluralist paradigm according to which individuals and civil society—interdependent on state actors—are fully-fledged players in a 'world society' (Burton, 1972). According to the perspective adopted, the increasing role played by mediation can be analysed in two different ways. The first hypothesis is that mediation strategies do not really break away from, but complement, traditional state action, as evidenced by the 'para-state' status of some NGOs. From that perspective, through a strategy of de-politicisation, the objective of these new players would be to facilitate the regulation of conflicts which directly 'concern' the most powerful states, by eclipsing the very intervention of these states. However, the second hypothesis is that the multiplicity of mediation initiatives 'from below', initiated by 'peacemakers' with heterogeneous legal statuses and fostered by 'beliefs' and interests which are not purely political, may eventually lead to defining new roles for peacemakers, thus blurring the frontiers between state and non-state actors. The analysis of the two hypotheses requires that we first clarify the contours of notions such as mediation and violent political conflicts.

At the early stage of our work, it should be mentioned that mediation belongs to the realm of peacemaking, which is different from peacekeeping and peace-building processes. The concept of peacekeeping, the best illustration of it being the deterring presence of UN Blue Helmets in conflict zones, is easy to define. It is somewhat more difficult to differentiate mediation from peace building which aims to reinforce economic and social development, set up new institutions and stage democratic elections.[4] Indeed, even though mediation may precede peace building, both processes can co-occur or be mutually interwoven.

It is also important to clearly distinguish mediation from negotiation. I adopt here a most uncommon position, insofar as the word 'mediation' is often synonymous with 'negotiation' in international relations. Such an undifferentiated usage is conspicuously visible in many scholarly works and in the way specialised data banks refer to peace processes.[5] One of the innovative objectives of the present volume is to focus exclusively on mediation.

[4] On the topic of peace building and its contradictions, see Paris and Sisk (2009).
[5] Peace Process Yearbook (Escola de pau) (Barcelona, Icaria, 2009).

Admittedly, any attempt at differentiating between the two notions is hampered by the diversity of the negotiation and mediation patterns. However, it may be contended that negotiation can be carried out without the intervention of a third party, whereas the role of the third party is essential in the mediation process. Negotiation aims to find a quick solution to an explicit conflict contrary to mediation which is a long-term process with a view to restoring communication between protagonists. Negotiation is also a game of mutual compromises whereas mediation favours a win-win approach.

Confusion between conciliation and mediation is also quite common. The distinction between both concepts is not easy. It may tentatively be said that conciliation is etymologically defined by its objective (*conciliare* means 'to unite') whereas mediation is characterised by its methodology (*mediare* means 'to be in the middle'). It can thus be inferred that the conciliator has an obligation of results and adopts a more directive approach—that is by proposing solutions—contrary to the mediator who is more concerned with establishing communication between the players than with the resolution of the conflict. In an attempt to clarify the terms of the debate, I propose to define mediation as a consensual process of conflict regulation in which an impartial, independent third party without any decision-making power helps people or institutions to improve or set up relations through exchanges and, as far as possible, to solve their conflicts.

What differentiates political conflicts from the various forms of social conflicts is that they are closely related to issues which pertain to the quest for or the exercise of political power. Political conflicts occur in all forms of political organisation since confrontation between political and social groups for the control of power is a common feature in democracies. My area of research is thus delineated by such various modes of confrontation. I am more particularly interested in political conflicts in which protagonists—states, social protest movements, political parties—do not respect the rules of the democratic game and resort to armed struggle and illegitimate physical violence, for instance. Such conflicts may be territorial, identity-based, economic, or ethnic but their common denominator is the violent and non-regulated dimension of the modes of competition between protagonists. As an illustration of this definition, I regard as political the conflicts that have taken or are taking place in the Basque country, Northern Ireland, Cyprus, Timor or Sudan. They are often presented as ethnic conflicts as some groups with a high feeling of shared identity do not consider the ruling government to be capable of fulfilling their needs, especially on cultural issues (Bercovitch and Derouen, 2004). Many such conflicts take on an international dimension because of the problem of refugees fleeing to neighbouring countries, when some cultural groups are split up between several countries—as in the case of the Kurds—or when ethnic leaders set up their main operating bases in a foreign country.

These conflicts may oppose not only neighbouring groups or countries, but more or less well-defined coalitions—Palestine, Iraq, Afghanistan.

The analysis of political conflicts is generally the exclusive domain of international relations specialists—although more and more conflicts are national—whereas mediation is an area of research shared by various disciplines gathering political specialists, law sociologists and increasingly specialists of conflict resolution—mainly in the US, and more recently in Norway and the UK—who endeavour to make it an area of scientific research on its own and borrow their analytical tools from anthropology, social and experimental psychology, law and international relations. On account of the diversity of academic constructs, researchers who want to have a global approach to mediation have to break free from the existing 'schools of thinkers'. Theoretical and empirical knowledge of the various 'worlds' of mediation may contribute to furthering their analytical efforts.[6]

I will first propose a synthetic and critical assessment of the realist literature on mediation in political conflicts (I). I will secondly focus on a less common pluralist and comprehensive approach with a view to studying less visible configurations of players and modes of mediation (II). I will then endeavour to analyse the nature and political issues of the new forms of political mediation (III). I will finally present the main articulations of the volume and a synthesis of the various authors' research paths (IV).

I. THE BLIND SPOT OF THE REALIST SCIENTIFIC APPROACH

Scientific interest in mediation which may be traced back to the 1970s (Edmead, 1971; Ott 1972)—the word 'negotiation' being frequently in use at that time—really developed in the mid-1980s. It was most exclusively tackled by American scholars, with the more punctual collaboration of some Australian, Scandinavian, Dutch, Swiss and British researchers. Several synthetic analyses presenting a general assessment of academic research were published (Fisher, 1978; Touval and Zartman, 1985; Bercovitch and Rubin, 1992; Kleiboer, 1998), more particularly in the form of articles in specialised journals, the most active publications being the *Journal of Peace Research*, the *Journal of Conflict Resolution* and to a certain extent the *International Studies Quarterly*, the *International Studies Review* or *International Negotiation*. Several non-specialised publications such as the *American Journal of Political Science* or *Political Studies* may also be mentioned.

[6] My reflections are based on a collection of research work on mediation in political conflicts published in English and in French, on empirical research conducted in Europe on various types of mediation—social, legal, family, school—on my frequent contacts with international networks of restorative justice, on a long personal experience as a mediator in collective and interpersonal conflicts, as well as on information gathered during my numerous stays in many foreign countries, complemented with observations and interviews.

In this research literature the concept of 'mediation' was taken in a broad sense. Mediation was presented as 'a process of conflict management in which protagonists look for or accept the assistance of an individual, a group, a state or an organisation, to solve a conflict or settle their differences without resorting to physical violence or invoking the rule of law' (Bercovitch et al, 1991). Mediators could adopt whatever role was deemed most adequate to avoid physical or legal constraint and offer the best possibilities of influence and manipulation. This definition included the analysis of all peacemaking processes—which could sometimes be rather disconnected from the ethics of mediation—undertaken by heads of state and government or political elites, international organisations or traditional diplomacy.

This body of research work dealt jointly with case studies and quantitative analyses. We may even speak of a real fascination for quantitative studies which led numerous researchers to use sophisticated mathematical models to analyse samples ranging from 100 to more than 350 cases of mediation over periods spanning from 15 to 50 years. They also resorted to simulation models in order to test the effectiveness of the various modes of mediation (among others Smith and Stam, 2003). What clearly marked this literature was a globally conclusive obsession as researchers, following the tradition of the rational choice theories, were pursuing the golden formula that would bring peace to the world.

Finally the general orientation of this literature was clearly based on an ethnocentric Western vision of the world. It extolled the ultimate objective of peace without considering the potential positive dimension of conflict for countries or peoples under domination. It was mostly focused on international armed conflicts—which directly concerned the international order and consequently the interests of the Great Powers—to the detriment of so-called peripheral national conflicts, and on the action of governments, heads of state, major NGOs and official diplomacy. This state-centred literature pertained to the realist paradigm in international relations, essentially focused on high politics. It enhanced the technical contribution of the problem solving theory without tackling the problem of the role played by institutions, power relations or political and economic constraints.

In the following part I propose a synthetic presentation of this analytical approach through a study of the five main themes most frequently addressed by researchers, ie, conflicts, protagonists, the context, the mediator's position and an assessment of the effectiveness of mediation.

(a) Conflicts

Conflicts go through life cycles and different stages, some of which are more auspicious for the intervention of a third party. To be effective, mediation must be made at the ripe moment. The question is therefore to determine this moment precisely. For some authors there is not one ripe moment but two. In their view, mediation efforts are likely to be effective if they are made shortly after the dispute has broken out or after a long period of time. If the conflict is not solved rapidly efforts made during the intermediary period will probably fail, and mediation may even prove to be counterproductive (Regan and Stam, 2000). Other analysts refute the notion of 'ripeness' in conflict resolution and defend the concept of a mutually hurtful stalemate (Zartman, 2000). According to Zartman, a conflict may be solved only when each protagonist acknowledges the fact that they will not be able to reach a solution on their own or when they feel that escalation will lead to a catastrophe and that the costs are unbearable. Ripeness depends on internal political changes within conflicting groups, such as the emergence of new leaders or the breakup of a government. In other words, determining the ripe moment cannot be only rational but must take into account the psychological dimension and the nature and intensity of the protagonists' feelings. There would thus be a narrow window of opportunity for successful mediation. Even though the 'ripeness factor' may be instrumental in the successful negotiation of a ceasefire or to abate violence between warring parties (Mooradian and Druckman, 1999), distinct dynamics determine the short-term or long-term success of mediation (Greig, 2001). Kleiboer (1998) thinks that the notion of complete willingness is more relevant than the concept of ripeness. The perception and mindset of the warring parties play a more fundamental role than the intrinsic dynamics of the conflict.

(b) Protagonists

Starting from the principle that the mediation process cannot be imposed and essentially rests on the players' willingness, a great majority of authors think that this choice is dictated by strategic and tactical considerations, because peace is not always the ultimate goal of disputants (Richmond, 1998). From that perspective Richmond underlines the importance of analysing the way mediators are perceived and how mediation is conducted. Mediation may be used as a delaying tactic to play for time—the frequent ceasefire periods in Bosnia would thus have made it possible for the warring parties to build up their forces again before resuming the fight—as a strategic option to re-arm and redeploy troops on better positions—as in the case of Angola—or as a way to hide the depletion of one's resources and take advantage of a temporary favourable balance of power in order to concede as little as possible. Accepting mediation may also improve the image of each party and pave the way for new alliances or financial deals. Moreover, mediation may be explained by internal political reasons, such as keeping one's leadership or meeting the expectations of one's people.

This strategic conception of mediation is often a failure, as exemplified by the way Greece and Turkey have made use of mediation over the issue of Cyprus with a view to reaching mutually incompatible initial objectives (Richmond, 1998). In any case, the choice of mediation, which is not totally rational as players do not possess all information—one party may think that the other one has resources which in fact it does not have or may wrongly anticipate what the other will demand—would only be one strategy among a variety of options. It rests more on individual interests than on 'shared values' or 'converging interests' (Princen, 1992).

Protagonists with long-standing relations of friendship and cooperation are deemed more likely to defend them than protagonists who have only established more recent relations. Cultural proximity would thus facilitate successful mediation, especially when the protagonists share the same democratic political culture (Leng and Regan, 2003). Mediation efforts involving multi-party countries would be more successful in 35 per cent of cases compared with a mere 6 per cent when they concern single-party states (Bercovitch et al, 1991). However these authors challenge the effects of 'the clash of civilisation' (Huntington, 1996) considering that conflicts between Western and Arab countries, in spite of 'an intercultural clash between individualist and collective cultures' have led to no less favourable outcomes than conflicts between Arab countries. The only thing is that democratic countries tend to resort to mediation more often.

(c) Context

The international context shapes the mediation process, from its initial stage to its completion. Economic and political pressure exerted by other countries with a direct or indirect interest in the conflict has an impact, as well as the attitude of the countries affected by the waves of refugees entering their territory (Assefa, 1987). The occurrence of other events, such as the breaking out of a new conflict or a change in the diplomatic policies of influential neighbouring countries, may also change the course of things (Kleiboer, 1996).

The implementation of mediation is affected by the presence of peacekeeping forces—the UN for example—on the territory concerned. While such initiatives are naturally necessary to prevent escalation in the conflict, they may also hinder the efforts made by the protagonists to reach a negotiated solution. Cyprus is a good case in point of such a dilemma. The presence of peacemaking forces may also be favourable once the peace agreement has been concluded. They reassure protagonists and help them to consolidate their peacemaking efforts (Greig and Diehl, 2005).

Financial aid has a significant impact on the initial development and nature of mediation. Without the $60 million worth of aid from Norway, the 1993 Oslo agreement would never have been concluded. Mediation undertaken by Alexis Keller, which led to the 2003 Geneva agreement between the Israelis and Palestinians, would have failed without the financial support—although modest as it only amounted to $1.5 million—from two Swiss foundations. The private origin of these funds contributed to Keller's independence from his own government in his mediation efforts (Keller, 2004). Mediation in Mozambique conducted by the Sant'Egidio community was successful thanks to the support of the Vatican and Italy which was the main sponsor of the country at that time (Marret, 2001). Several authors insist on some necessary favourable organisational conditions for a serene mediation process, such as distance from the place of the conflict, or good, comfortable conditions which contribute to creating a positive atmosphere.

(d) The Mediator's Position

All specialists agree on distinguishing three distinctive types of mediators—facilitators, formulators and manipulators. Facilitators act as intermediaries between the warring parties and actually have little control over the negotiation process, as illustrated by the Norwegian mediators in the Israeli–Palestinian conflict in 1993. They are often associated with good offices. The best they can do is to organise the logistics of the process and facilitate communication. Formulators have a more significant role; they exert an important formal control as they choose where, how many and what types of meetings will be staged; they set the agenda, manage the information flow and may propose new solutions to the parties concerned, as was the case with George Mitchell in Northern Ireland.[7] Manipulators can not only put forward proposals, but make use of their power and persuasion position and resources, and present ultimatums—what Jimmy Carter did for the successful conclusion of the Camp David agreement in 1979. But only powerful mediators with the potential capacity of influencing the international environment may play such a role. Many authors think that mediators should not restrict their action to one of these specific roles, but adapt their mode of intervention to the necessities of the crisis or conflict.

The prevailing doctrine is that mediators' impartiality—often confused with neutrality[8]— is fundamental in a successful mediation as the only

[7] Maine Senator George Mitchell was the Democratic leader in the US Senate; he then became president of the International Crisis Group. He acted as the American envoy to Northern Ireland and took an active part in the signing of the Belfast Peace Agreement in 1998.

[8] These terms are often confused. Mediation specialists prefer to use the notion of impartiality which is an objective position which requires that mediators do not take sides, contrary to neutrality, a more subjective and probably impossible position as all mediators are 'influenced' by their own beliefs and values.

way to foster mutual trust among belligerents and give legitimacy to their mediating action. Even though Wehr and Lederach (1991) have shown that trust was a determining factor, it may not necessarily be coupled with impartiality in some Central American societies. On the contrary, mediators may be insider-partial, and not outsider-neutral, the acceptance of their action resting not as much on their distance or objectivity, but rather on their links with the conflict and their relations of trust with the warring parties. However, these authors underline the fact that this type of mediation may only occur in a specific cultural context in which political exchanges are still characterised by face-to-face relations and traditions have not totally been eroded by modernity.[9] For Touval and Zartman (1985) impartiality is subordinate to the power actually held by mediators, such as their capacity to use the carrot and stick approach or provide material support. In the same vein Bercovitch and Houston (1993) also upheld the idea that power carries more weight than impartiality. The more leverage mediators have the less impartial protagonists expect them to be. Kydd (2003) gives an interesting illustration of this point when he asserts that mediators may reduce the likelihood of a conflict by providing information to the potential protagonists. By so doing they indeed adopt a biased attitude, but, according to a model based on the game theory, 'biased' mediators are more credible in the eyes of the players concerned. In other words, mediators need not systematically be impartial, and the game theory model reveals that bias, to a certain extent, notably through sharing information, is not only acceptable but sometimes necessary.

The issue of the mediators' power is much debated. Indeed Rubin (1992) distinguishes six forms of power: the power to reward when mediators are in a position to offer protagonists some advantages in exchange for a favourable change in their respective behaviours; the power of coercion based on threats of sanctions; the power of expertise stemming from the mediators' expert knowledge of the problem; the legitimate power depending on the mediators' authority and charisma; the relational power based on the existing relations between mediators and protagonists; and the power to inform which turns mediators into 'go-between' message bearers. Conversely, Quaker mediators extol the 'power of powerlessness' (Princen, 1994). Their power is acceptable precisely because they have no power to constrain players and do not pursue their own objectives. They just have the possibility of applying one model and influencing the course of the exchanges. However, a majority of authors thinks that although 'genuine' mediators (the Norwegian type) may be somewhat successful at the initial

[9] We may also contend that impartiality is not always wished for by the party that feels it is in a position of strength. Likewise the party with an inferior status may expect the mediator to have an ethnic bias and support the weaker side thus contributing to bringing about a more balanced settlement of the conflict or influencing the opponent.

stage of the exchanges, only powerful mediators may bring about the favourable conclusion and enforcement of an agreement. In their view that is why the Oslo peace process failed (Siniver, 2006), which leads us to consider the recurring theme of the assessment of mediation.

(e) Assessing the Effectiveness of Mediation

The tricky question of determining how successful mediation may be is a real obsession among specialists even though it raises more methodological questions than provides definite answers.[10] It reveals an 'instrumental' approach to mediation which gives more importance to the short to mid-term objective result—signing a treaty, a ceasefire, an arrangement, opening talks, curbing violence—than to the operating mode or its mid to long-term subjective consequences—the quality of communication, a change in the populations' attitude, the building of common projects.

From their study of a sample comprising 364 cases, Bercovitch and Langley (1993) conclude that 29 per cent of mediations have led to an agreement in interstate conflicts. For his part Dixon (1996) in his analysis of 220 cases, shows that in 40 per cent of the cases the result is conflict de-escalation. In their work these authors try to determine what factors may contribute to bringing about settlements, especially the nature of the conflict, the mediator's characteristics, behaviour and style, or the duration of mediation. When Bercovitch and Derouen (2004) contend, from their study of 309 cases, that conflict regulation through mediation has roughly one chance in three of being effective, they take great care to make distinctions according to the nature of the conflict insofar as interstate conflicts are much more likely—roughly in two cases out of three—than ethnic conflicts—approximately 15 per cent—to come to a peaceful settlement (Stedman, 1991). In their view, mediation is 60 per cent more likely to be effective when mediation is started at the ripe moment by experienced mediators—they contribute to reaching the highest number of agreements, and the best ones (Bercovitch and Houston, 1993)—who use directive strategies. Directivity would thus have a positive impact on the likelihood of reaching an agreement and abating a crisis, which is confirmed by a study of the 94 mediation efforts conducted during the war in the Balkans between 1989 and 2000 (Gartner and Bercovitch, 2006). Siniver (2006) comes to the same conclusion in his analysis of four cases of mediation in the Arab–Israeli conflict—Bunche in 1948, Kissinger in 1973, Carter in 1979, the Oslo agreement in 1993. He is convinced that the most effective

[10] Eg, on the definition of what mediation is, what a mediator is, how comparable the conflicts sampled may be, what the criteria of success or failure may be, etc.

mediators are those who can mobilise the greatest resources—as in the case of Kissinger and Carter—to change the protagonists' attitude. If so, Kochan, however, fears that using active strategies untimely may ruin the credibility of the mediator (Kochan, 1981). Finally, non-directive positions would also be of interest as they contribute to durably easing tensions (Beardsley et al, 2006).

In short, this research work, which undoubtedly offers interesting instrumental tools, suffers from a considerable methodological bias. The main problem lies in the authors' very extensive conception of mediation. All forms of third party intervention are gathered under this term. The problem is that there is a significant qualitative difference between pressure exerted by the President of the United States and the non-directive action of a Swiss or Norwegian professor or of a small humanitarian NGO. The tendency of some researchers not to go beyond the great institutional appearances has led them to ignore the diversity of peacemaking initiatives. We must admit that it is no easy task to determine them as secrecy is part and parcel of these strategies.

II. THE EMERGENCE OF TRANSFORMATIVE MEDIATION

Deciphering political mediation is hampered by the very principle of confidentiality which characterises it. Indeed, many mediators think that secrecy is fundamental to their action. The invisibility of the mediation process, more than in interstate conflicts addressed by traditional diplomatic means, is a prerequisite in identity-based or ethnic conflicts whose complexity needs time and deftness. It is probably impossible to make a list of all these types of mediation, which invalidates any tentative quantitative methodological approach. A qualitative approach thus seems to be the only relevant way to apprehend the small world of political mediators, the way they operate and their links with other regulating arenas in conflict regulation.

(a) Various Forms of Mobilisation

Political mediators have heterogeneous statuses—small or big NGOs, moral and religious authorities, foundations, specialised university research centres. They may be state civil servants, NGO workers, professionals in conflict regulation, academics or even volunteers. Their common denominator is that they all belong to Western democracies. They are white North Americans in their vast majority but may also be found in some European countries (Norway, Finland, Switzerland, Italy, the United Kingdom, Ireland) or in more far away countries such as Australia and New Zealand. The reasons why they get involved in this type of activity are generally hidden, but a close study of the political history of their native countries shows that these reasons are ideological, religious or pertain to professional strategies.

The first American mediators came from the pacifist liberal left wing in the 1970s, who opposed the 'Establishment' and US foreign policy. From a conceptual corpus elaborated by the *Critical Legal Studies* academics, a considerable number of diversion programmes developed under the Alternative Dispute Resolution (ADR) banner. Thanks to some radical law specialists and social activists, notably in the Neighbourhood Justice Centres, new forms of mediation emerged on legal issues (victim offender mediation, family mediation), on social questions (the San Francisco community boards), on school problems (peer mediation) and, more generally, in all domains of social life. Their initial objective was to de-institutionalise and de-professionalise conflict resolution processes through citizens' empowerment with a view to developing their sense of responsibility and neighbourhood solidarity. New patterns of political mediation stemmed from this counter-cultural movement and the main promoters of mediation were deeply influenced by these pioneering initiatives, as for example Roger Fisher (Fisher and Ury, 1981)[11] who created the Conflict Management Group in 1984. But it would be erroneous to regard these initiatives as essentially 'leftist', as experts in political conflict resolution progressively gathered former Republican high officials, such as James Baker[12] to quote but one, diplomats or former presidents. For instance, Jimmy Carter with the Carter Foundation was most active in Sudan, Ethiopia, Uganda, Liberia and Haiti,[13] his personal involvement being fuelled by his Baptist faith.

Indeed, political mediation is also buttressed on philosophical and religious considerations. The involvement of numerous mediators cannot be understood if we do not take into consideration their non-violent convictions, inspired by Buddhism and the teachings of Gandhi, as in the case of Johan Galtung,[14] or their religious beliefs. Let us just mention that the Quakers were awarded the Nobel Prize for Peace for their action in favour of reconciliation among peoples. Their non-violent philosophy—coupled with the fact that Protestantism has no national or supranational

[11] A law specialist at the Harvard Law School, Roger Fisher became famous for his interventions during the Vietnam War, the hostage crisis in Teheran, the Israeli–Arab conflict and the questions of South Africa and Georgia. He also developed the so-called Harvard model which enshrined the win-win principle.

[12] James Baker was Secretary of State in the Bush senior and Reagan Administrations. He then became the UN representative in charge of the conflict in the Western Sahara.

[13] His activities at the University of Emory, Atlanta, in 1986, were numerous and varied. He made a series of conferences for peace, development, democracy and human rights, and personally supervised elections in some developing countries. His action, although non-official, subtly interacted with US diplomacy under Clinton's presidency.

[14] A Norwegian academic, Johan Galtung created the *Journal of Peace Research* and the International Peace Research Institute of Oslo (PRIO).

institutions—naturally prepared them to act as mediators. One of them, Kenneth Boulding, was one of the founding fathers of the Peace Studies. He created the *Journal of Conflict Resolution* and the conflict resolution research centre in 1957. As early as the 1970s Quakers got involved in the conflict opposing India and Pakistan (Yarrow, 1978), in Nigeria, Rhodesia, Sri Lanka and the Middle East. They developed a non-directive type of action based on people's education for peace. They also pioneered school mediation. Although the commitment of the Mennonites to peacemaking action took some more time on account of their long tradition of retreat and quietism, they also developed a theology of engagement thanks to their progressive social ideas, which led some of them to actively fight for peace in the 1970s. They were at the origin of the first initiatives for penal mediation in Canada. Howard Zehr (Zehr, 1990), among others, initiated the movement of restorative justice whose main philosophy in a process of participative democracy was to empower individuals and communities so that they could regulate conflicts in a responsible way and engage in dialogue with a view to finding their own solutions for the future. This pacifist philosophy, more widely promoted by authors such as Jean-Paul Lederach, came to influence all types of mediation. These efforts were then taken up by the Catholic movement which developed both internal action, through its religious orders or clergy, or external initiatives thanks to the various Christian organisations (Itcaina, 2007). For instance, Bishop Ruiz Garcia played an active role in the conflict between the Zapatist movement and the Mexican government in 1994 (Gil Tebar, 1997). Alec Reid, an Irish Redemptorist priest, significantly contributed to the signing of the 1999 Good Friday Agreement in Northern Ireland—he was also called as a mediator in the Basque conflict. But it was mainly the Sant'Egidio community, the 'secular international organisation of the Roman Catholic Church', which best illustrated this mediation activism. It progressively evolved from missions of assistance in the fight against poverty to more political mediation strategies as in Lebanon in 1982 or in Africa in the following years. Its main achievement was the signing of a peace agreement in Rome on 4 October 1992 which put an end to a 15-year-long conflict in Mozambique (Marret, 2000). The involvement of the Roman Catholic Church in this new form of interventionism may be explained by its political philosophy, extolling intermediary bodies as so many bulwarks against authoritarianism and totalitarianism, and the principle of subsidiarity according to which conflicts are not necessarily best regulated by the state but rather by qualified and competent social players who act locally. The issue of mediation is thus 'fundamentally linked to the balance of power in the internal functioning of the religious institution and in the relations between the religious and the political spheres' (Palard, 2006).

Such mobilisation based on conviction and religious beliefs was soon confronted with the technical and economic requirements imposed by the professionalisation of the mediators' action. Historical activists had to adopt a distanced and impartial position which was more in keeping with the ethics of mediation. They also had to assimilate more sophisticated techniques of intervention, become more legitimate in a competitive environment and acquire new know-how in fund raising at the international and national levels. As a consequence, a number of English speaking academic programmes, at Harvard Law School or the Massachusetts Institute of Technology for example, were set up in the United States, as well as in Europe, in order to train specialists in conflict resolution. This led to the creation of new specific diplomas, specialised courses, journals, networks—for instance the *Negotiation Network* comprising the *Carter Foundation*, the George Mason University, Harvard, Uppsala and the World Conference on Religion and Peace—and careers. National and international experts progressively came to work for both the most modest NGOs and the larger international organisations, and exported the concepts of peace and managerial logics they had been trained in. But the new organisation of mediation activities has not so far brought about any standardised concepts and practices.

(b) A Wide Range of Mediation Patterns

We have seen that there are three types of mediators in the traditional approach to mediation: facilitators, formulators and manipulators. But this typology tends to overlook the multiplicity of patterns engendered by the various types of social and political mobilisation. The relative confusion which characterises these different concepts of mediation may explain the contradictions and shortcomings of what was initially an alternative movement but progressively became more institutional while keeping its capacity to subvert vertical regulations. Indeed, the rhetoric extolling the virtues of individual empowerment and autonomy, the de-institutionalisation and relative disempowerment of both elites and professionals, the transformation of the cognitive links between antagonistic groups, the discovery of the 'Other', the development of deliberation more respectful of the cultural patterns of the populations concerned, runs counter to an approach which mainly focuses on ceasefires and formal agreements while enhancing the mediators' positive power of influence and the potential necessity of bypassing some principles of impartiality and independence.

There is indeed a wide range of mediation patterns. This diversity should not only be understood as evidence of the ideological variety of points of view, but as the consequence of an economic competition between specialists with a view to controlling the market of academic training and diffusing their own models. While many disciples have strictly followed the models taught by their mentors, quite a few have broken away from them and embarked on some 'conceptual tinkering' either by adopting a synthetic approach or alternately using one model or another depending on the characteristics of the conflict and its development. In academic international relations (IR) programmes, the reference model was, and still is, that of multitrack diplomacy (Diamond and McDonald, 1996).[15] This was a global approach which did not really concern mediation. It generally referred to the problem solving or settlement oriented model. Conflicts were problems which had to be solved. The mediator's objective was to seek an agreement which would solve concrete problems in amicable and realist terms. The mediator was bent on finding solutions and thus tempted to exert strong pressure on the whole process and adopt directive behaviour. This model was complemented and superseded by the model of 'principled negotiation' whose main contribution was to clearly differentiate between the protagonists' positions—which must be transcended—and their interests—which must be brought to the fore—with a view to conceptualising a win-win logic in the pursuit of solutions (Fisher and Ury, 1981). Then emerged the transformative model (Bush and Folger, 1994) mainly based on individual and group awareness of their capacity to master their own destiny—empowerment—and on the positive change in the way they conceive of each other—recognition. According to this model, conflicts were crises in human interaction. Mediators had to facilitate the efforts developed by protagonists to resume dialogue. Reaching an agreement was not the ultimate goal; what mattered was the quality of communication between the players. We could also mention other alternative models, such as the narrative approach (Monk et al, 1997), which have all contributed to the development of these doctrines.

In short, we may say that there has developed an opposition between the doctrine of conflict resolution and that of conflict regulation. The first doctrine is more directive than the second one which gives more leeway to subjectivity and emotions and requires a non-directive capacity to hear the other. Beyond this methodological quarrel it is in fact two worlds which oppose each other, the world of corporate professionals, legal and political specialists and the world of activist social science academics and social workers. All attempts at reconciling both approaches, such as the bifocal model according to which the mediator pursues the double objective of finding an agreement that guarantees mutual interests and building new

[15] This model is opposed to the hierarchical approach to conflict regulation. It shows that for durable peace it is necessary to take into account the links which exist between nine ways presented under the form of a compass: government, professional conflict resolution, market, citizens, research, training and education, activism, religion, financing, public opinion and communication. This 'systems approach to peace' favours a complementary process involving traditional diplomacy, economic and institutional action, partnerships with local authorities, women and entrepreneurs for peace with a view to developing the community's commitment and improving the conditions of community life thanks to local wisdom.

relations between protagonists (Mareschal, 2003), cannot alone hide this cultural divide.

Behind this methodological debate it is indeed the issue of peace which is at stake. To the idea that the peace process must necessarily be buttressed on official negotiations and the signing of formal agreements, is opposed the conviction that peace requires the building of relations between the civil societies concerned. According to Fisher (Fisher, 1978) and his disciples, it would be vain to expect diplomats to sign agreements before former tensions are appeased. The peace process must involve not only high officials and notables, but all the societal and cultural strata. This opinion is taken up by Galtung (1975) who makes a difference between what he calls negative peace which only means putting an end to a violent conflict—the European school of thinkers criticises the American conception of peace which they regard as too superficial and contends that all negotiations or mediation efforts must necessarily tackle the deeper roots of the conflict—and positive peace which includes relations of collaboration and mutual help between states or social groups. In order to avoid 'peace-making without reconciliation' (Duclos, 2006), Lederach (2005) asserts the necessity to set up sustainable and peaceful relations based on objective experiences of communication. If relations are at the origin of a conflict they are also the necessary condition for its resolution. In his view, without the building of dialogue and tolerance, the peace process in Northern Ireland would be too elite driven and not enough mass driven, the Irish population, strongly marked by communitarism, being but a passive spectator (Féron, 2002). So, in this particular case, it is very important to take in account the bottom up efforts to making peace (Hancock, 2008).

(c) Multiple Interactive Arenas

Any analysis focusing exclusively on mediation would be meaningless, in the sense that it overlooks the larger initiatives which shape it and make it effective. A global approach should therefore address all the interactions—which are not always visible—that may exist between various levels of intervention. Saunders (2001), for instance, defines four interrelated and complementary arenas. In his view the first arena is state diplomacy. The second one involves individuals or institutions working in collaboration with governments but without any official authority or status as, for example, Terje Rod Larsen and Mona Juul who worked for the Oslo agreement, Alexis Keller for the Geneva agreement or the Catholic clergy in the Irish and Basque conflicts. The third arena is public debate in which influential persons and opinion-makers are invited to deliberate by non-official players with a view to understanding the nature of the conflict, developing alternative scenarios and taking initiatives. The fourth arena concerns civil society as a whole, through non-violent initiatives for peace and education. To be effective peacemaking efforts must be carried on, through a comprehensive strategy, in all four arenas and interconnect them. However, multiparty mediation (Crocker et al, 1999), which mainly focuses on cooperation, transfer of information and shared resources, may paradoxically lead to undermining the necessary feeling of confidence between protagonists which essentially rests on confidentiality and runs counter to the desire of non-official actors (track two) to remain distinct from official mediators (track one).

From that perspective, the study of mediation should not be limited to the time of mediation only but incorporate all the interconnected and complementary strategies paving the way for peacemaking (Fisher, 2006). That was the case of the Sant'Egidio community whose legitimacy as a mediating actor in the Mozambique conflict was enhanced by its long presence in the country and its sustained efforts to help the local population. We may also quote the example of Herbert Kelman and his colleagues who organised about 60 workshops regrouping participants from Israel and Palestine following their model of interactive conflict resolution (Kelman, 2005), as well as the problem-solving workshops set up by some British academics in the Moldavian conflict (Williams, 1999) or by the University of Maryland in the frontier dispute between Peru and Ecuador (Kaufman and Sosnowski, 2005). That was the strategy adopted by 'Search for Common Ground', an American NGO, whose involvement in conflict resolution was based on promoting partnerships with local communities, training local mediators and developing initiatives for mutual understanding through magazines, TV programmes, radio serials, bilingual kindergartens in Macedonia, peace festivals or football matches between young Hutus and Tutsis in Burundi. In the same vein, we may also mention the Peace Brigades International (PBI) organising workshops on non-violent conflict resolution gathering groups of women, trade union members and teachers in Guatemala, Colombia, Mexico and Indonesia (Peace Brigades International, 2006). Likewise, the Elkarri (Dialogue) association has set up 'small round tables' for discussions, staged debates and public awareness campaigns in the Basque country since 1992, convinced as it is that an effective peace process must involve as many people as possible (Mansvelt-Beck, 2005). All these initiatives confirm Fisher's opinion (Fisher, 2001) that, as evidenced by the conflict in Cyprus where all official mediation efforts have failed, it is only through a comprehensive approach to a conflict that past trauma may be surpassed and each party's basic needs fulfilled. The unofficial efforts made by the *Cyprus Consortium* since 1996 and involving hundreds of influential persons in bi-community interactions, seem to be the only effective solution as they help build or rebuild a feeling of mutual respect.

III. THE POLITICAL STAKES OF MEDIATION

The most fervent advocates of mediation, who are sometimes inspired by messianic logics, give the impression that mediation is the missing link in the quest for human fraternity. Others are more clearly motivated by economic considerations insofar as the world of mediation has also become a real business (Nelson, 2000). Assessing the impact of mediation on peacemaking thus requires that both approaches are taken into consideration.

(a) A Mere Facelift of Diplomatic Action

If we consider the present development of mediation we might be tempted to conclude that what is taking place is 'a process of privatisation of diplomacy through the use of private intermediaries taking on functions which were previously state prerogatives' (Hibou, 1998). The strong links that exist between some American NGOs, such as the Institute for Multi-Track Diplomacy or the Conflict Management Group, and the US government would seemingly evidence the privatisation of large areas of the country's diplomacy. Such a transfer of competences in favour of bodies with no political accountability might be interpreted as a de-politicisation strategy in peacemaking (Lefranc, 2006). The problem is indeed to determine whether mediators and the NGOs they belong to may not be in fact the visible side of state interventionism. This hypothesis is relevant in the case of the United States, often discredited in its role as an impartial intermediary and thus bent on changing this negative image. It is confirmed by US diplomats' progressive acceptance of initiatives taken by non-official players (Chataway, 1998). It is also validated by the fact that some American NGOs are directly financed by their own government or by a coalition of Western governments roughly sharing the same vision of the world. In a word, mediation would be a 'soft way' of maintaining some form of global domination, a manifestation of soft power (Nye, 1990) pertaining to a neo-liberal ideology enshrining the supremacy of transnational networks over national states in matters of global governance.

The notion of privatisation may also be interpreted in a different manner. When Cana (1998) speaks of privatisation in the mediation efforts conducted to solve the conflict between Ossetia and Georgia, he means that the process was not initiated by the states concerned or any international organisations. It was only on his own initiative, supported by Roger Fisher from Harvard and financed by the Norwegian Council for Refugees, that mediation could be started and carried through.

We may thus say that in the first instance mediation merely reveals a change in the management of international order, whereas in the second case it deeply transforms the 'cast', the respective roles played by actors and our approach to mediation. The mutagenic function of track-two diplomacy in fact depends on the degree of independence of the mediators. Though most of them insist on their total independence from official strategic considerations, their positive rhetoric may be challenged by the very fact that some of their initiatives are conducted in parallel or in collaboration with these very states. A case in point is the 'Norwegian model'[16] characterised by joint action combining official actors and NGO representatives largely financed by state authorities. The creation of the Peace and Reconciliation Commission, an internal body within the Foreign Affairs ministry, in 2002, testifies to the state control of mediation. Likewise, the Sant'Egidio community is often presented as a 'para-public' player (Marret, 2000) dependent on and controlled by the Holy See. Since 1995 and their joint intervention in Guatemala, there has been sustained collaboration between Norway and the Vatican. Even though it is impossible to draw any definite conclusion on the evolution of mediation from the example of these two states—on account of their specificities and differences—it cannot be denied that the combination of political, economic and humanitarian action in various, interconnected arenas, and the multiplicity of actors may eventually undermine the independence of mediators. Indeed 'sovereignist overstatement on the one hand and stubbornly repressive positions on the other hand, in a context periodically marked by tragic acts of violence' have hampered all mediation efforts by the Catholic clergy in the Basque country (Itcaina, 2007).

If we uphold the alternative hypothesis that mediators and the organisations they belong to are structurally independent, there still remains the question whether their common socialisation in Western democracies and their education in the great American, and to some extent European universities, may not lead them to diffuse an ethnocentric vision of the world. If so, the role of the third party mediator would not only be 'to solve conflicts but also to export an order, through its own values and its economic, political, social, cultural and normative conception of society' (Richmond, 2001). Following the structural theory of Galtung (Galtung, 1971) who has analysed the reproduction of the overall core-periphery hierarchy, Hareide (2003) compares the old religious missionaries with the present-day peace missionaries, notably the Norwegians, and declares that

> the old missionaries preached God and salvation, the new missionaries preach peace and democracy. The old stayed for a long time with low pay and learnt the local languages. The young travel back and forth, have a high pay and speak

[16] The so-called 'Norwegian model' emerged during the Israeli-Palestinian conflict. It was also used in Guatemala, Sri Lanka, Haiti, Cyprus, Sudan, Uganda, Eritrea and Somalia. It is mainly characterised by joint action from both state actors and NGO representatives, secrecy and a conception of mediation based on mutual trust and not on power. Several reasons may be evoked to explain the emergence of this model. Norway is a peaceful country, with no colonial history. It has a long tradition of humanitarian aid, a relatively independent position in international affairs and an image of impartiality. On account of its size and resources, it cannot be regarded as a potential threat by the other nations.

English. What is similar is a well-developed sense for the macro theories about Good versus Evil ... Both have a gospel, even if they do not like to admit it, that someone from the West will save the Rest of the planet.

(b) An Ethical Metamorphosis of Peacemaking

The analysis of international mediation undoubtedly evidences the leadership of governments, which leaves hardly any room for manoeuvre to independent mediators or citizen interest groups. Mediation policies are still often elaborated 'from the top' (Faget, 2006a). But we cannot ignore the impact that mobilisation movements from the world of mediation may have. Neither can we ignore the symbolical and instrumental influence of the rhetoric of mediation. In fact, besides the 'complementarity' model we have just analysed, there are two other possible approaches.

First, mediation may have an alternative impact if it proceeds from a methodological rupture. Contrary to the problem-solving approach, the transformative model makes it possible to carry on mid to long-term work on the deep causes of a conflict and on the needs of the disputants, through deliberation not only between elites, but with the representatives of all the political, social or community forces concerned. This method is recommended for the regulation of deep-rooted conflicts and leads to sustainable reconciliation when the protagonists' claims in matters of identity and participation are fully addressed (Mars, 2001). Such mediation efforts must be apprehended within the framework of more global 'politics of recognition' (Taylor, 1994). In a 'post-socialist' environment where 'fundamental injustice is no longer exploitation but cultural domination' (Fraser, 2005), the need for recognition is at the origin of many conflicts. Mediation creates the conditions for 'equal participation' (Fraser, 2005) and can thus prevent 'offensive' behaviours by allowing people and groups 'to develop positive self inter-understanding through inter-subjectivity' (Honneth, 2002).

Secondly, mediation may also take place in conflicts which are of no real interest for the states. We may quote the example of poor countries ruined by civil wars, with little or no economic or strategic interests. Such mediation efforts which make up for political indifference are most inconspicuous and invisible and it would be interesting to develop a research programme to identify them, in collaboration with the humanitarian NGOs and the local populations.

The fact that mediation is often carried out by NGOs financially dependent on governments should not lead us to the hasty conclusion that they are subservient to state logics. Indeed they do not represent a homogeneous whole and do not have the internal coherence they are often deemed to have. We should not forget either that they are increasingly organised in networks, as for example the Sant'Egidio-Norwegian government axis or the Negotiation Network federation, whose functioning eludes all state organisation, thus illustrating the advent of 'a world with no sovereignty' (Badie, 1999).

Finally, it may be contended that the rhetoric of mediation has had some performative results. It has been championed by charismatic personalities such as Galtung, Fisher and Lederach, who have deeply marked the fields of mediation and international relations. They have played a fundamental role in the emergence of an increasingly influential epistemic community which has developed links with the decision-making spheres. The rhetoric of mediation is part of a 'real industry of democratic promotion' (Santiso, 1998) defining 'the contours of a global society where the diffusion of ethical values may stir people into action' (Colonomos, 1998). Indeed, this rhetoric conveys a message of political—participative democracy, self-determination, human rights; ethical—independence, impartiality; and philosophical values—respect of the 'Other', tolerance and respect—which attracts a large audience and may partly account for the strong mobilisation movements which further the advent, fragile though it may be, of a new international code of ethics.

IV. RESEARCH PATHS

The authors who have contributed to the volume have endeavoured to follow the perspectives described and analysed in the introductory chapter. Even so, the reader will find conflicting or diverging visions of what mediation is. However, the multiplicity of points of view does not challenge the coherence of this collective work; they rather enrich each other and show how difficult it is to apprehend the concept of mediation. It should also be mentioned that the authors have not given an exhaustive list of peacemakers—individuals or organisations—who have played a prominent part in the development of mediation. The analysis proposed is thus incomplete. It reflects a European approach, which is admittedly limited, developed by the French, Spanish, Swiss and German specialists who have jointly contributed to the present project.

The volume is divided into three parts. The first part focuses on the ethical problems met by mediators. The second part is devoted to the role and action of the Roman Catholic Church in peaceful conflict resolution. The third and final part proposes an empirical approach to the mediation processes implemented in North Ireland and Africa.

The first part regroups two chapters which deal with the ethical position of the mediator, from different but complementary perspectives. In chapter two, Manel Canyameres and Anne Catherine Salberg reveal that the ethical foundations of political mediation can be traced back to the very principles established, as early as the seventeenth century, by Fabio

Chigi, who became Pope Alexander VII, and Venetian ambassador Alvise Contarini who contributed to bringing the Thirty Years' War (1618–48) to an end, with the signature of the peace treaties of Münster and Osnabrück. The authors analyse some essential rules such as impartiality, confidentiality, independence, lack of power, and show that the modes of action, as described by Abraham de Wicquefort in his time, offer surprisingly topical and appropriate responses to current challenges while giving food for thought for modern specialists. In chapter three, Viola Boelscher uses her rich, first-hand experience of conflicts in Uganda, Afghanistan, the Philippines and Colombia to expose the contradictions between organised mediation and the necessary protection of human rights. She explores the question whether mediation may be regarded as successful if it means granting an amnesty to criminals responsible for rapes, homicides, femicides and other atrocities. She differentiates between positive and negative peace, positive peace including peace and justice, whereas negative peace means peace or justice. Is it enough to promote peace, ie, stop violence, or should the process include all social groups, especially those who have been victimised during the conflict? Can we talk about a peace-building process if basic human rights are not guaranteed? Viola Boelsher comes to the conclusion that the human-rights based approach should be the mainstream strategy for development and cooperative programmes.

The second part is entirely devoted to the mediating role of the Catholic Church in places as varied as the Spanish Basque country, Burundi and the Chiapas region in Mexico. In these cases, it is not the Catholic Church as an institution which is involved in the pursuit of peace, but local or transnational groups of players. In chapter four, Xabier Itçaina analyses the activities of the clergy in the conflict of the Basque country. Though the Catholic Church still suffers from its tarnished image on account of its former relations with Franco's regime in an environment characterised by a spectacular secularisation process, Catholic players have managed to leave their mark on the various initiatives for the promotion of peace which have contributed to compensating for the deficiencies and shortcomings of political parties and public institutions since the 1980s. As the Catholic Church has a well-defined social and political role as an institution—political life being deeply marked by left–right and territorial cleavages—Itçaina convincingly addresses the question of the impartiality and legitimacy of its action. These ideological constraints do not restrict the influence of the Catholic Church whose commitment to peace rests more on its members' individual activism than on its official role as an institution. The author concludes that the Basque case cannot be defined as a success story in mediation and warns that 'we should remain prudent over the real impact of the Catholic Church's action in matter of mediation'. In chapter five, Pierre Anouilh proposes an in-depth analysis of the intervention of the Catholic community of Sant'Egidio in the conflict between the regular army and a rebel group in Burundi. The

Sant'Egidio community, well known for its successful action in the civil war in Mozambique, offers some interesting and specific characteristics. The objective of the community created under the control of the Holy See by young men who belong to the '1968 generation' and are influenced as much by Marxist ideology as by evangelism, is to fight against poverty. Their excellent education and privileged family backgrounds, combined with their economic wealth, great social prestige and important social networking, confer a great symbolic capital on the community. On account of their disinterested fight against poverty, they enjoy a high degree of legitimacy in the eye of the local populations and authorities. They have won national and international awards for their action and the community has become a prominent player in the transnational space of peace building, evidencing what Pierre Anouilh calls 'transnational civil society' and the emergence of new private players in the 'market for peace'. In chapter six, Pilar Gil Tebar analyses the role of the Diocese of San Cristobal de las Casas in the mediation efforts in the conflict of Chiapas, Mexico. She describes a long history of exploitation, illegalities, cruelties, abuses from the government and the public administration against the indigenous population. Breaking free from the period when 'priests drank chocolate with ladies', when the Cathlolic Church was an ally of the political and economic powers, the local clergy has embarked on a theology of liberation, spurred on by Vatican II. This change took place during the first indigenous Congress held in San Cristobal in 1974. In an environment marked by growing mistrust for political, social or union authorities, Pilar explains that this new position has contributed to endowing the Catholic Church, or at least some of its members, with new legitimacy among natives and thus helped the clergy to play a major role, directly or indirectly, in the pacification of intra or inter-community conflicts. This example demonstrates that the Catholic Church can play an important role in an environment where there are no credible institutions, only if the clergy adopts a critical attitude towards the powers-that-be and wins the trust of the poorest social groups.

The implementation of different mediation programs of mediation in North Ireland, Burundi, Congo and Ethiopia constitutes the subject matter of the third part. In chapter seven, Elise Féron analyses the prevailing spatial segregation which remains vivid between nationalist Catholics and unionist Protestants and upholds the idea that conflict pacification in Northern Ireland is not effective in the urban interfaces, these zones of contact where poor populations generally live and which are still marked by inter-community violence. In an attempt to compensate for the consequences of a peace process mainly engineered at the political and institutional levels, Féron describes the mediation strategies locally developed in Belfast and Londonderry by social workers, local NGOs or government agencies promoting mutual recognition and respect of the 'Other'. These political initiatives are various and varied, as they have to adjust to different local environments. In the eighth chapter, Aurélien Colson and Alain

Pekar Lempereur focus on the same topic and insist on the difficulties of reconciling parties when conflicts are marked by serious human rights violations. Peace does not arise when war stops, the end of hostilities only marking the opening of a transitional phase in which efforts are necessary to prevent the return of violence. To prove their point they give a precise account of a mediation programme—in both peacemaking and peace building—which they have been conducting in two hot spots, Burundi and the Democratic Republic of the Congo. Building on Simmel's seminal reflections and inspired by Burton's work, their paper explores a model of action which requires local players' involvement and appropriation. They propose an eight-level analysis grid to evaluate the impact, in terms of reconciliation, of this process—which may be transposed to other post-conflict situations. In chapter nine, Monika Sommer expands on her empirical field experience in Gambella, a region in Ethiopia close to the frontier with Sudan, and addresses the question whether local customs in conflict resolution, although undermined by modernisation but still deeply-rooted in the cultural subconscious of local ethnic groups, may not prove more effective than imported Western mediation methods. While she highlights the frequent inadequacy of such traditional practices within contemporary conflict-solving strategies, she contends that 'a creative bottom-up approach' may bring the necessary legitimacy to mediation efforts and engage local protagonists in an effective mediation process.

REFERENCES

Assefa, H (1987) Mediation of Civil War: Approaches and Strategies—the Sudan Conflict (Boulder CO, Westview).

Badie, B (1999) *Un monde sans souverainetés* (Paris, Fayard).

Bauman, Z (2000) *Liquid Modernity* (Cambridge, Polity Press).

Beardsley, K, Quinn, D, Biswas, B and Willenfeld, J (2006) 'Mediation Styles and Crisis Outcomes' 50(1) *Journal of Conflict Resolution* 58, 86.

Bercovitch, J and Derouen, K (2004) 'Mediation in Internationalized Ethnic Conflicts: Assessing the Determinants of a Successful Process' 30(2) *Armed Forces and Society* 147, 170.

Bercovitch, J and Houston, A (1993) 'Influence of Mediator Characteristics and Behaviour on the Success of Mediation in International Relations' 4(4) *International Journal of Conflict Management* 297, 321.

Bercovitch, J and Langley, J (1993) 'The Nature of Dispute and the Effectiveness of International Mediation' 37 *Journal of Conflict Resolution* 670, 691.

Bercovitch, J and Rubin, J (eds) (1992) *Mediation in International Relations: Approaches to Conflict Management* (London, Macmillan Publishers).

Bercovitch J, Anagnoson, T and Wille, DL (1991) 'Some Conceptual Issues and Empirical Trends in the Study of Successful Mediation in International Relations' 28(1) *Journal of Peace Research* 7, 17.

Burton, J (1972) *World Society* (Cambridge, Cambridge University Press).

Bush, B and Folger, J (1994) *The Promise of Mediation. Responding to Conflict through Empowerment and Recognition* (San Francisco, Jossey Bass).
Cana, J (1998) 'La privatisation de la diplomatie. Une expérience caucasienne' 1 *Critique internationale* 169, 178.
Chataway, C (1998) 'Track Two Diplomacy: From a Track One Perspective' 14(3) *Negotiation Journal.*
Colonomos, A (1998) 'L'acteur en réseau à l'épreuve de l'international' in MC Smouts (ed), *Les nouvelles relations internationales* (Paris, Presses de Science Po) 203, 226.
Crocker, C, Hampson, F and Aall, P (eds) (1999) *Herding Cats: Multiparty Mediation in a Complex World* (Washington DC, United States Institute of Peace Press).
Darbon, D (1998) 'Autopsie du miracle sud-africain: le cas de la *Truth and Reconciliation Commission* sud africaine' 48(6) *Revue française de science politique* 707, 724.
Diamond, L and McDonald, JW (1996) *Multi Track Diplomacy: A Systems Approach to Peace* (Blomfield, Kumarian Press).
Dixon, W (1996) 'Third-Party Techniques for Preventing Conflict Escalation and Promoting Peaceful Settlement' 50 *International Organization* 653, 681.
Duclos, N (2006) 'Pacification sans réconciliation. Les apories de la politique de réconciliation conduite par les Nations Unies au Kosovo' in S Lefranc (ed), *Après le conflit, la réconciliation?* (Paris, Michel Houdiard).
Duss-von Werdt, J (2005) *Homo mediator. Geschichte und Menschenbild der Mediation* (Stuttgart, Klett-Cotta).
Edmead, F (1971) *Analysis and Prediction in International Mediation* (New York, Unitar Study).
Faget, J (ed) (2005) *Médiation et action publique: la dynamique du fluide* (Bordeaux, Presses universitaires de Bordeaux).
—— (2006a) 'Médiation et post-modernité. Légitimation ou transformation de l'action publique?' 2 *Négociations* 51, 63.
—— (2006b) 'The French Phantoms of Restorative Justice: The Institutionalization of Penal Mediation' in I Aertsen, T Daems and L Robert (eds), *Institutionalizing Restorative Justice* (London, Willan Publishing) 151, 166.
Feron, E (2002) 'Irlande du Nord: la paix en haut, la guerre en bas?' 16(3) *Critique Internationale* 24–30.
Fisher, R (1978) *International Mediation: A Working Guide* (Boston, International Peace Academy).
Fisher, R and Ury, W (1981) *Getting to Yes* (Boston, Houghton Mifflin Company).
Fisher, RJ (2001) 'Cyprus; The Failure of Mediation and the Escalation of an Identity-based Conflict to an Adversarial Impasse' 38(3) *Journal of Peace Research* 307, 326.
—— (2006) 'Coordination between Track Two and Track One Diplomacy in Successful Cases of Prenegociation' 11(1) *International Negotiation.*
Fraser, N (2005) *Qu'est ce que la justice sociale? Reconnaissance et redistribution* (Paris, La Découverte).
Galtung, J (1971) 'A Structural Theory of Imperialism' 8(2) *Journal of Peace Research* 81, 117.
—— (1975) *Essays on Peace Research* (Copenhagen, Ejlers).

Gartner, S and Bercovitz, J (2006) 'Overcoming Obstacles to Peace: The Contribution of Mediation to Short-lived Settlements' 50 *International Studies Quarterly* 819, 840.

Gil Tebar, P (1997) 'Entre la médiation politique et la recomposition sociale: l'Église catholique dans le conflit du Chiapas' 97 *Archives de sciences sociales des religions* 63, 72.

Greig, JM (2001) 'Moments of Opportunity. Recognizing Conditions of Ripeness for International Mediation between Enduring Rivals' 45(6) *Journal of Conflict Resolution* 691, 718.

Greig, JM and Diehl, P (2005) 'The Peacekeeping–Peacemaking Dilemma' 49 *International Studies Quarterly* 621, 645.

Hancock, LE (2008) 'The Northern Irish Peace Process: From Top to Bottom' 10 *International Studies Review* 203, 237.

Hareide, D (2003) 'Peace Mediator: The New Norwegian Missionary?' available at: www.nordisk, Forum for Mediation and Conflict Management, Peace Mediation (Norway, 26/07).

Hibou, B (1998) 'Retrait ou redéploiement de l'État' 1 *Critique internationale* 151, 168.

Honneth, A (2002) 'Integrity and Disrespect: Principle of a Conception of Morality based on the Theory of Recognition' 20(2) *Political Theory* 188, 206.

Huntington, SP (1996) *The Clash of Civilizations and the Remaking of New Order* (New York, Simon and Schuster).

Itcaina, X (2007) *Les virtuoses de l'identité. Religion et politique en Pays Basque* (Rennes, Presses universitaires de Rennes).

Kaufman, E and Sosnowski, S (2005) 'The Peru-Ecuador Peace Process: The Contribution of Track Two Diplomacy' in RJ Fisher (ed), *Paving the Way: Contributions of Interactive Conflict Resolution in Peacemaking* (Lanham MD, Lexington Books) 175, 201.

Keller, A (2004) *L'accord de Genève: un pari réaliste* (Paris, Seuil/Labor et Fides).

Kelman, H (2005) 'Interactive Problem Solving in the Israeli-Palestinian Case: Past Contributions and Present Challenges' in RJ Fisher (ed), *Paving the Way: Contributions of Interactive Conflict Resolution in Peacemaking* (Lanham MD, Lexington Books) 41, 63.

Kleiboer, M (1996) 'Understanding Success and Failure in International Mediation' 40 *Journal of Conflict Resolution* 360, 389.

—— (1998) *Success and Failure of International Mediation. The Multiple Realities of Third Party Intervention* (Boulder CO, Lynne Rienner).

Kochan, T (1981) 'Step by Step in the Middle East from the Perspective of the Labor Mediation Process' in JZ Rubin (ed), *Dynamics of Third Party Intervention: Kissinger in the Middle East* (New York, Praeger) 122, 135.

Kydd, A (2003) 'Which Side are you on? Bias, Credibility and Mediation' 47(4) *American Journal of Political Science* 597, 611.

Lederach, JP (2005) *The Moral Imagination: The Art and Soul of Building Peace* (Oxford, Oxford University Press).

Leng, R and Regan, P (2003) 'Social and Political Cultural Effects on the Outcomes of Mediation in Militarized Interstate Disputes' 47 *International Studies Quarterly* 431, 452.

Mack, A (ed) (2005) *Human Security Report, 2005. War and Peace in the 21st Century* (Human Security Centre, University of British Columbia).
Mansvelt-Beck, J (2005) *Territory and Terror: Conflicting Nationalisms in the Basque Country* (London, Routledge).
Mareschal, P (2003) 'Solving Problems and Transformative Relationships. The Bifocal Approach to Mediation' 33(4) *American Review of Public Administration* 423, 448.
Marret, JL (2000) 'Les ONG et la médiation de la paix: l'exemple de la communauté Sant'Egidio' 1 *Annuaire français de relations internationales* 1, 11.
—— (2001) *La fabrication de la paix, nouveaux conflits, nouveaux acteurs, nouvelles méthodes* (Paris, Ellipses).
Mars, P (2001) 'Ethnic Politics, Mediation and Conflict Resolution: The Guyana Experience' 38(3) *Journal of Peace Research* 353, 372.
Monk, G, Winsdale, J, Crocket, K and Epston, D (1997) *Narrative Therapy in Practice: The Archaeology of Hope* (San Francisco, Jossey Bank).
Mooradian, M and Druckman, D (1999) 'Hurting Stalemate or Mediation? The Conflict over Nagorno-Karabakh 1990–1995' 36(6) *Journal of Peace Research* 709, 727.
Nelson, J (2000) *The Business of Peace: the Private Sector as a Partner in Conflict Prevention and Resolution* (London, Prince of Wales, Business Leaders Forum).
Nye, J (1990) 'Soft power' *Foreign Policy* 80, 153–171.
Ott, MC (1972) 'Mediation as a Method of Conflict Resolution: Two Cases' 26(4) *International Organization* 595, 618.
Palard, J (2006) 'Médiation et institution catholique' 133 *Archives de sciences sociales des religions* 9, 26.
Paris, R and Sisk, TD (eds) (2009) *The Dilemmas of Statebuilding. Confronting the Contradictions of Postwar Peace Operations* (London, Routledge).
Peace Brigades International, *Annual Review* 2006–07, available at: www.peacebrigades.org.
Princen, T (1992) *Intermediaries in International Conflict* (Princeton NJ, Princeton University Press).
—— (1994) 'Joseph Elder. Quiet Peacemaking in a Civil War' in DM Kolb (ed), *When Talks Works: Profiles of Mediators* (San Francisco, Jossey-Bass) 428, 445.
Regan, P and Stam, A (2000) 'In the Nick of Time: Conflict Management, Mediation Timing and the Duration of Interstate Disputes' 44(2) *International Studies Quarterly* 239, 260.
Richmond, O (1998) 'Devious Objectives and the Disputants' View of International Mediation. A Theoretical Framework' 35(6) *Journal of Peace Research* 707, 722.
—— (2001) 'A Genealogy of Peacemaking: The Creation and Re-creation of Order' 26(3) Alternatives 317, 348.
Rubin, J (1992) 'International Mediation in Context' in J Bercovitch and J Rubin (eds), *Mediation in International Relations: Approaches to Conflict Management* (New York, St Martin's Press) 249, 272.
Santiso, J (1998) 'Circulation des idées et relations internationales' in MC Smouts (ed), *Les nouvelles relations internationales* (Paris, Presses de Science Po) 227, 251.

Saunders, H (2001) 'Prenegotiation and Circum-negotiation: Arenas of the Multilevel Peace Process' in C Crocker, F Hampson and P Aall (eds), *Turbulent Peace: The Challenges of Managing International Conflict* (Washington DC, United Institute of Peace Press) 483, 496.

Siniver, AP (2006) 'Impartiality and Timing: Three Hypotheses on Third Party Mediation in the Middle East' 54(4) *Political Studies* 806, 826.

Smith, A and Stam, A (2003) 'Mediation and Peacekeeping in a Random Walk Model of Civil and Interstate War' 5(4) *International Review Studies* 115, 135.

Stedman, SJ (1991) *Peacemaking in Civil War* (Boulder CO, Lynne Rienner).

Taylor, C (1994) *Multiculturalism. Examining the Politics of Recognition* (Princeton NJ, Princeton University Press).

Touval, S and Zartman, W (eds) (1985) *International Mediation in Theory and Practice* (Boulder CO, Westview Press).

Wehr, P and Lederach, JP (1991) 'Mediating Conflict in Central America' 28(1) *Journal of Peace Research* 85, 98.

Wicquefort van, A (1680–81) *L'Ambassadeur et ses fonctions* (The Hague, J & D Steucker).

Wilkenfeld, J, Young, K, Asal, V and Quinn, D (2003) 'Mediating International Crises. Cross National and Experimental Perspectives' 47(3) *Journal of Conflict Resolution* 279, 301.

Williams, A (1999) 'Conflict Resolution after the Cold War: The Case of Moldavia' 25(1) *Review of International Studies* 71, 86.

Yarrow, CH (1978) *Quaker Experiences in International Conciliation* (New Haven CT, Yale University Press).

Zartman, W (2000) 'Ripeness: The Hurting Stalemate and Beyond' in PC Sternand and D Druckman (eds), *International Conflict Resolution after the Cold War* (Washington DC, National Academy Press) 225, 250.

Zartman, W and Touval, S (1996) 'International Mediation: Conflict Resolution and Power Politics' in C Crockett, F Hampson and P Aall (eds), *Managing Global Chaos* (Washington DC, United States Institute of Peace Press).

Zehr, H (1990) *Changing Lenses, a New Focus for Crime and Justice* (Scottdale, Herald Press).

Part I

Ethical Stakes of Mediation Practices

2

Historical Contribution to the Ethical and Methodological Principles of Mediation

MANEL CANYAMERES AND ANNE CATHERINE SALBERG

I. INTRODUCTION

IN THE FINAL quarter of the twentieth century, the figure of the mediator as a professional that plays a role in conflict management and intervention emerges. In his introduction, Faget (2005) emphasises the broad definition of mediation in the field of political conflicts and its close relationship to the ethics of mediation.

This issue of the variety of models of action for mediation, and of ethical and methodological principles, occurs in all fields of mediation. The typologies that classify the role of the mediator as *facilitator*, *interventionist* (negotiator, formulator) or *expert* (therapist for the family mediators (Roberts, 1988), evaluator for commercial mediators or manipulator for political mediators (Slim, 2007)) are noteworthy. In this last model, the *expert mediator*, regardless of his field of intervention, focuses on the agreement to be reached with great risk of instrumentalisation, while the *facilitative mediator* is oriented towards the process and emphasises communication between the 'parties to the conflict'[1] more than the result to be obtained.

Is it possible, within this diversity of models and practices of mediation in different contexts, to establish ethical principles and deontological common rules?

There is a European tradition of mediation of political conflicts that is firmly rooted in history, which defines the ethical principles of a mediation practice that is similar to the meaning of the definition proposed in the introduction to this book: 'a consensual process of conflict regulation in

[1] According to the terminology used by Duss-von Werdt, J, *Einführung in Mediation* (Heidelberg, Carl-Auer Verlag, 2007).

which an impartial, independent third party without any decision-making power help people or institutions to improve or set up relations through exchanges and, as far as possible, to solve their conflicts'.

This chapter will consider the figure of the mediator in European history (I) and the links that can be established presently with the ethical stance of the mediator (II). Across the centuries, European political history has been replete with wars, the handling of which has happily culminated in the form of treaties. These treaties, in turn, have had a tremendous impact, as they have been the source of nations' legislation, a topic that been widely studied in the work of Lesaffer (2004). But what is of most interest to us here is not so much their impact but the *process* of their gestation, and specifically the advance work of mediators in reaching their conclusion.

II. THE FIGURE OF THE MEDIATOR IN HISTORY

This short historical overview of the figure of the mediator will be mainly based on the work of Professor Duss-von Werdt (2005), one of the rare authors with Murray and Lacey (2008), to our knowledge, who has conducted in-depth research on the written sources of the European history of mediation.

(a) On the Traces of the Homo Mediator

According to Duss-von Werdt, mediation in Europe can be documented back 2600 years, with the first hard copies of the action of Solon, 'mediator and archon',[2] in the sixth century BC. Admittedly, such research can lead to a-historical considerations, since the author is not a historian but rather a mediator and a philosopher, and the sources are insufficient to explain all. Therefore, his line of work is to seek 'the spirit of mediation' and show how a *homo mediator* develops. He is committed to emphasising a constant: they are always human beings who are called on to work, whether or not they have a personal interest, encouraging dialogue between human beings, sometimes successfully. The continuous development of a concept that would lead to improvement of mediation cannot be identified. However, it can be shown that in European history there is a practice that, for twenty-first century mediators, allows one to become aware that the current deontological standards have already been applied for over two millennia.

[2] Aristotle in 'State of Athenians' in Athens.

In this study we will be analysing two chapters in history that have left us with documentary evidence written by direct witnesses of the work that took place in the lead up to peace treaties. The first of these was the Treaty of Münster and Osnabrück (1648) which marked the end of the Thirty Years' War, which was sparked off in 1618 as a result of a 'local' dispute in Prague (the Kingdom of Bohemia) between the Catholic king and the Protestant princes and then mushroomed into a Europe-wide war. And the second treaty, though not quite as significant as the first, was the Treaty of Ryswick (1697) which put an end to the Grand Alliance war involving England, Spain, the Holy Roman Empire and the United Provinces, also known as the Nine Years' War.

Before going into the methods used to put these treaties together, it is necessary to make a few observations on their scope and subsequent impact. First, we need to start by looking at the massive complexity of the underlying causes that spark off wars. A broad-ranging study (Holsti, 1991) shows that in many cases the reasons, or 'issues' as he calls them, are not fully considered in the treaty agreements and therefore the original conflict is not properly resolved, breaking out again at a later date. Holsti says that we need to go beyond the question 'Why war?' and ask ourselves 'What are they fighting about or over'. The explanation then becomes teleological: wars occur not 'because of' but 'in order to'. He therefore believes that if the end objectives being sought by the war are not achieved, they will emerge once again.

In his study, Holsti analyses wars between 1648 and 1989, obviously including the two wars that led to the treaties we will be looking at later on, and he concluded that in most cases peace treaties only achieve the objective of ending the war (armistice) and do not envisage any possible future conflicts. To quote him: '(peace treaties) provide a pause until the next round of war', and he finishes his work by stating quite categorically: 'peace then becomes the father of war'. While respecting his conclusions, and accepting the limitations of peace treaties, this gives us no reason to underestimate the work that goes into their preparation and the role of the mediators who, as we know, are not responsible for the content of these agreements which is incumbent upon the parties who sign them.

Having put forward these considerations, we will now take a look at how mediators intervene in the process of reaching agreements that lead to peace treaties. On 24 October 1648, the treaties of Münster and Osnabrück marked an end to the Thirty Years' War. This was the first time that the relations between the states with regard to the absolute sovereignty of each state were defined (the principle of non-interference). After extensive preparations, this peace, which was known as the Peace of Westphalia, inaugurated a new era; that of the balance of powers and the coexistence of several Christian faiths. It was also the time of emergence of the Nation States with their corollary, the principle of national sovereignty.

(i) Alvise Contarini and Fabio Chigi, Mediators of the Peace of Münster

The modalities of success of this treaty were remarkable: this peace was concluded thanks to mediation rather than on the battle field by the triumph of one party and the defeat of the other. The negotiations were conducted for several years (1643–48) by two mediators, the nuncio Fabio Chigi (1599–1667, the future Alexander VII), a cardinal mediator designated by the Pope and the ambassador Alvise Contarini (1601–84), designated by the Republic of Venice. The former was to conciliate the Catholic powers, the latter to manage the United Provinces, Sweden and the German Protestant princes. Contarini, who worked on this conflict from 1636,[3] settled in Münster in 1643, where he remained for six years. The nuncio Chigi was only named later—although he also arrived in Münster in 1643—because the French remained strongly opposed to the idea of mediation and were wary of the mediators proposed by the Pope. Contarini succeeded in negotiating the ongoing presence of Chigi in Münster. If Contarini received his instructions from the Venetian Senate in 1643, 'interposition and mediation to facilitate and remedy the difficulties arising that could be opposed to the conclusion of peace' (Duss-von Werdt, 2005: 272), Chigi only received his instructions in 1644.[4] His mission was not clearly defined. He was to encourage the Catholic interests and could not negotiate with the 'heretic' Protestant princes, although he himself was assigned to negotiate a 'European *pax universalis*'. Chigi received the following specific instructions:

— To maintain an even temper (*indifferentia*) towards the parties in order to never lose their confidence.
— To avoid proposing solutions to the parties.
— To maintain secrecy about what one party said, except about that which he was authorised to communicate to the other party to support peace (at the time of the shuttle mediation).
— Not to agree to arbitrate, either on his own behalf or in the name of the Pope, in order not to renounce the idea that His Holiness is the Father of all.
— To seek the peace of religions, the good of each Catholic prince, and fight together against the common enemy, the Turks.
— To overcome difficulties with patience and forbearance.
— To propose that the weapons be laid down in order to better negotiate

[3] The Pope and the Republic of Venice attempted mediation from 1636 and proposed that a peace conference be held in Cologne; this did not take place due to lack of agreement by the parties to the conflict. The structure was nevertheless maintained, and Contarini worked on it until the conclusion of peace in 1648.

[4] In fact, Rome initially gave this instruction about mediation to its legate (Cardinal Ginetti) to prepare the Cologne conference in 1636.

The working method of the two mediators can be summarised as follows:

Shuttle Mediation

It was usual that the mediator would meet the parties to communicate the negotiation offers of the other party. It is believed that Contarini held over 800 individual interviews with this method.

Diplomatic Communication

Contarini, a career ambassador, was an experienced negotiator. He held talks between 'four eyes' in his residence in order to advise the parties on negotiation tactics. Chigi worked skilfully in his role of negotiator with regard to specific issues and his mission of mediator, in which he maintained a distance from representation of the political interests of the Church.

Co-Mediation

Contarini and Chigi worked together a great deal, shuttling between the parties to the conflict. They followed the same rules, particularly that of showing complete impartiality. They never accepted gifts, nor invited the parties to their table. Nevertheless, since both of them were Italian, they were regularly subject to judgement by France, which reproached them for failing to oppose Spain. As a result, they made proposals to overcome the rivalries (for example, in 1645 Contarini proposed that the future Louis XIV and the Spanish Infanta should marry).[5]

Contarini was about to abandon his role on several occasions. However, he always maintained the will to be a mediator of peace. Finally, he was very proud of his work and reported that these 12 years of pre-mediation and mediation were a 'singular period in the world'. Indeed, it can be said that since the Peace of Westphalia, 'the principle of mediation for peace by one or more third parties not involved in the conflict can be valued ... as a European standard' (Duss-von Werdt, 2005: 43). Chigi had received a mission of mediation, which he considered incompatible with the arbitration that the parties wished him to endorse. Like Contarini, he found it difficult to work in a climate of mistrust, intrigues and diplomatic falsification, and to follow his principles when the parties continuously attempted to instrumentalise the mediators.

With Duss-von Werdt we can conclude retrospectively that these two mediators succeeded in developing political mediation by establishing new

[5] Peace between France and Spain was not concluded until 10 years later, in 1658, and the marriage between Louis XIV and the Spanish Infanta in 1660 sealed the peace.

requirements between the states and the faiths. These developments are still valid today and take on new dimensions of interculturality with regard to the need to regulate common life and activities on the local as well as the global level, while negotiating the diversity of traditions and cultures.

(ii) Abraham de Wicquefort—A Theoretician of Practice

We will continue this journey with a Dutch seventeenth-century author, Abraham de Wicquefort (1606–82) who theorised about the practice of the mediators of his time in his posthumous work, *L'Ambassadeur et ses fonctions* (1686). Diplomat and 'trainer' of diplomats, he worked primarily at the service of France, where he lived for over 30 years. His highly rigorous relationship with the authorities led him to be sent to prison on several occasions. Nevertheless, he was a successful posthumous writer. His work was written in ancient French, republished several times and translated into German.

This book includes a chapter entitled 'On Mediation and Ambassador Mediators'. This contribution to the practice and theory of mediation included many examples from the fifteenth to the seventeenth century. The value of his writing lies in development of a specific theory about the activity of mediation and evaluation of the practice of this theory. He refers particularly to the peace treaty of Westphalia. As a Brandenburg diplomat in France, it is likely that he witnessed the treaty. His work comprises specific examples of the difficulties encountered at the time of the peace of Münster and proposes an extensive reflection on mediation. It contains deontological elements that are used regularly by present-day mediators. In this respect, it represents the first handbook for mediators. Therefore, it seems to us to be particularly interesting to reproduce lengthy excerpts that, after more than 300 years, are still highly topical for contemporary mediators, regardless of the type of conflict they must deal with. Quotations from the original text of the main rules of mediation are shown below.

The Absence of Power of the Mediator

> Power is not required by the Mediator at all, and these two ministers had none of it. The word Mediator expresses the function quite well: it consists strictly of intervention in the situation to bring together the parties that have become distant.
>
> The position of Mediator is one of the most difficult that the Ambassador must hold: and Mediation is one of his most tiresome tasks. The Prince that he represents must be disinterested, and his Minister should lack passion, which is neither effortless nor very common (...) That is why one must be extremely cautious in offering to intervene, and adjust one's behaviour so that there can be no suspicion of bias in any way.
>
> He should gain the confidence of the parties, so that that they discover their true sentiments.

> The instruction ... [given] ... recommends moderation and patience.
>
> It can be truthfully said that it is not the Mediators that make the treaties: it is the goodwill of the parties that allows them to be concluded.

The Independence of the Mediator

> The Princes did not always accept the proposed mediation (...) the real reason was that the Emperor did not wish to have a Mediator between himself and the Protestant Princes, since he considered them to be subjects.
>
> The Minister Mediator should be as disinterested as the Prince that assigns him this task (...) In fact, the Mediators had great difficulty in Münster, with little success, and even less honor. Their intentions were good, but they encountered animosity from all sides, which the strongest reasons in the world were unable to temper (...) they were considered as suspects by some and unpleasant by others.
>
> He should not arbitrate nor allow the matter to be undertaken by the Pope as, instead of a Mediator, he would become a judge.

The Impartiality of the Mediator

> And in fact, it was only the Papal nuncio, who received all the written statements, proposals, responses and replies, and kept them in his home: it was he that communicated them to the parties, and signed only the replies.
>
> He should maintain secrecy, and only communicate to one of the parties that which the other party wishes.
>
> If the Mediators are required by one of the parties to make a proposal to the other party, they must not hesitate, although it may be misinterpreted. (...) The Office of the Mediator obliged them to report promptly to one of the parties the proposal that the other party had instructed them.
>
> The Mediators (...) told them that they were not able to judge the content of the proposals. That the duty of the mediation allowed them only to report faithfully what was said, not to judge the fairness or righteousness of the proposals, or make proposals in order to facilitate conclusion of the treaty, as this would exceed the power of their mission.
>
> [The instruction ... given] recommended first and above all, indifference, [so] that no partiality would be seen in his conduct, and no meaning would be attached to the words and actions of the servants.

(iii) François de Callières—French Diplomat

Almost 40 years after the Münster Treaty, the Ryswick Treaty was signed (1697) and hence the end of the war known as the War of the League of Augsburg. A direct witness of the preparation process of that treaty was the French diplomat and cabinet secretary to King Louis XIV, François de

Callières (1645–1717). As a result of his experience with this treaty, he left an invaluable work that also has merit today: *De la manière de négocier avec les souverains* (de Caillères, 1716).

In this work, he describes in meticulous detail the method of dealing with a prince, taking into account both political and personal factors. Issues as specific as 'the natural pride inherent in their status as princes' can be translated in the present day to mediation between two parties between which there is an obvious imbalance of power. The ethical stance of the mediator in these situations is a complex one, and has given rise to many doctrinal discussions on the limits of mediation. De Callières is illuminating on this point, although in a different historical context, but one which can be seen today in nations with different degrees of power.

Meanwhile, the process that leads to obtaining a satisfactory treaty is a laborious one, and requires meticulous preparation, the result of which is its efficacy—in other words, that it endures. However obvious this may seem, it is important to state the following:

> It is impossible for a treaty to exist unless it is based on reciprocal benefits; and when this maxim is not fulfilled, these agreements will not endure and will end up self-destructing. Thus the big secret… entails knowing how to find the means to allow benefits to be shared and, given these circumstances, to try to increase them at an equal rate for both parties.
>
> (de Caillères, 1716: 90)

From this we can extrapolate a maxim that is a factor in present-day mediation: focusing more on the process, 'letting common interests prosper' than worrying too much about the end result. And from the two authors mentioned above, whose words we have used as an example though others could be found in the details of the treaties, we take the leap into the present day.

(b) Lessons to be Learnt from History?

Called on to handle an international conflict, dealing with many states, kingdoms, principalities and paramilitary organisations, the mediators worked for five years without departing from certain standards of action, namely:

- To maintain impartiality (impartial neutrality).
- To refuse to be used by the parties and not assume any role other than that of mediator—not to become an arbitrator.
- To not be involved in the conflict, nor to have any course of action other than accompanying the parties in finding a peace agreement.
- To gain the trust of the parties by ensuring confidentiality.
- To never make proposals and to report the proposals made by either of the parties without judging them.

— To be without power, to handle the in-between position to attempt to bring together the parties that have become distant.
— To believe in the good faith of the parties in order to reach an agreement.

As a result of this, at the time of the Hague Peace Conference in 1907, a declaration in favour of just mediation in order to prevent wars was drafted within the framework of the Convention for the Pacific Settlement of International Disputes. This Convention provided a whole part dedicated entirely to good offices and mediation:

> [I]n case of serious disagreement or dispute, before an appeal to arms, the Contracting Powers agree to have recourse, as far as circumstances allow, to the good offices or mediation of one or more friendly Powers (....) The part of the mediator consists in reconciling the opposing claims and appeasing the feelings of resentment which may have arisen between the States at variance.[6]

In connection with this Convention, Nicolas Politis, in his article entitled 'The Future of Mediation' (1910) estimated that for mediation to be successful, it was necessary above all for the mediator to gain the confidence of the two parties and the recognition of his impartiality and wisdom. The author considered that such qualities were so rare that in most cases it was not possible to find a mediator.

III. THE ETHICAL POSTURE OF THE MEDIATOR

Is this figure of the wise and impartial mediator impossible to find nowadays? Other fields of mediation such as family, commercial or civil mediation, which have consolidated over the past decades, are supported by ethical principles that are not much different from those described above. While drawing a historical parallel, we will reconsider the three ethical subjects dealt with in the first chapter 'The Metamorphosis of Peacemaking' that should play a central role in any mediation: independence, impartiality and the lack of decision-making power of the mediator (often described as the principle of neutrality in many deontological codes) and set these against some present-day mediation situations in political conflicts.

(a) The Independence of the Mediator

We saw that the choice of mediators for Münster was crucial and was the object of extensive negotiations. What occurs at present in political mediation? Who are the mediators? What sort of independence do the mediators

[6] Permanent Court of Arbitration, 1907 Convention for the Pacific Settlement of International Disputes, arts 2 and 4.

claim? How can they guarantee such independence if they have financial or political ties to a state that has geostrategic interests at stake in the area of conflict? Quite often, even the mediating NGOs impose a Western model. As mentioned ironically, we have evolved from the figure of the missionary that arrived, settled and learned the local language to the mediator that arrives, leaves and only speaks English.[7]

The mediator or team of mediators should guarantee sufficient autonomy to the parties in order to be able to intervene, as mediators, in the process of conflict management. The potential transformation of the conflict will be greater if the mediator is independent and freely accepted by all parties, outside any political pressure. The independence of the mediator means that he should not have any direct or indirect interest in the controversy and the financing for his activity should respect his autonomy of action. An obvious example is the community or citizens' mediation involved in disputes between neighbours, a service provided by a town council or public administration. The community mediator maintains his independence in managing the dispute, although he is paid by the public administration which evidently has an interest in resolving the conflict.

The question of independence is crucial for the mediator. The more his mission depends on powerful institutions (such as the public ministry for a penal mediator), the more the mediator will have to ensure that he will be above any partisan interests and not accept instructions from anyone. The mediator should be free to examine any relevant issue without seeking approval of governmental or international bodies.

Chigi and Contarini took years to gain the acceptance of the parties, although in some cases they remained wary until the end. However, while refusing to abandon their role as mediators, and not seeking to arbitrate the conflict, they maintained their independence in spite of their proximity to the Roman Catholic Church, which was a major actor of the conflict. Their only aim was that the parties would conclude a peace agreement on their own, in spite of the extremely complex nature of this political and religious conflict that kept Europe in blood and fire for 30 years.

This ethical principle of independence guides active mediators in all fields of mediation. Could it not be adopted nowadays by political mediators, regardless of their model of intervention and the complexity of the conflict considered?

(b) The Impartiality of the Mediator

To arrive at a peaceful and negotiated solution, the mediator should guarantee that his role will be that of an impartial third party. This impartiality

[7] This is mentioned by Faget in his chapter quoting Dag Hareide.

will allow him to gain the confidence of the parties and ensure his legitimacy. Our experience shows that the mediator is in danger, and with him the process of mediation, when the parties involve him in the conflict. In this case, the mediator is 'jointly responsible' for the conflict and, as a result, the process itself becomes distorted. The dynamic is lost and the risk of failure increases. Although it is difficult to remain outside the conflict, the mediator should always maintain his posture of a non-involved third party. He must resist, on the one hand, being part of the conflict, and on the other, judging it.

In order to achieve this, the mediator should preserve the confidentiality of the process. Confidentiality is a key element in the processes carried out by mediators of civil or criminal conflicts. The information obtained in mediation is confidential and cannot be used except by express agreement of the parties. The mediator is bound to secrecy with regard to third parties. He should not testify nor summon to testify before a legal body, or report to the governing institution. He should inform the parties of the limits of confidentiality, whether ethical or legal.

Nowadays, in the case of mediation in major business conflicts where confidential information is at stake (know-how, technology, patents, etc) that could put the actual continuity of companies at risk, it would be unthinkable for this mediation not to be based on the strict principle of confidentiality. This is exactly the same model as that described by de Wicquefort, which emphasises the absence of initiative and power of the mediator (often referred to by modern mediators as neutrality) as well as the confidentiality guaranteed to the parties.

In many political conflicts, peace talks are given a very prominent role in the media with enormous stakes in communication. Would political mediators not achieve a better result by maintaining the media at a distance and keeping strict confidentiality about the processes they carry out?

Slim (2007: 27) proposes balancing the principles of confidentiality and transparency. He recommends distinguishing between the general information about the process and the work of the mediator. Any information that is made available to the parties by the mediator should obtain the explicit consent of each of the parties involved, unless it is in the interests of the peace process. Lastly, the mediator, because of his duty of independence, should be free to establish contacts with all organisations or states that are likely to support the current peace process, while maintaining his duty of confidentiality.

In modern political conflicts, a link can be established between the figure of the mediator and his popularity. The more the political mediator bases his action on his personal notoriety, the more he will be tempted to value his role publicly and to make proposals to achieve the success of his mission quickly.[8] Organisations such as the Centre for Humanitarian Dialogue, on

[8] We think particularly of the role of mediator played in 2008 by the President of the European Union in the Georgian conflict.

the other hand, base their effectiveness on the absolute secrecy of the peace processes they direct, and even refuse to reveal the conflicts they are dealing with. They only report them when the peace agreement has been signed. Should a good mediator not be modest and humble regardless of his notoriety since, as recalled by de Wicquefort, 'in fact, the Mediators had great difficulty in Münster, with little success, and even less honor'? Should not the only role of the mediator be mediation?

(c) The Lack of Power of the Mediator

The question of the power of the mediator arises particularly depending on the model chosen and the status of the mediator. However, self-determination is an essential principle of mediation that is based on the capacity of the parties to conclude a voluntary arrangement without constraints, within the framework of the mediation process.

The experience of many mediators—regardless of their model of intervention and the complexity and gravity of the conflict they are dealing with—shows that the parties often wait for the mediator to resolve the conflict by providing the solution. Therefore, beginning the process of legitimisation from the posture of an expert and interventionist, as believed by the parties, is not ethically incompatible, if this leads to initiate the process of mediation and subsequently this legitimisation is transformed into the role of facilitator as the process develops. The mediator, as an expert in the process and without expertise in the contents of the agreements to be reached, will be very directive at the beginning of mediation. He will not negotiate the structure of his intervention, which he will impose on the parties especially if they consider the conflict cannot be resolved. At the same time, the lack of willingness decreases the involvement of the parties significantly, not only in development of the dialogue of mediation, but in that the future agreement will lack the guarantees required for fulfilment.

It may occur that even the willingness of the parties participating in a mediation process cannot be considered, due to a situation in which there is no protection of human rights, or in dictatorial states where intervention by a third party is limited or politicised. This is part of the mediator's ethical responsibility to plan his role, and decide whether if he must persist or desist with regard to the feasibility of the mediation, if his intervention may also be counterproductive.

The parties to the conflict should accept their responsibility and obligation to deal with the conflict, since it is theirs. The mediator is there to help them do so by facilitating dialogue. However, he cannot and should not take on a prominent role. An excess of support has a negative effect on assuming responsibility for the conflict, as well as the possible final agreement.

Finally, we would like to emphasise the power of the mediator in terms of directing the process, and not taking responsibility for the contents of the agreement, which corresponds solely to the parties. A peace process managed within the framework of mediation should aim to reach an agreement that is acceptable for all the parties to the conflict, without the mediator imposing his solution by force or constraint.

If we consider the conditions of the conclusion of the Treaty of Westphalia and the words of de Wicquefort: 'It can be truthfully said that it is not the Mediators that make the treaties: it is the goodwill of the parties that allows them to be concluded' can we not say they seem to be remarkably modern, regardless of the field of action of the mediator of conflicts and his model of intervention?

IV. CONCLUSION

Over 300 years ago, Chigi and Contarini, as mediators of the peace of Münster, developed a model of mediation that offers an appropriate response to current challenges. The work of de Wicquefort has left us a testimony of this, and other authors, such as de Callières, have added complementary elements. Admittedly, like many present-day political mediators, Chigi, as nephew of the Pope and future Pope, was a powerful mediator. However, in spite of his prestigious stature, he had to continuously ensure his legitimacy—particularly with regard to the French, who sought to use him in their conflict with Spain. As papal legate, he refused to arbitrate the conflicts between the Catholic powers. The sole objective of these two mediators was for the parties themselves to arrive at a peaceful resolution without resorting to coercion. They maintained a rigorous ethical stance of independence, impartial neutrality and absence of power to impose solutions. They believed that an agreement can only be reached as a result of the 'willingness of the parties'.

The ethical standards developed by de Wicquefort and used by the mediators Chigi and Contarini are still of interest for many twenty-first century mediators. These rules can be found in the deontological codes or European reference texts followed by most mediators of conflicts.[9] Ethical principles such as impartiality, confidentiality, independence and the lack of power of the mediator, which are the key elements of any mediation and are required to ensure successful development of a mediation process, are weak in many political 'mediation' processes. We might ask why the mediators of modern political conflicts could not also refer to this model of action developed by

[9] We are thinking particularly of the recommendations of the Council of Europe on family mediation (Rec 98(1)); mediation in criminal matters (Rec 99(19)) and civil matters (Rec 2002(10).

two of their counterparts, with regard to a conflict whose scale, difficulty and duration have few equivalents in the modern day world, in order to give a true chance to mediation.

REFERENCES

Callières de F, (1716) *De la manière de négocier avec les souverains* (Pour la Compagnie, Amsterdam).

Duss-von Werdt, J (2005) *Homo mediator. Geschichte und Menschenbild der Mediation* (Stuttgart, Klett-Cotta).

—— (2007) *Einführung in Mediation* (Heidelberg, Carl-Auer Verlag).

Faget, J (2005) *Médiation et action publique, la dynamique du fluide* (Bordeaux, Presses Universitaires de Bordeaux).

Holsti, KJ (1991) *Peace and War: Armed Conflicts and International Order 1648–1989* (Cambridge, Cambridge University Press).

Lesaffer, R (ed) (2004) *Peace Treaties in International Law in European History: From the Late Middle Ages to World War One* (Cambridge, Cambridge University Press).

Murray, W and Lacey, J (2008) *The Making of Peace: Rules, States, and the Aftermath of War* (Cambridge, Cambridge University Press).

Politis, N (1910) 'L'avenir de la médiation' *Revue générale de droit internationale public* 136–63.

Roberts, S (1988) 'Three Models of Family Mediation' in R Dingwall and J Eekelaar (eds), *Divorce Mediation and the Legal Process* (Oxford, Clarendon Press) 144–50.

Slim, H (2007) *Guide de la médiation. Conduire des processus de paix lors de conflits armés* (Genève, Centre pour le dialogue humanitaire).

Wicquefort, de A (1686) *L'ambassadeur et ses fonction* (Veneur, La Haye).

3

Human Rights and Mediation—A Much Discussed but not Resolved Relationship: Views on International Cooperation

VIOLA BOELSCHER

THIS CONTRIBUTION TO the subject of 'mediation of national and international political conflicts' will focus on the complex relationship between human rights and mediation—based on the author's experience of working in several conflict and post-conflict countries and countries in transition—as well as on the means of practitioners working in this field.

In this case, the term 'mediation' will be used in a broad sense, based on conflict-transformation including pre-conciliation, conciliation and reconciliation phases and the whole area of peace building. In the same broad sense, the terms of 'international community' and 'international cooperation' will be used. The examples used for this chapter have to be restrained to a general level so as to obey the declarations of confidentiality.

The challenges for peace do not stop after signing peace agreements; they grow even more due to the beginning of the complicated phase of implementation: the efforts for peace building. The pre-conciliation phase can take years, several countries or groups of countries to accompany these processes and support talks of strengthening the preconditions for peace negotiations, such as safe places, travel guarantees etc as well as the assignment of mediators. These high diplomacy efforts can be supported through assistance from international cooperation for micro and meso-level activities to give some 'motivation' from the bottom to the top. Protection and support for peace communities are possible development strategies.[1]

[1] Eg, The Peace Brigades International, tries to protect Colombian peace communities through their presence.

On signing peace agreements or ceasefire agreements, long-term efforts for peace building can be undertaken, whereby international cooperation needs a special commitment to continue this support on a long-term basis. In a war and conflict-affected society the question is how and when to provide support without doing harm and without giving priority to peace at the expense of fulfilling human rights. Verification missions[2] and peace builders face this problem quite often although in theory the institutions claim for 'Peace *with* Justice'.[3]

I. HUMAN RIGHTS AND MEDIATION

Some mediation principles are worth highlighting in the context of peace negotiations so as to make them useful for the implementation of peace-building strategies and to relate them to human rights. Although the specific context is different from the mediation processes, the same important principles should be adhered to. It appears to be necessary to redefine some of the terms which will be referred to in the following text.

The first principle to be discussed is the participation in peace negotiations. As known from mediation processes, it is crucial to discover and involve all essential parties at the different stages during the development of a peace agreement as well as its implementation and the peace-building process; if this does not happen, the probability of long lasting peace will decrease (Galtung, 2003). Besides considering widespread participation as necessary for the success of the mediation process, it is possible to understand this objective as fulfilling the human rights of political participation guaranteed through Article 25 ICCPR.[4] This means that people have the international protected human right to participation. Using this human-rights based approach it is possible to change the way peace talks will be organised in the future.

The second important issue to tackle is the concept of *impartiality*. Impartiality is one of the central principles of a mediation process. But is it possible and is it ethically correct to be impartial in a situation with numerous human rights violations and crimes against humanity, involving strikingly high numbers of individuals and groups who have been victims of those actions? To be impartial facing these kinds of situations may be

[2] Specific UN missions as UNAMA or regional institution such as the Organization of the Islamic Conference (OIC) or Organization of American States (OAS).

[3] Eg, the Carter Center Peace Programme.

[4] International Covenant on Civil and Political Rights, 1966.

understood as a new human rights violation by the victims since their trauma and suffered harm does not seem to be recognised. To be neutral and impartial, or even to be empathetic seems to be too aloof when listening to certain human rights violations. It is possible to be impartial concerning actors, when referring to the international human rights framework, but not regarding acts. Human rights can be understood and recognised as a perfect catalogue of transcendence (Galtung 2003). The concept of '*Allparteilichkeit*' (impartiality) offers the possibility of debating values and violated values. Universal human rights are the valid benchmark for every party within the conflict. Based on these universal rights, it is possible that criteria for affirmation or criticism can grow—even for partiality in asymmetric conflicts.

The third important point to be highlighted here is the need to agree on the agenda. In every single mediation process, one of the first steps is to agree on an agenda for the mediation process (Farré Salvá, 2004). It may be worth assigning the same principle to peace processes and to decide on the relevant time frame. This means it is possible that the first step after having signed a peace agreement is to ensure security and only later begin talks about the prosecution of former human rights perpetrators and reconciliation between the divided groups.

A peace agreement officially puts an end to an armed conflict, recognises former agreements on the cessation of hostilities and should therefore stop violence and mass human rights violation. Yet, in reality severe problems are faced in fulfilling that expectation. The case of Guatemala[5] and its recent history and development can make the issue more understandable. The alarming Guatemalan figures on homicides and femicides explain the urgent need for reaction. Since 1995, one year before the peace agreements were signed, until 2006, the rate of homicides and femicides per 100,000 inhabitants increased from 38 to 47.[6] Only 2 per cent of these cases have been resolved by the police. One reason for the rise in violence is the fact that since the war ended clandestine groups have continuously operated in close proximity to governmental and state institutions. The battle against impunity is nearly impossible, since these structures have not been tackled within the peace agreements or further peace-building activities.[7] The so-called 'amnesty law' declared a broad amnesty except for genocide, torture and forced disappearances. To this formalised amnesty, the amnesty de facto due to threats, attacks and pressure against human rights activists

[5] The author lived in Guatemala from 1999 to 2003 and worked in different non-governmental human rights organisations and for the United Nations Human Rights Commission.

[6] UNDP, 'Informe estadístico de la violencia en Guatemala (Guatemala, 2007).

[7] *Ibid.*

in Guatemala must be added (Álvarez, 2007). Guatemala is considered to be a country in peace, but the criminal statistics reflect a quite different situation. The peace agreement provided a broad amnesty for alleged human rights violators and perpetrators. Only in December 2006, was an International Commission against Impunity established and started work.[8] The amnesty law and the informal amnesty politics have caused the continuity of illegalised criminal groups and the incapacity of the police to fight against them, and therefore the high level of impunity even in cases of homicides and femicides.[9]

Finally, one may ask why it was not possible to include a broader aspect of justice into the peace talks and later peace agreements. As simple as it seems, due to the fact that former human rights violators participate in negotiating peace, it is quite challenging to be able to tackle the point of justice and human rights violations within the peace talks and peace agreements. To achieve it later depends on the power relation within the society and government. The 1999 elections in Guatemala were won by the party of the dictator who was in power in the early 1980s when the worst massacres against the indigenous population occurred. This former dictator, Rios Montt, was president of the Guatemalan Congress between 1999 and 2004 (Goldmann, 2004). This means that conflict transformation has to handle a critical level of power imbalances.

Of the lessons that have been learnt, which could be adopted by the international cooperation when working in a post-conflict country with approaches based on human rights *and* peace agreements?

One possible point of view is that the dynamics of dialogue, mediation and peace negotiations are the '*conditio sine qua non*' for reaching peace and human security and therewith for improving the human rights situation in countries experiencing war, armed conflict or post-conflict situations. Nevertheless, the same processes do guarantee reaching the full implementation and respect for human rights. For the latter purpose a second component may be necessary, supplementing processes of dialogue, mediation and peace negotiations and adding substance to the improvement of the human rights situation by reaching a positive and sustainable peace. This conclusion has not always been shared by the different actors working in the field of international relations or development cooperation (Mertus and Helsing, 2006). Politicians and those who are involved in peace talks have been struggling with human rights activists and advocates. Interestingly, human rights advocates do not necessarily identify

[8] See: www.humanrightsfirst.org/defenders/hrd_guatemala/hrd_cicig.asp.

[9] Recently a critical level of femicide has been added to the alarming proportions of homicides. A new law for combating these phenomena has passed the parliament. BBC Mundo, 'Femicidio' en Guatemala: ¿solución?' (23 April 2008) available at: www.bbc.co.uk/news/hi/spanish/latin_america.

mediators as an indispensable group of professionals when developing human rights and searching for peace. The 'human rights community' on the one hand and the 'mediation community' on the other, seem to follow different priorities and approaches. First, the human rights actors advocate for justice, truth and reparation as a means of building sustainable peace, therefore they are considered to be following an outcome-oriented approach. Secondly, the 'mediation community', working on conflict resolutions, is believed to use a more process-oriented approach and to understand the end of violence as the first step towards the beginning of peace. Mediators and negotiators have accused the 'human rights community' of complicating dialogue and aggravating the reaching of peace agreements by putting human rights at the front of the process, thus focusing on the prosecution of human rights violations during war or armed conflict. However, those who advocate for human rights accuse the mediators of being responsible for the development of a high level of impunity by accepting broad amnesty laws for former perpetrators of serious human rights violations (Mertus and Helsing, 2006). One of the most important objectives of conflict transformation is to get mutual respect and recognition between the struggling parties. Human rights in fact are the result of the international and collective recognition of some basic values such as human dignity. Therefore, using human rights as a framework for conflict transformation after a civil war or armed conflict could bring international recognition to the suffering of the victims. The main questions emerging from this are: do human rights on the one hand and mediation concepts on the other hand help or hinder each other's efforts, or do they do both?; is it possible to recognise the importance of both approaches, and although the relationship between both has often been highlighted as complicated, is it possible to build bridges and reconnect two systems which should not hinder but give mutual support to each other and to each other's objectives?; is it possible to reconcile these two opposing concepts or to overcome these problems by implementing a complementary approach?; if so, how is it possible to bring both concepts together, in a way that recognises the contribution of the different approaches so that they can help each other? The theoretical discussion seems to be advancing in this aspect although the implementation in specific cases creates still new questions (Parlevliet, 2009).

(a) The Conflict Phase

(i) The Relation between Human Rights and Conflict

It is highly important to analyse the several facets of the relationship between human rights and conflict to be able to identify the connections between human rights and peace, too. In the following table, the different options are depicted: human rights and conflict:[10]

Relation	*Description*
1. Demand for human rights as a cause of conflict	Demands—for self-determination, fair access to resources, an end to forced acculturation and discrimination—involve violent conflict between groups
2. State's inability or unwillingness to protect human rights as a cause of conflict	Domestic policies (especially in ethnically divided societies) that ignore minority rights increase social and political tensions until conflict erupts Even in stable polities, structural oppression increases the danger of future confrontation and violence
3. Instrumental use of human rights violations	Manipulation of collective memory of human rights abuse to create a sense of revenge
4 Human rights violations as a conflict escalator	The sustained denial of human rights causes repressed/oppressed groups to react and may prompt intervention, intensify conflict
5. Human rights violations as direct symptoms of violent conflict	Warring parties torture, rape, mutilate and summarily execute both combatants and non-combatants
6. Human rights violations as a direct or indirect consequence of violent conflict	War adversely affects the environment and the ability of people to sustain their livelihoods, thereby affecting related human rights Ceasefires and peace agreements that ignore human rights often perpetuate inequities and denial of human rights, leading to greater suffering and violence. Sustainable peace depends on the assurance of human rights

The first possible relationship includes demands for both, political/civil rights and for economical, social and cultural human rights. This situation can be found in Guatemala and Colombia where the core causes of conflict have been the lack of access to land, limited possibilities for the active and secure political participation and discrimination of the indigenous population. The second case can be illustrated by the difficult situation of the Ogoni people in Nigeria, when the government neither protected them from the threats of the extractive petroleum industries nor stopped the (extra) judicial killings.

[10] Adapted from Mertus and Helsing (2006).

The third case is exemplified by the horrifying experiences of the genocide in Rwanda and Yugoslavia. The fourth case for instance was South Africa during the apartheid system or currently Mindanao/Philippines, where systematically and historically oppressed groups have reacted or may react violently in the near future while justifying armed violence as self-defence (Diaz, 2003). In Guatemala, it could be seen that human rights violations were not only the core cause of conflict, but a direct symptom of the armed conflict, too, which refers to the fifth case. The inherent logic of a violent and armed conflict generates cruelty and crimes against humanity. The armed conflict was transformed into genocide against the indigenous population of Guatemala.[11] The sixth possible relation can be observed as a consequence of violent conflicts. The population living in a warring context is not able to follow their economic and social activities such as work, studies, health care etc, which means that the social human rights are severely affected by war or armed violence. Fear of leaving the home, a lack of economic opportunities and stability or the situation of displacement impedes the enforcement of economic, social and cultural human rights.

These six facets of relationships cannot be understood as mutually exhaustive or alternative. It has been frequently found that during the development of an armed conflict, the dynamics of the conflict change and, unfortunately, accumulates more than one form of the presented options. What can be evidenced using this systematisation of relationships is the fact that the human rights situation in a country or region does impact on the onset of conflicts or the aggravation of a violent situation. The human rights situation and the conflict itself influence each other and the cause of one becomes the result of the other and therefore following a circular process where the conflict negatively affects the human rights situation and vice versa. Identifying this situation may modify the mediation approach in practice.

(ii) The Relation between Human Rights and Mediation in Practice

Uganda

Starting peace negotiations with Uganda's President Yoweri Kaguta Museveni has been rejected so far by Joseph Kony, the leader of the rebel group Lord's Resistance Army (LRA). The LRA is charged with mass killings of the civil population and mutilation (such as cutting off limbs, lips, ears, noses etc). The violations committed by the LRA have been classified as crimes against humanity by the International Criminal Court (ICC) which issued arrest warrants for five top LRA leaders in 2005. The overall effect of the LRA

[11] The mass killings between 1981 and 1983 have been declared as genocide against the Mayan population. Comisión para el Esclarecimiento Histórico (CEH), 'Guatemala, Memoria del Silencio, Informe de la Comisión para el Esclarecimiento Histórico' (Guatemala, 1999).

activities and the war in Uganda has been social and economic disruption on a massive scale; schools, hospitals, health centres and trading centres have been drastically affected. Livelihoods have been disrupted through the destruction of crops, houses and stores. Women and children have been raped, displacement took various forms. Despite the militaries' presence in refugee camps, the camps remain targets for the rebel attacks. As a result, Northern Uganda has been facing an acute humanitarian crisis. Thousands of people have been killed and currently more than 1.7 million civilians remain displaced. In August 2006, the government of Uganda and the LRA signed the landmark Cessation of Hostilities Agreement (CHA), which has resulted in improved security conditions and humanitarian access. It appears that the peace talks depend on the question whether Joseph Kony will be granted amnesty or extradited to face the ICC. The issue seems to be either peace *or* justice but not peace *and* justice. President Museveni has proposed to abandon the report issued to the ICC against Joseph Kony if he accepts a peace agreement. A population-based survey in Uganda concludes that 66 per cent of those interviewed favour formal punishment of perpetrators; 22 per cent opt for forgiveness and reconciliation; 2 per cent for confessing to the community and 1 per cent voted for compensation to victims. Twenty-nine per cent would reject peace if amnesty were the precondition for signing a peace agreement.[12]

Similar situations can occur in other countries too, thus the critical questions emerging from the case of Uganda must be examined. The main problems are related to the precondition for mediation or negotiation.

Putting Joseph Kony on trial in The Hague is not the main objective from a human rights perspective; it is a means to achieve justice, to prepare further social reintegration of perpetrators and to promote prevention through deterrence. The inviolable victims' rights are: the right to truth; the right to justice; the right to reparation and the right to the guarantee of no-repetition (Álvarez, 2007; Hayner, 2001). These are not only the core and therefore inviolable rights of victims, but they are also considered to be necessary for building a lasting peace. Switching from the rights approach to the needs approach, it could be concluded that peace is not to be achieved for free and one could argue that it might be an option to stop the international prosecution of Joseph Kony and his collaborators. But is peace exchangeable for the end of violence and murder? In this context, it is worth distinguishing between negative and positive peace. According to Galtung (2000) negative peace is the absence of direct violence (physical, verbal and psychological) between individuals, groups and governments, while positive peace means the presence of social justice through equal

[12] International Centre for Transitional Justice and the Human Rights Centre, 'Forgotten Voices, a population-based survey on attitudes about peace and justice in Northern Uganda' (Berkeley, University of California, 2005) 4–5.

opportunities, a fair distribution of power and resources, equal protection and impartial enforcement of law. Perhaps there are more choices than just two and it is possible to find a way out without following one of these two options. Finally, the ICC accusation can be considered by Joseph Kony and the other accused leaders of the LRA to be the worst alternative to a negotiated agreement (WATNA) and therefore a medium to promote peace talks and not to be an obstacle to it, as he should know that without any approximation he will end in an international judicial process. Using the principle of subsidiarity and experiences of different national penal mediation approaches,[13] it may be possible to agree on the procedures. Instead of considering the ICC prosecution as an obstacle to peace talks, it can be strengthened and therefore utilised as an incentive for Joseph Kony to start taking the ICC and international approaches seriously, and thus embark on peace talks. It is therefore possible to pause the ICC intervention if Ugandan actors deal with the situation in a way which accords with international (human) rights standards.[14]

Afghanistan[15]

Much can be said about the recent history of Afghanistan and the role of the international community. However, only the most relevant points will be highlighted here. The power of the Taliban ended with the US-led military intervention in Afghanistan in 2001, after which the Afghan government, and later the Afghan Parliament, took power. The still ongoing conflict has been classified as an armed conflict with high intensity and a tendency to worsen. Even though it is impossible to classify the Afghan situation as an organised peace process, the Afghan Parliament passed an amnesty law in 2007. Before that, there had been various attempts to integrate transitional justice and accountability in the efforts to build peace. It was stated that:

> In making such a decision, attention should be paid to this reality that considering the clear Koranic verses and the international law, no amnesty should be

[13] Usually according to the national proceedings, the penal prosecution stops during mediation and if the conflicting parties agree on a result, the criminal process does not necessarily have to go ahead until the parties stop following its own agreement. In this case, the agreement should include a national criminal prosecution to allow the ICC to stop or freeze its investigation and prosecution. This way could offer a solution between the maximum and minimum of human rights based expectations.

[14] Recently, the ICC has called for help from the international community to find the LRA leaders. ICC, 'Prosecutor calls for renewed efforts to arrest LRA leader Kony in wake of new attacks'. (The Hague, 6 October 2008) available at: www.icc-cpi.int.html.

[15] The author worked in 2006 with the Afghan Independent Human Rights Commission and in April 2008 for the Gender-Mainstreaming Project within the Ministries in Afghanistan.

provided for war crimes, crimes against humanity and other gross violations of human rights.[16]

The action plan on peace, reconciliation and justice was approved by the Afghan government before the parliamentary elections in September 2005. Following the Bonn Agreement (2001) the Afghan transitional government, led by Harmid Karzai, committed itself to early elections, although conditions were not very supportive. Former so-called warlords formed part of the Parliament—the legislative body—and this is perhaps one of the reasons why the amnesty law passed the legislative body, despite pressure on the Parliament and government from national and international human rights and transitional justice organisations not to vote in favour. As the elections of 2005, resulting in the strengthening of this disputable parliament, were carried out with the financial support of the international community, it may be criticised for promoting peace even if the victims' basic rights have not been addressed. Karzai won the second elections, although cases of election fraud are assumed to have occurred.[17] The question is, what options exist that can be applied by the international community in a situation like that? Is it worth ceding justice, ceding victim's rights for the implementation of a formal but disputable democracy?

The Afghan contradiction is seen more clearly on the micro level. In the rural part of Afghanistan it is a tradition that the so called 'shura'[18] assumes conflict management activities. It is a common and promising strategy of the international community to strengthen local and existing capacities and structures for peace. Peace building on the micro level means identifying connectors and people/institutions that support peace and conflict transformation processes.[19] Although there are many attempts to integrate a gender perspective or women's rights perspective into the recently so-called 'peace shura', only infrequently do women participate as members in the common 'shura', and it seems it would be more challenging if they participated in specific women shura (El Samam, 2008). Even worse, it is a common tradition to hand over the youngest girl of a family to another family to compensate for murdering a member of the latter, thus further violence between the families involved comes to an end. The price for stopping new violence is the nullification of all the rights to that youngest girl—the

[16] Action Plan of the Government of the Islamic Republic of Afghanistan on Peace, Reconciliation and Justice, key action four, 2005, available at: www.aihrc.org.af/actionplan_af.htm.

[17] See: www.iec.org.af/results/leadingCandidate.html, uncertified final results 16 September 2009.

[18] Council of recognised religious men.

[19] Several international cooperation agencies support the development of the peace shuras. An interesting overview of the projects, structure and approach of the peace shura can be found in El Samam (2008).

currency with which the 'peace' between the families is paid can be called 'human rights'.

Due to the security situation in Afghanistan there exists a large distance and several intermediaries between the international donor's office in Kabul and local implementing organisations. Therefore, it is difficult to monitor whether the supported 'peace shuras' maintain human rights' violating practices in order to promote peace in the place of stopping violence.

The Philippines[20]

The Philippines, and even more so the island of Mindanao, have been suffering a multipart and multifaceted armed conflict with numerous intentions of peace dialogues and mediations. Movements of the Muslim population for independence, the Maoist New People's Army and the Philippine National Army form part of the violent conflict. Others, such as the indigenous population, are conflict actors too, but don't form another armed group. The core cause of the conflict in Mindanao is the sense of injustice and discrimination experienced by several groups within the population for their religious, ethnic or social belongings. International organisations, such as the Centre for Humanitarian Dialogue and several countries have been trying to support peace talks and offer the conditions for secure meetings.

Only recently has the approach of the international community switched from a traditional poverty reduction programme towards a conflict transformation and peace building programme to respond to the population's needs and to address social groups which have been highly affected by the armed conflict.[21] It is primarily the young, women and indigenous displaced population which have suffered due to the conflict-forced displacement and domestic violence. In the specific case of Mindanao it is even more important to address the needs and the rights of the indigenous population; since they have not been integrated as a dialogue partner in the peace talks, they do not feel represented by the Islamic indigenous population who participate in the talks. This means that human rights violations and discrimination are a core cause of conflict in Mindanao. If the peace talks exclude certain groups of the population, it will be understood as replicated discrimination and the consequence will be that future peace agreements will not fulfil the expectations of the excluded groups and thus conditions for future (armed) conflicts will be created. The indigenous population has not become a member of the peace talks because they do not appear as a single armed group. But this does not mean that they do not have their own and different interests. As mentioned above, the composition of the

[20] The author worked in the Philippines/Mindanao in 2007.

[21] See: www.kfwentwicklungsbank.de/DE_Home/Laender_Programme_und_Projekte/Asien/Philippinen/Foerderschwerpunkte.jsp.

members of peace talks is highly critical for the success of those processes. Although the indigenous people do not claim independence for their people, some of their human rights have been violated in the past and therefore they become part of the multifaceted violent conflict in Mindanao. The structural and general poverty of the indigenous people is not so much the reason for the conflict, but the result. Many of them have lived as displaced people for years. The structural violation of political and civil rights leads to incomplete economic, social and cultural human rights. Work on human rights would lead to positive developments in crisis situations and would improve the lives of displaced people.

Colombia[22]

Colombia is politically a highly sensitive and complex case. The country has been suffering a long-lasting and fluctuating armed conflict. Recently the international community's attention has been attracted by events such as the dramatic liberation of Ingrid Betancourt or the military attack against a guerrilla camp in Ecuador where members of the Colombian guerrilla movements were killed. Both actions have been conducted by Colombian armed forces. The current situation in Colombia is much more multifaceted. The most important actors within the armed conflict have been the two guerrilla movements (*Fuerzas Armadas Revolucionarias de Colombia* (FARC) and *Ejército de Liberación Nacional* (ELN)), the paramilitaries, the drug traffickers and the Colombian armed forces. Some of these groups are interrelated and are connected to the national or regional political elite. One of the examples of those interrelations is the so-called 'parapolítica',[23] that is, the policy influenced by the paramilitaries. According to official Colombian interpretation, the armed conflict terminated. The government declared that after the demobilisation campaign in 2005 all paramilitary members have been demobilised, the guerrilla movements are declared terrorists and the new illegal armed groups which arose as a result of the demobilisation are now ordinary criminals without any paramilitary structure. Parts of Colombian society and parts of the international community disagree with this interpretation of the current situation. They highlight the ongoing existence of the paramilitary structure and its influence on the political structure, as well as the ongoing armed conflict with the guerrilla movement, only the war-strategy changed from open combats to individual killings

[22] The author has worked in different projects regarding human rights and peace building in Colombia since 2007.

[23] Corporación Nuevo Arco Iris, 'PARA Política—la ruta de la expansión paramilitar y los acuerdos políticos' (Intermedio, Bogotá, 2007). The editor, a non-governmental organisation founded after a peace agreement between the government and the former guerrilla group M19, received life threats after publishing this book. (Interview May 2008 with the director of Corporación Nuevo Arco Iris).

on both sides. Even though a peace agreement has not yet been signed and peace talks have not advanced, the Colombian government has implemented specific post-conflict laws and instruments such as the Peace and Justice law;[24] establishing state institutions such as the department for peace and justice within the Public Attorney's Office and within the Defensoría del Pueblo[25] (ombudsperson for human rights); creating the Commission for Reconciliation and Reparation (CNRR) and conducting exhumations of massacre victims, sometimes accompanied by the Colombian armed forces, even though the latter have been part of the armed conflict.

The emerging question is whether it is possible to meet the goals of post-conflict, transitional justice and reconciliation if the armed conflict and violence is still continuing and the minimum conditions have not been met for the security of the victims of human rights violations. Is it possible to build a lasting peace if none of the economic, social, political and civil human rights are addressed through the post-conflict activities? It has been mentioned above that one of the core causes of the Colombian armed conflict has been the systematic violation of all kinds of human rights and the lack of access to land property. Colombia is the only Latin American country which has not implemented a land reform.

What effects does this situation cause for the international community and international cooperation? Colombia is classified as a lower-middle-income economy, it is not a poor country although most of the population live in poor conditions. Most of the donor countries focus their programmes on peace building, good governance, security and human rights.

International cooperation faces the problem that it wants and needs to support the peace-building measures taken by the government, although the relevant conditions are still weak and the necessity of improving the human rights situation is still high. Furthermore, the conditions established by the agreements between the government and paramilitary groups have not been fulfilled completely by the demobilised paramilitary groups' members. The handing over of all children forced to be soldiers or to take part in paramilitary groups in other ways was one of the most important duties. During the demobilisation phase, only seldom were child soldiers handed over to the governmental institutions. It is not known whether child soldiers have returned to their families, if they have got lost in the mountains or if they have died or been killed. Even though it was a precondition for the paramilitaries to hand over the child soldiers to be able to enjoy the advantages of the Peace and Justice Law (important reduction of penalty) they still remain accused under the special transitional justice law and not under the normal penalty law which would have meant an increase in imprisonment

[24] Diario Oficial 45.980 LEY 975 / 2005 (julio 25), available at: www.altocomisionadoparalapaz.gov.co/justicia_paz/documentos/Ley1_975.pdf.

[25] See: www.defensoria.org.co/.

years, although the child soldiers are still missing. The second problem faced by the implementation of the transitional justice law is that during the 'free version'[26] the alleged paramilitaries do not mention the high number of mass rapes and other sexual abuses against women as a war strategy, but they should expose without exception all the human rights violations they have committed in relation to their membership of the paramilitary groups. For different reasons,[27] female victims of rape do not usually denounce their abuse, yet it is known that

> underreporting is also a significant barrier to justice. Many women feel shame and fear rejection from their husbands, families, and communities if they report having been raped. The threat of divorce or the possibility of being considered 'unmarriageable' causes many women's reluctance to report their experiences. The economic and social dependence of women on men in many societies contributes to their fear of reporting rape.[28]

This means that the paramilitaries judged under the Peace and Justice Law should not be granted any exemption if they have not fulfilled their duties. Who is able to resolve this contradiction and to question the success of Colombian efforts to obtain peace? The same question arises again, who is able to participate in the peace negotiation, and who has the power to cede justice and rights (their own rights and not other's rights) for peace? Even though former forced child soldiers or women agreed to accept this price in return for peace, they would not be asked for their opinions or be integrated into the peace talks. Women only rarely take up arms but they do pass their trauma on to the next generation and this would generate an emotional barrier for reconciliation and reconstruction of a country and its population (Op den Velde, 1998). What should be the position and actions to be taken by the international cooperation[29]?

It seems that the process in Colombia—even if it is recognised that the armed conflict has ended—still presents so many problems and deficiencies regarding human rights that it is difficult to support these efforts without asking for serious improvements in the human rights situation and inclusion of all victims' groups, particularly child soldiers and women. One technical but serious problem caused by the statement that the armed conflict is over is that several international human rights instruments (for example, children's rights in armed conflicts) or international humanitarian law can

[26] 'Free version' means that the accused person has the right to explain what he or she did without any interventions and has the duty to admit all his or her actions carried out under the armed conflict.

[27] Eg, shame or fear.

[28] Amnesty International, USA. 'Stop Violence Against Women', available at: www.amnestyusa.org/women/rapeinwartime.html.

[29] Including all the activities done by the UN or national agencies, DFIF, EU, OECD, Spanish cooperation agency, GTZ for Germany etc.

no longer be applied because a conflict situation is the legal condition for the implementation of those international laws. This apparently formal or juridical problem represents serious consequences for the civil population and particularly for the child soldiers involved in the activities of the new illegal armed groups. They are treated as normal criminals and lose all the protection offered by the optional protocol on children in armed conflict to the children's rights convention and Security Council resolution 1612 on children's protection in armed conflicts.[30] Child soldiers are considered to be victims of war and have several rights related to joining reintegration, education and protection programmes (Santiago, 2008). Young members of illegal groups are considered as criminals by law and not as victims. This change of the legal definition of a social group—one actor of the conflict—is quite difficult for human rights advocates and peace mediators to respond to.

IV. CONCLUSIONS

The main conclusion to be drawn from these cases is that attempting to apply the basic mediation principles based on a human rights approach may facilitate finding a strategy for peace building programmes to pursue both human rights and peace. The human rights based approach as a method on the one hand supports participation, empowerment and non-discrimination of the population, and on the other, related to state actors, responsibility for their actions. The first three principles are the basic ones for any mediation process, which means that the main difference between the mediation and human rights approach is related to the question of legal and/or ethical responsibility.

It is obvious that every single conflict or war situation needs special treatment; there is no common formula of response. The multitrack approach (Lederach, 1997) is, as always, valid in these situations. To design a programme for a post-conflict country includes analysing on which level, with which kind of instruments and with which partners and rights holders work must be done. Traditional approaches to conflict management should be supported if and when human rights standards are respected or the goodwill for change is expressed.

If core causes of conflict, economic courses or competition related to the use of natural resources and land cannot be tackled during peace talks, the further peace-building process will suffer a lack of creditability and sustainability (Davis, 2009). The current situation in Guatemala shows, besides the high level of impunity, an aggravation of the economic situation of the rural and indigenous population.

[30] See: www.unhcr.org.

The next important point to highlight is the complex issue of neutrality and impartiality. Of course, during a peace building and reconciliation process it is indispensable that former combatants get some kind of attention and inclusion in programmes—but without granting them special privileges. Still, The main focus—financial, psychological, social and political—should still be on the victim groups. In particular, with regard to mass human rights violations, extremely cruel crimes against humanity and war crimes, neutrality would not be understood as neutrality but as partiality in the interest of the people who are responsible for those atrocities. This does not mean forgetting that those responsible have been shaped by a specific historical moment, and that they need to be treated differently than they would under the normal criminal law. Transitional justice unifies some known criteria from restorative justice, but it is still different (Bell and O'Rourke, 2007). The approach is more collective; however, individual cases and experiences are tackled. The main focus that exists within restorative justice is based on apology. But in a post-conflict context those who have suffered human rights violations were victims in one specific moment and as members of a group or society, but not as specific individuals. It was the historical moment that caused the framework for making them victims, thus being a victim is not a permanent condition. To reach this transformation within the society, the rights-based approach needs the support of a communication-based mediation process. A transitional justice strategy has to be able to meet the needs and rights of the people who have suffered human rights violations and support them so as to overcome the condition of being a victim.

The last important point is the integration and participation of all groups besides the armed groups. To be able to build a fair and long lasting peace, it is indispensable to integrate all groups in society and furthermore, participation is the one way to respect their human rights.

In summary, decisions on the funding of specific activities, the support for identified institutions and organisations and the question of maintaining programmes or leaving a country, etc has a significant impact on post-conflict situations. Due to its involvement, the International Development Cooperation is taking on great responsibility for the development and the dynamics in these contexts, especially as it is not acting in a political vacuum. Political, economic and security interest impact on the scope of action of international cooperation. If the human rights-based approach is the general mainstream strategy for sectional development and cooperation programmes in these contexts, it should be the fundamental for mediation and peace-building programmes, too. Even if the practical implementation is challenging and a specific strategy for every single conflict and peace-building approach is necessary, the theoretical background for a complementary approach is developing.

REFERENCES

Álvarez, J (2007) *Derecho Internacional y transiciones a la democracia y la paz* (Madrid, Partenón).
Bell, C and O'Rourke, C (2007) 'Does Feminism need a Theory of Transitional Justice? An Introductory Essay' 1 *International Journal of Transitional Justice* 23–44.
Davis, M (2009) 'Why Should Mediators consider the Economic Dimensions of Conflict?' Center for Humanitarian Dialogue.
Diaz, PP (2003) *Understanding Mindanao Conflict* (Davao City, MindaNews Publication).
El Samam, R (2008) *Linking Formal and Informal Conflict Resolution Mechanisms in Afghanistan: A Survey of the People's Perspective* (Friedrich-Ebert-Stiftung).
Farré Salvá, S (2004) *Gestión de conflictos: taller de mediación* (Barcelona, Ariel).
Galtung, J (2000) 'A Structural Theory of Imperialism' in D Barash (ed), *Approaches to Peace: A Reader in Peace Studies* (Oxford, Oxford University Press).
—— (2003) 'Demokratisierung der Mediation als Beitrag zu einer Friedenskultur und: Hintergründiges zum 11 September' in *Mediation und Demokratie* (Heidelberg, Carl-Auer-Systeme Verlag).
Goldmann, F (3 November 2004) 'Guatemala's Fictional Democracy' *New York Times*.
Hayner, PB (2001) *Unspeakable Truths. Confronting Terror and Atrocity* (New York, Routledge).
Lederach, JP (1997) *Building Peace. Sustainable Reconciliation in Divided Societies* (Washington DC, United States Institute for Peace).
Mertus, J and Helsing, J (2006) 'Exploring the Intersection between Human Rights and Conflict' in J Mertus and J Helsing (eds), *Human Rights and Conflict, Exploring the Links between Rights, Law and Peace-building* (Washington DC, USIP).
Op den Velde, W (1998) 'Children of Dutch War Sailors and Civilian Resistance Veterans' in Y Danieli (ed), *International Handbook of Multigenerational Legacies of Trauma* (New York, Plenum).
Parlevliet, M (2009) *Rethinking Conflict Transformation from a Human Rights Perspective* (Berghof Research Centre for Constructive Conflict Management).
Santiago, L (2008) *Nacido para triunfar—Testimonio de un adolescente desvinculado de un grupo armado ilegal* (Colombia, Unicef).

Part II

The Catholic Church as Political Mediator

4

The Power of Powerlessness: Religious Actors' Peaceful Mediation in the Basque Conflict

XABIER ITÇAINA

Bakea uzten dauzuet, ene bakea emaiten[1]

POLITICAL SCIENTISTS HAVE shown renewed interest in political conflict mediation over the last few years. Their work, mainly conducted from the perspective of international relations, has also been marked by a sociological bias focusing on an in-depth socio-historical analysis of conflict-building rather than on a more comparative approach. The aim of the present chapter is to illustrate and discuss, from the example of the Basque country, one of the recent studies on changes in peaceful regulation as developed by Jacques Faget (Faget, 2008). Starting his analysis from a comprehensive review of the specialised literature, Faget points to the emergence of new actors in mediation and peace building in violent political conflicts and argues that mediation is now making up for the shortcomings of the international order, as states and traditional national or international diplomacy have proved unable to address the issue of conflict resolution. These initiatives do not really break away from, but rather complement, traditional state action, as evidenced by the para-state status of some NGOs. Through a strategy of de-politicisation, the objective of these new actors is to facilitate the regulation of conflicts by eclipsing the very intervention of the states. However, the multiplicity of such initiatives from below, initiated by

[1] 'Peace I leave with you; my peace I give you' (John, 14:27). This chapter is the revised version of a paper presented at the workshop *La mediación en los conflictos políticos nacionales e internacionales* (International Institute for the Sociology of Law, Oñati 5–6 June 2008). The author wishes to thank Jacques Faget for his invitation and comments, the two anonymous referees for their extensive and useful comments and JF Allafort for his precious help in the translation of this chapter.

peacemakers with heterogeneous legal statuses and fostered by beliefs and interests which are not only political, may eventually lead to defining new roles for peacemakers thus blurring the frontiers between state and non-state actors (2008: 310).

Beyond the traditional distinction between mediation and negotiation, Faget proposes a new definition of mediation which he clearly differentiates from the more classical approach developed by international relations specialists in peace studies programmes. In his view, mediation is different from global peacemaking processes, state or supra-state UN-style diplomacy, etc, in so far as it is

> a consensual process of conflict management, in which a third party who is impartial, independent and without any decision-making capacity, tries to solve or to moderate conflicts through the organisation of exchanges between persons and institutions.
>
> (Faget, 2008: 312)

Faget applies his approach to mediation in his study of violent political conflicts, ie, 'political conflicts in which protagonists—states, social protest movements and political parties—do not respect the rules of the democratic game and resort to armed struggle and illegitimate physical violence, for instance' (2008: 313). While we may question the true mediating dimension of the various solutions tentatively proposed so far, the violent nature of the Basque conflict, even if deemed of 'low intensity', is beyond any doubt. Since *ETA* (*Euskadi eta askatasuna*, Basque Homeland and Freedom) resumed its bombing campaign in December 2006, which led the authorities to adopt a repressive stance as a response, a new cycle of violence has spread all over the Basque country. Quite obviously, the so-called 'Basque question' should not be restricted to its most radical manifestations, but the fact is that violence has had major political consequences and contributed to destabilising the democratic game, if we consider the sufferings it has generated and the mediation efforts it has prompted.[2] The persistent use of violence as a political instrument, especially in light of the peace process in Northern Ireland, makes the Basque country an exception in Western Europe. What it clearly evidences, beyond the tentative explanations focusing on the historical genesis of an old conflict, is the incapacity of institutional and political actors to propose any durable solution. The question of the Basque identity, hinging on antagonistic values, is indeed buttressed on irreconcilable moral positions. As a consequence, today's Basque society is highly politicised,

[2] In order to limit the scope of the present analysis, examples will be taken mostly from the Spanish Basque Autonomous Community. Navarre and the French Basque country have different historical profiles. For a comparative study on religion and politics between both sides of the border, see Itçaina (2007).

as illustrated by the findings of anthropologists working on such distinct domains as art, sports or even cooking (MacClancy, 2007). Continued violence has prevented this conflict from evolving into a pacified confrontation of values in a stabilised political game, as is the case in Quebec or Catalonia. Since the mid-1980s, the difficulties met by institutional actors who have proved unable to provide solutions have led the organised civil society to take initiatives with a view to solving this enduring conflict, thus breaking the 'spiral of silence' (Funes, 1998). To take up Bernard Enjolras' categories, horizontal governance of the conflict by civil society has compensated for the shortcomings of vertical governance by public institutions (Enjolras, 2008).

Religious actors play a specific role in the world of mediation, not only in the Basque country, but in other places (Smock, 2006). According to Faget, religious actors have long represented the second largest group of political mediators in the world, together with the pacifist and liberal left wing in the United States in the 1970s. In his analysis of the Quakers in the 1970s, the Roman Catholic Church in Latin America and various other Catholic organisations, the best known of which being Sant'Egidio in Africa, Jacques Palard—who adopts a wider definition of mediation—has shown how the Catholic Church could justify its intrinsic capacity to act as a mediator from its own theological foundations, privileging subsidiarity as a way for intermediary bodies to propose solutions to conflicts without systematically resorting to state regulation (Palard, 2006). The case of the Basque country offers a good illustration of this thesis, the Catholic Church and other actors close to it being particularly active in the *making* rather than in the *process* of peace—which would require some basic social agreement on the way to follow (section I). However, the Church's commitment to mediation in the Basque conflict has not gone smoothly, notably on account of the controversy over its supposed impartiality, independence and absence of decision-making power. Two contrasting perceptions of the Catholic Church have emerged—the Church as an expert in mediation at both local and global levels, and as the guardian of the memory of an old conflict of identity, thus conferring an *insider-partial* status on it. Promoting peace, reconciliation and pardon has necessarily led to questioning the responsibility of the Church in the historical crystallisation of the identity cleavage. Though its expertise in mediation has been widely acknowledged, the Catholic Church in the Basque country has also been forced to come to terms with history, as though the burden of memory periodically acted as a nemesis for the religious, political and social actors (section II). Finally, and from a more global perspective, the Catholic Church's contribution to peacemaking can only be apprehended through the double perspective of the secularisation of Basque society and the redefinition of the relationships between religion, the public space and democracy in the Basque country (section III).

I. THE CHURCH'S DUAL MEDIATION IN THE BASQUE COUNTRY

Although case studies may prove to be too specific, they nevertheless offer the possibility of proposing an in-depth historical perspective. In the case under scrutiny, we uphold the hypothesis of a redefinition of the mediating activities of the Basque Catholic Church in the history of the modes of action adopted by the Basque clergy. From this perspective, contemporary mediation would be the fourth stage of a long process of interaction between religion and the 'Basque question' which started in the mid nineteenth century. Broadly speaking, we may discern four successive periods on both sides of the frontier: a first period marked by *tradition* during the nineteenth century (Carlism and political traditionalism), followed by a period of *filiation* (some members of the clergy were close to the first expressions of Basque nationalism and its Christian-Democratic, personalist development) and a period of *rebellion* (secularisation of Basque nationalism and radicalisation of a segment of the Basque clergy in the 1960–70s). The reorientation of the activities of a part of the Basque clergy towards peacemaking mediation, in addition to its traditional concerns for social action and more specifically religious questions, evidences the emergence of a fourth mode of action—*mediation* (Itçaina, 2007). Though Catholic actors do not hold any monopolistic position, they seem to have incorporated the pacifist third sector which has developed in the Basque country since the mid-1980s.

Catholic mediation is multifaceted, thus placing the Basque Catholic Church in a position somewhere in between mediation and committed activism. Some authors have analysed it from the wider perspective of political mediation (Itçaina, 2005; 2010) notably drawing on the findings of the research work conducted by Andy Smith and Olivier Nay who differentiate between the 'mediator-broker' and the 'mediator-generalist' (Nay and Smith, 2002). In apparent opposition to the stricter definition of mediation proposed by Faget, such a concept makes a distinction between the activities of the general mediator who tries to build some common meaning between institutions which may not share the same knowledge and representations—the *cognitive* dimension of mediation—and the activities of the broker who looks for acceptable solutions for opposing groups who may find an advantage in co-operating even though they do not pursue the same objectives and do not have the same interests—the *strategic* dimension of mediation. The Catholic Church in the Basque country has clearly acted in both ways, more successfully in its activities as a general mediator than as a broker.

(a) General Mediation or the Making of a Culture of Peace

In terms of *general mediation*, the Church, in its capacity as an expert in peace-making, has shown its know-how when it comes to staging negotiations and smoothing out differences. In its internal organisation, the Church has put the theme of peace at the top of its agenda, especially in its network of dioceses (Pagola, 1995). The best illustration may be found in Guipuzcoa, a province where nationalist radicalism is deeply rooted. Within the diocesan structure—the social Secretariat created when Monsignor Setién became Bishop of San Sebastián in 1979[3]—top priority was given not only to the nagging problem of unemployment, but to the restoration of peace. From 1992 onwards, the *Gentza* diocesan committee has taken reflective and symbolical action on this issue and staged highly publicised demonstrations, as, for instance, the March for Peace to the Arantzazu sanctuary, which gathered nearly 10,000 people, or the Rally for Peace in Armentia (Alava) on 13 January 2001 under the aegis of the four Basque and Navarre bishops. Prelates have urged ETA to lay down its arms and politicians to open negotiations. The leadership of the San Sebastián bishops, Monsignor Setién (1979–2000) and Monsignor Uriarte (since 2000), has played an essential role in mobilising local people and neighbouring dioceses, with the support of the Bishops of Bilbao, Vitoria and Tudela-Pamplona.

In a more acute way, some groups, notably religious orders, have regarded the reorientation of their activities towards the promotion of peace as an opportunity for them to reactualise their former and time-honoured specialisation. The Jesuits could thus use their long experience in peace studies and peace building, from Loyola to the entire Catholic world. The Franciscans could invoke the theology of their founder, Saint Francis of Assisi, to support their peacemaking activities along with their old and firmly grounded commitment to the Basque culture in the Guipuzcoan sanctuary of Arantzazu. Arantzazu, a highly symbolical place, was first and foremost a Marian sanctuary which traditionally had a symbolical and identity function in the province of Guipuzcoa. It was also a *locus* of memory in commemoration of the Basque cultural resistance against Franco's regime. The year 1956 marked a revival of this symbolical dimension. *Euskaltzaindia*, the Academy of the Basque language, convened in Arantzazu to lay the foundations of a movement for the unification of the Basque language. On that occasion, the Arantzazu seminarians distributed the first issue of *Jakin* ('knowledge') which was soon to become a major journal in philosophy and social science published in the Basque language. The sanctuary, which was rebuilt by contemporary Basque artists under the guidance of Oteiza, became the symbol of Basque cultural creativity and emancipatory religious feelings clearly at odds with official national Catholicism (Zulaika, 1988). The Arantzazu sanctuary thus acquired a specific and highly symbolical dimension in the Basque country. In an attempt to restructure its pastoral project around the question of peace, the

[3] Monsignor Setién was first auxiliary bishop in San Sebastián between 1972 and 1979.

pastoral council of Arantzazu—which brought together both priests and laypersons—started to take training and advisory initiatives in 1992, with the help and support of the diocesan authorities. The sanctuary regularly became an arena where representatives of the peace movements and political parties could meet and discuss. Together with symbolical moves such as prayers for each violent death and marches for peace, the Franciscan community significantly contributed to the emergence of new *loci* where each party could express their views, in spite of the methodological differences that occasionally cropped up between the Church and the peace movements. Its action rested on the belief that intermediary bodies were presumably more efficient. As expressed by a friar from the Arantzazu community, 'we must not leave it only to politicians to find the solution, we must show them the way, hence the importance of pardon'.[4] Through the promotion of peace and pardon, the radicalism of this religious order, which initially originated from an internal and Utopian protest against the institutional Church (Séguy, 1984) has thus been rejuvenated and updated.

The general dimension of the mediation efforts conducted by Catholic actors is also evidenced externally through their commitment to structuring the peace movements. It was not so much through the avowed implication of the Catholic Church as an institution, but rather through the individual activism of Christians that their commitment for peace was to express itself visibly. For instance, *Gesto por la paz*, an association for the promotion of peace, was from the start helped and supported by the diocese of Bilbao and by young Christian organisations from Biscaye. However, Christian activism within the peace movements proved to be a very delicate task as they gathered members from various political origins. Jan Mansvelt Beck, for instance, distinguishes six peace activist groups according to their objectives—*Asociación de victimas contra el terrorismo, ¡Basta ya!, Elkarri, Foro de Ermua, Gernika Gogoratuz, Gesto por la paz*—founded between 1981 and 1999, and emphasises the differences—and the shortcomings—between their respective initiatives (Mansvelt Beck, 2005: 214). Funes (1998) highlights the contrasting strategies of the two main organisations, *Gesto por la Paz* and *Elkarri*. Indeed the vast majority of *Gesto* members accepted the political regime after the democratic transition, gathering under their name a wide spectrum of political activists, mainly from the PNV (Basque Nationalist Party) but also the PSOE (Spanish Workers' Socialist Party). From a cognitive perspective, *Elkarri* was closer to the radical nationalist left wing, though it refused violence (Funes 1998: 508). Some organisations were mostly concerned with the problem of financial and moral compensation for the victims of ETA and excluded the approach adopted by Basque nationalists. Other groups originated in some radical factions within the

[4] Interview with Brother E (Arantzazu, 1998).

Basque nationalist left wing. Some were supported by the 'constitutionalist' parties whereas others were more firmly rooted in their territory, etc. The Basque Catholic Church thus found itself in a very delicate position among fragmented peace movements, all the more so as most of these pacifist movements expected the Church to adopt a clear stance as if, unconsciously, they still saw the Catholic institution as a reference *par excellence* in its capacity as a mediator.

(b) Christian Personalities as Mediator-Facilitators

It is undoubtedly in the second register of action that the Catholic Church has been able to act as a true mediator, according to Faget's approach. If we adopt the conceptual distinction made by Smith and Nay, the Church has played the role of mediator-broker in the Basque country. Several times since the establishment of the Autonomous Community, members of the Catholic Church have been called, or have proposed, to act as intermediaries between the most radical parties. Their mediation efforts have mainly, but not exclusively, concerned the Spanish government and ETA. The Church has also been active in the promotion of dialogue, not only between the moderate Basque nationalists and the Spanish authorities, but among the Basque nationalists themselves. Though we lack precise data on the Church's mediation activities, on account of the necessary confidentiality of the negotiations, we may still find evidence of the interventions of some high-ranking religious personalities as mediators in secondary sources such as chronicles, testimonies or press articles, which points to the fact that their mediation efforts were anything but anecdotal.

The Church's function as a mediator seems to date back to the transition period. In his memoirs, Carlos Garaikoetxea, the former president of the Basque Autonomous Community (1980–85) and now a member of the moderate nationalist party *EA* (*Eusko Alkartasuna*, Basque solidarity) mentions an initiative undertaken by the Society of Jesus in 1984 with a view to initiating new negotiations (Garaikoetxea, 2002: 179–80). The Basque episcopal authorities regularly proposed their help, as, for instance, the Bishop of San Sebastián, Monsignor Setién, in 1986–87,[5] then in November 1997,[6] or the Bishop of Bilbao in October 1996. After a failed attempt to resume talks, ETA made public the names of four intermediaries who had taken part in the organisation of meetings with the Spanish government. Under the Socialist government, it was the former 1980 Nobel Peace Prize laureate, Argentinian writer Adolfo Pérez Esquivel, who assumed

[5] 'Entrevista realizada por Francisco Mora a Mons. Setién' *Interviú* 569 (9 April 1987) 19–23.

[6] 'La Iglesia vasca está dispuesta a mediar en el conflicto' *Egin* (2 November 1997).

this charge. When the conservative Popular Party came to office in 1996, Harry Barnes, a member of the Carter Foundation, took on the role of intermediary.[7] According to ETA, the representatives of the Spanish government were reluctant to accept this type of mediation which could eventually turn the domestic conflict into an international one. The extradition of two ETA representatives from Santo Domingo to Spain put an end to negotiations in August 1997. The Roman Catholic community of Sant'Egidio also offered its mediation services. Specialised in conflict management as in Mozambique for example, Sant'Egidio allegedly held secret meetings with ETA and the Spanish minister of the interior. The rumour of a potential police operation ended these talks. During the ETA ceasefire in 1998–99, Monsignor Uriarte, then Bishop of Zamora before becoming the Bishop of San Sebastián, is also said to have taken part—unsuccessfully—in negotiations between the armed organisation and the Popular Party government.[8] As the fragile success of such mediation efforts essentially depended on the actors' discretion, the official announcement of Monsignor Uriarte's mediation by the Spanish government in October 1999, ie, a few days before the truce was broken, may have contributed to weakening this mediation process.

Some representatives of the Church did not limit their mediation efforts to bilateral contacts between ETA and the Spanish government, but also acted in order to further dialogue between the moderate nationalists and the Spanish executive, as well as between moderate and radical nationalists. This initiative was undertaken by senior members of the Catholic hierarchy. In late September 2000, on the occasion of the canonisation of María Josefa

[7] The Carter Center Conflict Resolution Programme started showing interest in the Basque conflict in the early 1990s. In 1994, *Elkarri* and the Basque Studies Programme of the University of Nevada in Reno approached the Carter Center to inquire about its possible commitment as a mediator, should there be negotiations between the parties. On 14 November 1995, in San Sebastián, *Elkarri* and the Basque Studies Programme signed an agreement creating the *International Committee for the Basque Peace Process*. In 1995, Harry Barnes, a former diplomat and member of the Carter Center, established contacts with Basque political parties, representatives of the Socialist party (PSOE) and ETA. In 1996, after the victory of the conservative *Partido Popular* (PP) at the Spanish general elections, the foundation tried to inaugurate a new round of contacts, but in December, President Aznar and the minister of the interior, Jaime Mayor Oreja, prevented a meeting between PP members and the Carter Center. In May 2003, members of the Carter Fundation had their first contacts with the associations of victims of terrorism (*Fundación de víctimas del terrorismo*, *Fundación Miguel Angel Blanco*, FAES, *Fundación por la Libertad*, *Basta Ya*) and with the department of the Basque government in charge of the victims of terrorism (Fernando Lazaro, 'la fundación Carter contactó con las víctimas del terrorismo a finales de Mayo' *El Mundo* (6 July 2003, no 4960). Harry Barnes also joined the permanent group of international advisors to the peace process set up by JJ Ibarretxe, president of the Basque Autonomous Community, in January 2007, together with Joseba Azkarraga (Basque minister for Justice, Employment and Social security), Javier Madrazo (Izquierda Unida), Albert Reynolds (former Irish Taoiseach), Joanna Weschler (Human Rights Watch), Rolf Meyer (South Africa's former defence minister). (*Le Journal du Pays Basque*, 30–31 January 2007).

[8] *Gara* (1 May 2000).

del Corazón de Jesús Sancho de Guerra, talks were held between the head of the Holy See's diplomacy, Monsignor Tauran, and the president of the Basque government, Juan José Ibarretxe (PNV) on the one hand, and the Spanish minister of the interior, Jaime Mayor Oreja (PP) on the other. Their main objective was to analyse 'the present and future prospects of a peaceful solution [...] together with the potential contribution that the Catholic Church can offer'.[9] For the Spanish foreign affairs minister, Josep Piqué, this proposed 'collaboration' did not mean that the Church was to act as a mediator, as 'nobody can serve as a mediator between a democratic State and murderers'.[10] Beyond the political controversy, the Vatican acted in its capacity as an expert in peace seeking, which it had already done in other circumstances.

The new political context after the banning of the Basque radical nationalist party *Batasuna* (Unity) in June 2002 in Spain, favoured the emergence of a new form of mediation. Talks took place within the nationalist camp between the moderate PNV and EA parties, the ELA (*Euskal langileen alkartasuna*, Union of Basque Workers) and LAB (*Langile abertzaleen batzordeak*, Union of Patriot Workers) trade unions, political, cultural and economic actors and social movements close to the ideas of Basque leftist and radical nationalism, the association of *Udalbiltza* municipalities and some *abertzale* lawyers. These talks were symbolically initiated by religious actors, notably an Irish priest, Alec Reid, who, as a member of the Redemptorist Roman Catholic missionary order, had played a significant part in the 1998 Good Friday Agreement in Northern Ireland.[11] The initiative of Alec Reid evidenced the strategy of the Irish Catholic Church which had maintained contacts with the Republican leaders though it had forcefully and openly condemned the IRA's military campaign (Rafter, 2003). He proposed a 'tactical ceasefire' to ETA in order to put forward a common proposal for the resumption of negotiations with the Spanish State. He was helped in his task by members of the Bilbao diocese and supported by the Bishop of San Sebastián. Alec Reid had previously taken part in the peace conference organised by *Elkarri* in October 2001 and 2002, as a guest expert, together with a member of the Sant'Egidio community.[12]

[9] See: archimadrid.es/princi/menu/notdirec/notdirec/oct2000/03102000 (3 October 2000).

[10] *Ibid.*

[11] Resumen diario de prensa, Arzobispado de Pamplona (28 May 2003). See: iglesianavarra.org/hemeroteca/20030528.

[12] In the last stage of the Conference for Peace, in June–October 2002, Elkarri staged another seminar bringing together international experts in conflict resolution, with A Bartoli, the head of the International Centre of Conflict Resolution, Columbia University, and a member of the Sant'Egidio Community, WD Weisberg, a member of the Programme for the Resolution of International Conflicts, Harvard, H Barnes, the former head of the Conflict Resolution Programme in the Carter Center and Alec Reid.

The Church resumed its activism after ETA's announcement of a ceasefire on 22 March, 2006. On 3 April 2006, Monsignor Uriarte, the Bishop of San Sebastián, presented to the Vatican the efforts made by the Church of the Basque country in favour of peace. Two days later, Pope Benedict XVI exhorted the congregation gathered in Saint Peter's square 'to pray in order that everybody will intensify their efforts for the consolidation of the horizons of peace that seem to appear in the Basque country and in Spain, and to overcome the obstacles that could appear'.[13] Despite a very cautious attitude—promoting peace is *not* mediating in the conflict—the intervention of the Pope had a considerable symbolical impact, as it contributed to putting the Basque issue on the Catholic agenda. However, hope for a peaceful resolution of the conflict vanished when ETA resumed its violent campaign of assassination in December 2006.

The role of religious mediators is more akin to the position of facilitators than to the position of formulators or manipulators. Faget (2008: 318) has clearly shown that there was a consensus among specialists on three types of mediation. *Facilitators* act as intermediaries between the warring parties and actually have little control over the negotiation process. Such diplomacy of 'good offices' at best contributes to organising logistic support in the negotiation process and facilitating communication. *Formulators* have a more significant role in so far as they exert an important formal control as they choose where, how many and what types of meetings will be staged; they set the agenda, manage the information flow and may propose new solutions to the parties concerned. *Manipulators* can not only make proposals but also use their power of persuasion and their resources, and present conflicting parties with ultimatums. The Catholic Church mediators in the Basque country have mainly played the role of facilitators, furthering dialogue between the various parties. The fact that they have no decision-making power is most probably the reason why their action may be seen as legitimate by the warring factions, much in line with the 'power of powerlessness' extolled by the Quakers. 'Their power is acceptable precisely because they have no power to constrain actors and do not pursue their own objectives. They just have the possibility of applying one model and influencing the course of the exchanges' (Faget 2008: 320).

We should remain cautious at this stage of the analysis. It seems a priori that the Church has proved to be more efficient as a general mediator than as a broker, according to the precise definition of mediation proposed by Faget. The scarcity of information available, on account of the very secret nature of talks and negotiations, makes it impossible to delve further into this question. However, we have to address the question of the impartiality

[13] Luis R Aizpeolea, 'El Papa apoyó el proceso de paz tras la mediación del obispo Uriarte ante el Vaticano' *El País* (22 October 2006).

of the Church as a general mediator acting for social peace, and redefine the relationship between religion and politics in the Basque country.

II. IMPOSSIBLE IMPARTIALITY?

(a) Mediation in Context

The Church's activism on the theme of peace has generated open and politically-oriented controversies over the impartiality of the institution on both sides of the borders. The Church of the Basque country—the very expression 'the Basque Church' is much debated—has been confronted with a double problem of internal divide over the territorial issue within the Spanish collegial institutions, especially the Episcopal Conference, and within the Basque clergy. In Spain, the internal cleavage within the Church mirrors the various cleavages that have shaped Spain's political life, in some form of political isomorphism: left–right divide and territorial divide. The Spanish Episcopal Conference, for instance, has not always been in a position to adopt a consensual position on the question of territorial identity and Nation-State, as evidenced by the declaration of Monsignor Uriarte, the Bishop of San Sebastián, who publicly expressed his reservations[14] about the memorandum 'On Nation and Nationalism'[15] published by the Episcopal Conference on 7 January 2005 in which a clear distinction was made between legitimate and illegitimate forms of nationalism, and secessionist positions were condemned. Such a plurality of opinions has also been perceptible among the Basque-Navarre bishops, since the democratic transition. The activism of Guipuzcoan bishops in terms of general mediation has run counter to the more reserved position adopted by the bishops of Navarre over the concept of shared territoriality between the Basque and Navarre provinces. The clergy and the various secular movements have also split over the identity question. The *abertzale* ('patriot') tendency has been most perceptible in three organisations, which are both close to each other yet quite distinct—the Coordination of the Priests of the Basque Country (*Euskal Herriko Apaizen Koordinaketa*, EHAK) founded in 1976 and present on both sides of the border as early as 1977, the Popular Christian Communities (CCPs) and the magazine *Herria 2000 Eliza* ('people/country 2000 Church'). These movements have been studied in depth by Felix Placer in his PhD thesis in theology (Placer Ugarte, 1998) in which he highlights the fact that they have periodically expressed their own positions, sometimes at odds with the official views of the Church, over questions

[14] *La Vanguardia* (23 January 2005).

[15] 'Sobre nación y nacionalismo' *OICEE, nota de prensa, sobre nación y nacionalismo* (Madrid, 7 January 2005).

such as the theology of liberation, the status of political prisoners or the nagging problem of the territorial reorganisation of the ecclesiastical provinces of the Basque country and Navarre. The identity-oriented movements within the Basque clergy have been most active in the social forum over the question of peace, creating new debating arenas (Goñi Alzueta, 2003). In spite of their systematic, open opposition to all forms of violence, their views in favour of a shared Basque identity and territoriality have regularly been the butt of criticism, owing to their alleged partiality towards Basque nationalists.

The action of the Vatican, as the central institution of Roman Catholicism, initially took on a special meaning in this specific context. Different voices emanating from very distinct sectors of the Basque society appealed to the Vatican—Catholics asking for the official recognition of a Basque ecclesiastical province, or, conversely, victims of terrorism asking for a clearer condemnation of violence *and* of Basque nationalism, pacifists, etc. Periods of ceasefire unilaterally decided by ETA were favourable moments for the expression of more global messages from the Vatican in favour of peace in the Basque country. Pope Benedict XVI's exhortation in April 2006 testifies to this trend. The fact that he should have made an explicit reference to the Basque conflict, though in a very cautious manner, contributed to internationalising the Basque question, despite all the efforts developed by some actors who tried to keep it a purely domestic issue. The strong presence of clergymen of Basque origin in the Roman curia and in the missionary orders may also have had some influence on the Holy See's positions on the Basque question. However, we lack solid data to go further in that direction and analyse better the role played by key figures of Basque origin in Rome with strong experience as mediators in other conflicts.[16] Nevertheless, it clearly appears that the few implicit or explicit calls for the intervention of the Vatican's diplomacy were undoubtedly tainted by recurrent references

[16] Two figures, one from the Spanish Basque country and the other one from the French Basque country, typically represent such expert mediators. Born in San Sebastián, Monsignor Laboa acted as a mediator in many conflicts in Uruguay, Libya and Panama where, in his capacity as an apostolic nuncio, he liaised between General Noriega and the US government. According to *El Pais* (15 October 2000) he was also active in a case of extradition of some presumed ETA members between France, Cuba and Panama in the late 1980s. Monsignor Roger Etchegaray, who was born in Espelette (French Basque country), chaired the Pontifical Council Justice and Peace under John Paul II. A close advisor to Benedict XVI, he took part in a number of missions on behalf of the Vatican, notably with Saddam Hussein in 2003 or in Rwanda, etc (Etchegaray, 2007). According to *El Pais*, Basque political parties would have used Monsignor Etchegaray in order to gain access to the Vatican. In May 2004, he was asked by the Spanish Socialist party and by *Batasuna* to act as a mediator in the talks between the Spanish government and ETA. The prelate refused, as he did not want to involve the Vatican in these negotiations (*El Pais*, 22 October 2006). In October 2007, various media revealed Monsignor Etchegaray's 'indirect mediation' between ETA and the French authorities, an allegation that he denied. He seems to have adopted a very cautious attitude on the Basque question, although he was deeply concerned by the situation in his region of origin.

to the awkward positions of the Holy See on the Basque cause in recent history, notably during the Civil War (1936–39) and Franco's regime (Iztueta, 1981). The heavy burden of history visibly pervaded every reference to the Roman institution.

(b) Constraints and Resources of the 'Biased Mediator'

The question is therefore to know whether the Church's impossible neutrality can be seen as an obstacle to its efforts for the promotion of peace. From a comparative approach, the impartiality of the mediator as a necessary condition has been much debated. In his analysis, Faget has taken up the research work conducted by Paul Wehr and John Paul Lederach (Wehr and Lederach, 1991) who contend that, although trust in the mediator is a prerequisite, it is not necessarily coupled with impartiality, at least in the societies of Central America that they have studied. On the contrary, they uphold the hypothesis of the existence of an *insider-partial*—and not *outsider-neutral*—mediator whose acceptability and legitimacy rest not as much on his distance or objectivity but rather on his links with the conflict and his relations of trust with the warring parties. However, these authors underline the fact that this type of mediation may only occur in specific cultural contexts in which political, economic and social exchanges are still characterised by face to face relations and where traditions have not totally been eroded by modernity. A 'biased' mediator may thus appear to be more credible in the eyes of the actors, especially if he has some leverage. 'In other words, successful mediators need not systematically be impartial, and the game theory model reveals that bias, to a certain extent, notably through sharing information, is not only acceptable but sometimes necessary' (Faget, 2008: 319).

Can we thus say that the Catholic Church has been a biased mediator? This is the criticism levelled at the Church by the most radical and polarised parties. For instance, ETA has criticised the Rally for Peace organised in April 2001 by the Basque-Navarre bishops in Armentia, accusing the Church of trying to 'depoliticize the conflict' in order to go back to the period 'before the Lizarra Pact', while recalling the mediating role of the Church during the 1998–99 ceasefire. Organisations of prisoners' families (*Senideak*—the families) and the *Gestoras pro-amnistia*, close to the nationalist left, have regularly invited the Church to air its views on the problem of political prisoners, either by staging hunger strikes with the support of some priests, or by directly questioning the diocesan authorities. On the other side of the political spectrum, the organisations of the victims of terrorism have systematically blamed the Basque Church for its lack of concern for the families of the victims of ETA, and its guilty complacency for the most radical nationalists. Controversies have hinged on the problem of the funerals and services in memory of the victims who had met a violent death. Criticism has generally merged into a single but ambiguous message: the Church has been blamed for both its partiality *and* impartiality, deemed politically biased because it was based on some hypothetical equivalence of violence (on the part of the Spanish State and ETA).

Acting as a regulator between the various and diverging positions defended within his own diocese, the bishop is undoubtedly the religious personality who is the most exposed to criticism. This is particularly the case of the Bishop of San Sebastián in Guipuzcoa, a province where radical nationalism, though a minority movement, has historically been firmly rooted. In a recent book which updates previous research work on the subject (Setién, 1998), José Maria Setién (Setién, 2007), the Bishop of San Sebastián between 1972 and 2000, reveals how complex the pressure exerted on the Church has been in his diocese. He delves into the controversies over the positions of the Basque Church which rejected both ETA's violence and the purely repressive stance adopted by the state authorities—the bishops' visits to *all* the prisoners, the rights of the victims, the question of the funerals and commemorative services, the Basque and Spanish bishops' diverging positions during the 2006 ETA ceasefire, the debate over the equivalence of violence. Peace, according to Monsignor Setién, cannot be reduced to a mere issue of public order. In his view, there is a close link between the Church's predominantly religious vision of reconciliation and pardon and its call for the recognition of the fundamentally political dimension of the conflict which cannot be restricted only to the question of violence:

> From this perspective, dialogue, agreements and negotiations must encompass a wider spectrum than the relations with *ETA*. In other words, the solution to the 'conflict' and the achievement of peace must be attained, with or without *ETA*, by the political choice of negotiations.[17]
>
> (Setién, 2007: 197)

According to Monsignor Setién, the two processes—the end of violence and political normalisation—have to be distinguished and considered together in order to attain real pacification (Setién, 2007: 197). Such a stance is clearly at odds with the views of the armed organisation claiming for the recognition of the so-called inalienable rights of the Basque people, and with the positions of those who assimilate all claims for identity with terrorism. In the same vein, Monsignor Setién (2007: 202) challenges both the 2002 law on political parties—which banned Batasuna as a legitimate party—and Batasuna's persistent refusal to condemn ETA's violence. This ethical approach to the conflict has been perceived by the Basque radical

[17] This quotation and the following one were translated from Spanish.

nationalists and by their more radical opponents as abusively liberal, since it reaffirms the legitimacy of all ideologies—or as too overtly committed—because Monsignor Setién acknowledges the political nature of the conflict (Bastante Liébana, 2006). In his conversation with political specialist Francisco Garmendia (Garmendia and Setién, 2003) Setién exposes his pluralist approach to a democratic state, respectful of cultural diversity, a theory which may apply to the pluri-national Spanish State as well as to a hypothetical Basque state. The 'state' and the 'nation' must be distinguished and the recognition of citizens' rights need not necessarily be linked with any adhesion to 'national' feelings:

> From the perspective that he belongs to the political community, according to what we have just defined, any 'citizen' who has stable relations with a territorially well-defined Basque State should be regarded as a fully-fledged 'Basque citizen', even though he may not feel he is part of the Basque 'Nation'. For that matter, it is only through the mature and respectful acceptance of all the 'differences' born out of 'freedom' that political *convivencia* ('living together') may emerge, the necessary condition so that tolerance, assumed as a fundamental value in a modern and pluralist society, and solidarity, in a society made up of and shaped by national 'differences', may guarantee political and social cohesion.
>
> (Setién, 2003: 135)

Setién's reflections are complex, oscillating between a liberal *and* pluralist approach to citizenship and the political acknowledgment of national identities. His views, which according to some observers (Bastante Liébana, 2006: 113–33) may have influenced the sovereignty-association plan promoted by the president of the Basque Autonomous Community Juan José Ibarretxe in 2003–05, were to shape the debate in the Basque public arena in the years 1990–2000. The accusations of partiality regularly levelled at him were also the price to pay for his intellectual and ethical commitment. Setién's positions—which were in fact far from being consensual—were challenged by those, even among nationalists, who contended that the only conflict in the Basque country was the radical violence imposed by a group of criminals to the whole society.

III. SECULARISATION AND PEACE BUILDING

We will now tackle the issue of the social and political response to the Church's commitment to peace. Broadly speaking, the involvement of religious actors in mediation activities evidences the redefinition of the relationship between religion and the public sphere in the Basque country from a double perspective—the role of religion in Basque society and the influence of the multiple conceptions of the Church's mission on the peace movements and on the democratic debate.

(a) Trust in the Church and Secularisation

The involvement of religious actors in the promotion of peace is multifaceted. By renouncing any monopolistic position on this issue, the Church has found itself sharing the same public space with a multitude of other social and political movements. The Catholic Church may have been seen as one of the main models for political protest against Francoism (Iztueta, 1981) but it is no longer the case today. In his recent PhD thesis on environnmental protest in the Spanish Basque country, Mario Zubiaga Garate (2008) underlines that many of today's pacifist movements borrow their line of action—in terms of protest *and* mediation—from the environmental mobilisation movements of the early 1990s, rather than from the Church. For example, *Elkarri*, founded in January 1995, followed the initiative of the *Lurraldea* (territory) collective group, created in 1986, to oppose the planned Irurtzun-Andoain motorway. The stance adopted today by the Church, notably via the *Batetik* Centre, along with other pacifist movements, confers on it the role of a 'civil society' actor among others in its mobilisation for the building of a more global movement for peace.

The Church's acknowledgement of plurality is all the more significant as its positions in Basque society have evolved over the last decades. According to a *Euskobarometro* study published in November 2007 on the degree of trust in the main institutions as expressed by the citizens of the Basque Autonomous Community,[18] the Catholic Church only ranked eleventh out of a total of 17, behind the Basque Parliament, the government of the Autonomous Community, the European Union, the unions, *Ertzaintza* (the autonomous police force), the King, managers' organisations, the Spanish government, the Congress of Deputies and the Senate. However, the Church was cited before the Constitutional Court, the political parties, the *Guardia Civil* and the national police force, the Justice department, the armed forces and NATO. Generally speaking, there was an approval rate of 3.7 for the Church on a scale ranging from 0 to 10. Most analysts explain these results by a general feeling of *desconfianza* ('mistrust') for the institutions in the Basque society—only the Basque Parliament and government had scores higher than 5 out of 10. Such results should of course be apprehended with all the necessary caution as they do not reveal much on the exact state of public opinion on religion. However, they reveal a new trend: the end of the social prevalence of the Church in Basque society, historically shaped by the structuring role of Catholicism.

This phenomenon is not new. Indeed, the secularisation process was already more pronounced in the Basque country than in the rest of Spain

[18] Euskobarometro, *Estudio periódico de la opinión pública vasca*, Leioa, Euskal Herriko unibertsitatea, November 2007.

by the end of Franco's regime, as though opposition to the dictatorship was necessarily coupled with growing estrangement from a religious institution regarded as the main support of the regime. The *Law on Historical Memory*, voted by the Congress of Deputies on 31 October 2007, had reactivated the debate on the role of the Spanish Church—and the specificities of the Basque clergy—during the Civil War and Franco's dictatorship,[19] a debate which had conspicuously been silenced during the democratic transition period in the name of national reconciliation.[20] However, and despite this new politicisation of religion, in the Basque country and Navarre, two provinces with the highest ratio of church-goers and clergymen until the early 1970s, there has been a significant and regular loss of interest for the Church, as regularly confirmed by CIS (*Centro de investigaciones sociológicas*) polls. The Basque country may still be an exception in Spain, but it can be explained by the persistence of the secularisation process today, contrary to the rest of the country (Pérez-Agote and Santiago Garcia, 2005). The hypothesis developed by Pérez-Agote (1986) at the end of Francoism, who argued that the central role of religion had been replaced by politics, is thus confirmed. Nationalism and the linguistic issue have gradually become more important than religion in a now secularised Basque society. The Basque radical nationalists' rejection of the Church has thus contributed to furthering disinterest or even hostility towards religion among the younger generations.

As a consequence, there are now very few seminarians in the Basque dioceses which used to be the main purveyors of young priests, a phenomenon confirmed by data published by *Comisión episcopal de seminarios y universidades* in 2007. The number of seminarians dropped by 30 per cent between 1987 (1997 seminarians) and 2007 (1387) in Spain. The trend is even more pronounced in the Basque country. In the diocese of Vitoria, which played such a significant role in the history of the Church, there was only one seminarian in 2007 against 119 in the diocese of Madrid (Bellido, 2007).[21] We can thus speak of an ever-growing gap between the loss of social influence exerted by the Church as an institution and a high level of politicisation among the religious actors in their public activities. The perception of the major role of the Catholic Church by the political world and the media seems to be increasingly disconnected from the reality

[19] The *Ley de la memoria histórica* or *Ley de extensión de derechos a los afectados por la Guerra civil y la dictadura* is a law initiated by JL Zapatero's Socialist government for the recognition of the victims of Francoism. This much debated law was approved by the Council of Ministers on 28 July 2006 and by the Congress of Deputies on 31 October 2007. It finds its origin in the creation of an inter-departmental committee in charge of rehabilitating the victims of Francoism (Decree, 10 September 2004).

[20] Sandrine Lefranc has highlighted the ambivalent rhetoric of repentance used by the Churches of Argentina and South Africa after the end of the dictatorial regimes (Lefranc, 2002: 179).

[21] J Bellido, 'Creciente caída del número de vocaciones en España', *Camineo.info, Noticias católicas en Internet* (19 February 2007).

of its eroding social influence. However, there is still mutual recognition among institution. Political parties and institutional actors acknowledge the importance of the Church as a meaningful and legitimate reference in a public sphere lacking stability.

(b) A Catholic Methodology of Peace?

The religious dimension of the Catholic institution both brings together and singles out the various initiatives undertaken by the clergy within the multifaceted world of peace movements. The Church's commitment to the promotion of peace is made, as we have just explained, in the name of a conception of democracy in which the notion of subsidiarity prevails. More fundamentally, this form of interventionism betrays a critical approach to democracy. The Church rejects a purely *procedural* conception of democracy, according to which political decisions are legitimate first because they are made by a majority. From a critical perspective, the majority rule may be useful for the adoption of temporary compromises, but can hardly initiate any durable solutions to deeply-rooted conflicts such as the ethno-nationalist Basque one. Some mobilisation movements, notably those inspired by Monsignor Sétien's reflections, also level criticism at the *constitutional* conceptions of democracy, in which the institutional arrangements of rules and procedures are essential for the achievement of political and social stability. In the Basque country, the institutional order which emerged after the 1978 Constitution of Spain has been unable to address the issue of the recognition of Basque identity in a completely normalised and pacified way. If we follow Funes (1998) other movements such as *Gesto por la paz* are conversely supported by citizens who adhere to the institutional order based on the Constitution and calling for the end of violence. Through its promotion of a wider social debate hinging on the question of peace, the Church promotes a *deliberative* conception of democracy in which dialogue should precede decision-making. Contrary to the majority system in which the objective is to assess the balance of power without eventually changing the actors' respective viewpoints, the deliberative model makes it possible to solve moral conflicts which, according to Gutmann and Thompson (2004) always imply irreconcilable positions.[22] In the deliberative process, every single dimension of the problem becomes essential and can be discussed. As identity conflicts are both political *and* ethical cum moral conflicts, purely

[22] These authors define deliberative democracy 'as a form of government in which free and equal citizens (and their representatives) justify decisions in a process in which they give one another reasons that are mutually acceptable and generally accessible, with the aim of reaching conclusions that are binding on all citizens in the present and open to challenge in the future' (Gutmann and Thompson, 2004: 7).

procedural democratic approaches do not seem to the best tools to initiate any durable or viable solutions.

The Catholic Church seems to have adopted the same critical approach to procedural democracy in the Basque country as it had already done in other domains, notably on ethical problems. In Spain, the electoral victory of the Socialist party after the Madrid bombings on 11 March 2004 was an opportunity for the Church and some conservative milieus to reactivate their critical positions, especially against the new social reforms on same-sex marriage or education. Barreiro (2001) has shown how the various conceptions of democracy—deliberative, constitutional, majority—could be mobilised and opposed on ethical and moral issues such as abortion in Spain and Italy. Politically-committed Christians have to overcome the inherent contradiction of the logic of democratic public deliberation—laws are the expression of the citizens' collective will—and the binding religious law which must prevail over all, whether they adhere to it or not (Hervieu-Léger, 1996). There are indeed superior Christian values which cannot be constrained by the majority rule. In the Church's view, the *nature* of the law is often of more importance than its *form*, in accordance with the Catholic conception of common good. During the democratic transition in Spain, some values of democratic governance such as tolerance and acceptance of the 'Other' were encouraged by the Church while others were ethically challenged even though they had been institutionalised (Anderson, 2003). It is thus from the perspective of the complex positioning of the Catholic Church towards the democratic regime that its pacifist activism in the Basque country must be apprehended.

The deliberative option is at the core of the methodology promoted by the Baketik Centre in Arantzazu, the Church's latest initiative for the promotion of peace. According to Philippe Braud, it evidences the Catholics' deep and structural reluctance towards any politicisation of the conflict (Braud, 1998: 39–40). Historian Ludger Mees highlights the fact that the diverging opinions in the political sphere on the nature of the conflict may account for the different positions adopted by the peace movements. Contrary to *Gesto por la paz*, *Elkarri*, for instance, considers that the debate is political, not ethical (Mees, 2003: 97). The source of violence thus finds its origin in the conflicting opposition between a significant part of the population and the Spanish State on issues such as power sharing and self-determination. Mees also points out that there is a double risk in the openly political dimension of *Elkarri's* action, since its efficiency depends on the support of political parties. *Elkarri* is also criticised by all those who object to the intervention of non-elected organisations.

Some Catholic mobilisation movements have tried to smooth out differences with a view to initiating some common and converging positions. This is the case with the pacifist movement in Arantzazu in the years 1999–2000. Its approach to peace was based on the teachings of St Francis of Assisi and Monsignor Sétien's reflections. The Baketik Centre has reaffirmed such references since its creation in 2006 under the auspices of the Franciscan community, by giving priority to the promotion of a generalist method of 'ethical elaboration of conflicts'. Between 2006 and 2007, 3500 people, including local representatives and civil servants, took part in the training sessions staged by the Arantzazu centre for peace. We may speak here of an implicit division of work—organisations such as *Elkarri* or *Gesto por la paz* are entrusted with the task of looking for concrete solutions among the most polarised parties in the conflict, while Baketik conducts preliminary training work on more global societal problems, without forgetting the religious dimension. In other terms, pacifist organisations are active in the 'pre-conciliation' and 'conciliation' stages, and Baketik is in charge of post-conflict 'reconciliation'.[23] Through the expression 'ethical elaboration' rather than 'resolution', Baketik insists on the complexity of some conflicts, with no specific solution, which may continue even after the end of violence. Baketik proposes to work on three themes: (1) reappraisal of the perceptions of the conflict and of the opponent; (2) personal links with the conflict (desire for and perceptions of the outcome) and (3) methodology of empathy. Such an approach, inherited from a long experience of mediation in the Basque conflict (Fernandez, 2007) is presented by Baketik as an instrument which can be used in other conflicting situations, notably in matters of inter-cultural and inter-religious dialogue. For instance, the 'Arantzazu Assisi Proposal', a collection of prayers and quotations which Baketik published in six languages in 2008 (Baketik, 2008) and sent to all Basque schools, evidences this new global approach, just like the organisation of solidarity weeks for the African continent. By so doing, Baketik intends to reconcile an ethical approach to conflicts globally apprehended and take into account the emergence of new identity problems linked to the transformation of Basque society, notably because of immigration. At the same time, such an inter-cultural approach should probably be related to the new context of the professionalisation of mediation, especially in a society with a high social capital and a dense network of community life groups, NGOs and social movements (Mota and Subirats, 2000).

IV. CONCLUSION: TOWARDS A RESEARCH AGENDA

In the closing lines of this chapter, we should remain prudent about the real impact of the Catholic Church's action in matters of mediation. We may

[23] Intervention of Jonan Fernández, workshop *La mediación en los conflictos políticos nacionales e internacionale* (Baketik Centre, Arantzazu, 5 June 2008). The affiliation with *Elkarri* has been reinforced by the personal history of the Baketik centre leader who was the former leader of *Elkarri* and an environmental and political activist in the early 1990s.

indeed express some reservations about the consequences of the Basque clergy's mediation-facilitation efforts *stricto sensu*. However, the Church's activism in order to attract public attention to the urgent necessity of peace cannot be denied. A more detailed analysis should focus on the way Catholic actors intervene in each of the three stages which characterise the construction of political problems, according to Pierre Lascoumes and Patrick Le Galès. The first stage is the transformation of some social facts into public problems, after a process of categorisation: 'The problem only becomes a public one when the mobilised actors manage to make it emerge in the public space, ie, when it becomes a cause of public attention, even of controversies, and when positions oppose each other in order to define its contours, scope and causes' (Lascoumes and Le Galès 2007: 69). In such a process, politicians do not necessarily play an essential role. The Church's contribution to the first stage of the transformation of the peace issue into a public problem has been significant, especially in the Basque country where whole segments of society still refuse to use the expression 'peace process' to qualify a conflict perceived as merely pertaining to public order. A public problem then becomes a political one when mobilisation 'is strong enough to make it sufficiently visible and challenging for actors who were initially reluctant to take position and debate for or against it' (Lascoumes and Le Galès, 2007: 80). The problem 'becomes political when the solution envisaged concerns public authorities' (Lascoumes and Le Galès: 70). We have seen that part of the Catholic mediation efforts converge on the recognition of the political dimension of the conflict and on the necessity of a social, political and institutional response to it.

However, we have not addressed the question of the Catholic 'third sector' in the third stage of the process. There are indeed three necessary conditions for the incorporation of a problem into the government's agenda: actors must first acknowledge that there is a problem pertaining to general interest and calling for governmental action. The problem must then be presented in terms compatible with the government's domain of competence and in keeping with its ideological positions. Finally, there is no systematic call for the actors' intervention and involvement on account of the difficulties of adjusting their respective agendas. In the Basque country, the institutional response to the conflict has taken the form of extremely diverging politically-oriented initiatives, ranging from the Ajuria Enea Pact in 1988 (together with the PP-PSOE anti-terrorism Pact in 2000 in Spain) and President Ibarretxe's project for new statutes in the Basque Autonomous Community, voted by the Basque Parliament in December 2004 but rejected by the Congress of Deputies in Madrid in March 2005, to sovereignist initiatives such as the Lizarra-Garazi Pact in 1998. Daniele Conversi (2006) has highlighted the potential threats at each of the three stages in the process: the persistence of a culture of violence at the local level, the central government's uncompromising positions and the influence of the international context and notably the 'war on terror' in the US since 9/11. In such an environment, the Basque regional Parliament[24] voted a resolution on 27 June 2008 in favour of a new referendum supporting the peace process in the Basque country. Presented by President Ibarretxe amid a new campaign of political violence, the text was welcomed by the usual chorus of protest and support. The proposed text has recently been invalidated by the Spanish Constitutional Court, after an appeal lodged by the central government. What will the impact on public opinion of these pacifist initiatives be amid such diverging and discordant positions? How will the Catholic Church manage to reconcile its acknowledged expertise in peaceful mediation and the historical burden of its role in the genesis of the conflict? Catholic mediation is more than ever at a watershed, permanently exposed to the changing winds of political passion.

REFERENCES

Anderson, J (2003) 'Catholicism and Democratic Consolidation in Spain and Poland' 26(1) *West European Politics* 137, 156.

Baketik (2008) *Points de rencontre interculturelle et interreligieuse. Une proposition, 80 prières et des textes pour la paix* (Arantzazu, Baketik).

Barreiro, B (2001) Democracía y conflicto moral: la política del aborto en España e Italia (Madrid, Istmo).

Bastante Liébana, J (2006) *Setién. Un pastor entre lobos* (Madrid, La esfera de los libros).

Braud, P (1998) *Etes-vous catholique?* (Paris, Presses de Sciences Po).

Conversi, D (2006) 'Why do Peace Processes Collapse? The Basque Conflict and the Three-spoilers Perspective' in E Newman and O Richmond (eds), *Challenges to Peacebuilding: Managing Spoilers during Conflict Resolution* (Tokyo, United Nations University Press) 173, 199.

Enjolras, B (2008) 'Deux perspectives théoriques sur la gouvernance' Working paper, groupe de recherche CIRIEC France (Paris, CIRIEC France, unpublished manuscript).

Etchegaray, R (2007) *J'ai senti battre le coeur du monde: conversations avec Bernard Lecomte* (Paris, Fayard).

Faget, J (2008) 'Les métamorphoses du travail de paix. Etat des travaux sur la médiation dans les conflits politiques violents' 58(2) *Revue française de science politique* 309, 333.

Fernandez, J (2007) Being Human in Conflicts. An Ethical Reflection after Direct Experience of the Basque Conflict (Arantzazu, Baketik).

Funes, MJ (1998) 'Social Responses to Political Violence in the Basque Country: Peace Movements and their Audience' 42(4) *The Journal of Conflict Resolution* 493, 510.

[24] This chapter was written before the 1 March 2009 elections to the Basque Parliament which led to the first non-Basque nationalist autonomous government since Madrid had granted self-government in 1980.

Garaikoetxea, C (2002) *Euskadi: la transición inacabada. Memorias políticas* (Barcelona, Planeta Singular).
Garmendia, F and Setién, JM (2003) *Pueblo vasco y soberanía. Aproximación histórica y reflexión ética* (Lasarte, Ostoa).
Goñi Alzueta, J (ed) (2003) *Tiempo de Soluciones, Proyectos políticos, Análisis y Sugerencias* (Bilbao, Herria, 2000).
Gutmann, A and Thompson, D (2004) *Why Deliberative Democracy?* (Princeton, Princeton University Press).
Hervieu-Léger, D (1996) 'Croire en modernité : au-delà de la problématique des champs religieux et politiques' in P Michel (ed), *Religion et démocratie* (Paris, Albin Michel) 361, 381.
Itçaina, X (2005) 'La médiation vaine ? L'Église catholique et la question basque' in J Faget (ed), *Médiation et action publique. La dynamique du fluide* (Pessac, Presses Universitaires de Bordeaux) 117, 134.
—— (2007) *Les virtuoses de l'identité. Religion et politique en Pays Basque* (Rennes, Presses universitaires de Rennes).
—— (2010) 'Between Mediation and Commitment. The Catholic Church and the Basque Conflict' in J Haynes (ed), *Religion and Politics in Europe, the Middle East and North Africa.* (London, Routledge) 91–113.
Iztueta, P (1981) *Sociología del fenómeno contestatorio del clero vasco 1940–1975 (análisis de las causas de la radicalización del clero vasco en el período 1940–1974)* (Bayonne, Elkar).
Lascoumes, P and Le Galès, P (2007) *Sociologie de l'action publique* (Paris, Armand Colin).
Lefranc, S (2002) *Politiques du pardon* (Paris, Presses universitaires de France).
MacClancy, J (2007) *Expressing Identities in the Basque Arena* (Oxford, James Currey).
Mansvelt Beck, J (2005) *Territory and Terror. Conflicting Nationalism in the Basque Country* (London, Routledge).
Mees, L (2003) *Nationalism, Violence and Democracy. The Basque Clash of Identities* (London, Palgrave Macmillan).
Mota, F and Subirats J (2000) 'El quinto elemento: el capital social de las Comunidades Autónomas. Su impacto sobre el funcionamiento del sistema político autonómico' 1(2) *Revista Española de Ciencia Política*, 123–58.
Nay, O and Smith A (2002) 'Les intermédiaires en politique. Médiation et jeux d'institutions' in O Nay and A Smith (eds), *Le gouvernement du compromis. Courtiers et généralistes dans l'action politique* (Paris, Economica) 1–21.
Pagola, JA (1995) *Una ética para la paz, los obispos del Pais Vasco (1968–1992)* (San Sebastian, Idatz).
Palard, J (2006) 'Médiation et institution catholique' 133 *Archives de sciences sociales des religions* 9–16.
Pérez-Agote, A (1986) 'The Role of Religion in the Definition of a Symbolic Conflict: Religion and the Basque Problem' 33(4) *Social Compass* 419–35.
Perez-Agote, A and Santiago García, JA (2005) *La situación de la religión en España a principios del siglo XXI* (Madrid, CIS).
Placer Ugarte, F (1998) *Creer en Euskal Herria: la experiencia creyente de las Comunidades Cristianas Populares y de la Coordinadora de Sacerdotes de Euskal Herria, 1976–1996* (Bilbao, Herria 2000 Eliza).
Rafter, K (2003) 'Priests and Peace: The role of the Redemptorist Order in the Northern Ireland Peace Process' 28(1) *Etudes irlandaises* 159–76.

Séguy, J (1984) 'Pour une sociologie de l'ordre religieux' 57(1) *Archives des sciences sociales des religions* 55, 68.

Setién, JM (1998) *Obras completas. 1. Dios, política, paz* (San Sebastian, Idatz).

—— (2003) 'Función del estado y de la soberanía en una sociedad plurinacional. Reflexión ética' in F Garmendia and JM Setién (eds), *Pueblo vasco y soberanía. Aproximación histórica y reflexión ética* (Lasarte, Ostoa) 65, 195.

—— (2007) *Un obispo vasco ante ETA* (Barcelona, Crítica).

Smock, DR (ed) (2006) *Religious Contributions to Peacemaking. When Religion brings Peace, not War* (Washington, United States Institute of Peace).

Wehr, P and Lederach JP (1991) 'Mediating Conflict in Central America' 28(1) *Journal of Peace Research* 85–96.

Zubiaga Garate, M (2008) *Boteretik eraginera: mekanismoak eta prozesuak Leitzarango eta Urbina/Maltzagako liskarretan* PhD, Dpto. de ciencias políticas y de la administración (Leioa, Euskal Herriko Unibertsitatea).

Zulaika, J (1988) *Basque Violence. Metaphor and Sacrament* (Reno, University of Nevada Press).

5

From 'Charity' to 'Mediation', From the Roman Suburbs to UNESCO: The Rise of the 'Peace Brokers' of the Community of Sant'Egidio

PIERRE ANOUILH

All together we'll be one
We where gathered by His world
To be a family of love
'cause a new time has come
you can start to dream, now ...
'Il Vangelo Della Pace' Song of the Community of Sant'Egidio

IN 1995, DURING an official visit to Italy, Sylvestre Ntibantunganya the President of Burundi and his diplomatic advisors met the community of Sant'Egidio. After the official visits, a meeting was organised at the headquarters of the community in the Trastevere. Following discussion, the president asked Sant'Egidio to do something for Burundi.[1] In 1995, Sant'Egidio launched a series of preliminary contacts among the Burundian political forces. In 1996, the idea of a direct negotiation between the government and the rebellion emerged.[2] On 10 March 1997, the government agreed to open negotiations with Leonard Nyangoma's CNDD (National Council for the Defence of Democracy). From 27 February to 10 March 1997, the headquarters of Sant'Egidio was the place for the negotiations.[3]

[1] Interview with Président Ntibantunganya (Bujumbura, Burundi, June 2006).

[2] But in the same year, the government was victim of a coup. The new president, Pierre Buyoya agrees to negotiate with the CNDD in exchange for a cancellation of the international sanctions against Burundi.

[3] Voluntarily secret, the negotiation process suffered serious leaks and a rumour began to spread in Bujumbura. On 13 May 1997, President Buyoya confirms the rumour. His declaration provokes a huge scandal among the Burundian political force. The mediation is perceived

All Burundian political key actors in contact with the community, despite their antagonistic political goals, recognise Sant'Egidio's 'experience, skills and charisma'.[4] Sant'Egidio appears as 'an efficient pool of diplomats without any material interest at stake'. A few years earlier, in Rome on 4 October 1992 (the feast day of St Francis of Assisi, patron saint of Sant'Egidio) following 27 months' of heavy and delicate negotiations held in the local seat of the community, the Mozambican General Peace Accord was signed. Four mediators assisted the belligerents towards peace: Mario Raffaelli, the deputy who represented the Italian government, His Grace Jaime Gonçalvez, Archbishop of Beira and Andrea Riccardi and Matteo Zuppi of Sant'Egidio. Armando Emilio Guebuza, Minister of Transport and Communication and current President of Mozambique, directed the delegation of the FRELIMO (Liberation Front of Mozambique); Raul Manuel Domingos, Chief of the Department of Foreign Affairs for his party, directed that of the RENAMO (Mozambican National Resistance).

The headquarters of the laymen's Catholic community of Sant'Egidio would appear to have become a place where one should seek a truce to conflicts. Discussing peace has now become an important identity marker for Sant'Egidio. The 'work for peace' holds a strategic place concerning both the later internal developments of the community and the way Sant'Egidio is perceived. Created to assist the most impoverished and vulnerable people of the Roman suburbs, Sant'Egidio was not predestined to peacemaking (or diplomacy), if it were not for its unique *Weltanschauung* and operatives modes (Anouilh, 2005). This original spiritual community has now become a legitimate actor in peacemaking and conflict resolution.

But for many observers, Sant'Egidio embodied either a good example of 'track 2 diplomacy' or another transnational actor dedicated to 'mediation' and 'good offices'. For others, it symbolises the rise of a 'transnational civil society' through the medium of a 'parallel diplomacy'. Sant'Egidio's work for peace would then be a topical example of the rise of a 'faith-based diplomacy' inaugurating an ethical shift in the international arena where states are bypassed by 'skilful individuals'. Part of a larger PhD research focusing on Sant'Egidio's commitment for peace in Mozambique and Burundi and grounded on several fieldworks in Africa and Italy, this chapter wishes to avoid these 'zero-sum/win-lose perspectives' concerning the patterns of interaction between states and non-state actors and would also like to avoid the substantialist point of view embedded in the mainstream 'globalist'

as high treason. From now on, the regional mediation takes the leadership. Nevertheless, Sant'Egidio will reintegrate the peace process as an expert during the Arusha negotiations in Tanzania (1997–2000). As vice-president of the third commission, Sant'Egidio was in charge of the ceasefire.

[4] Interviews with representatives of Burundian political forces involved in the negotiation process (Bujumbura, Burundi, 2006).

literature of international relations theory. What is really at stake with the rise of Sant'Egidio as a legitimate peace broker?

Sant'Egidio is, above all, a Catholic organisation. But observers should be aware of situating the 'religious' and its weight and role in the right place. Using the sociology of Pierre Bourdieu and the interrelated concepts of 'social capital' and 'symbolic capital', this chapter provides an empirical case study, which aims to understand how, why and in what way a Roman lay Catholic community became a 'legitimate actor' in the 'transnational space of peacemaking'. The first part will focus on certain features, often overlooked, but essential for a full understanding of the action of this transnational community, suffused with a missionary spirit. The second part will provide an analysis of the contemporary emergence of a 'transnational space of peacemaking' in relation to the phenomenon of the 'privatisation of diplomacy' and the dynamics of a state's redeployment in a context of globalisation. The third part will provide an analysis of Sant'Egidio as a symbolic capital to explain the social conditions of their success.

I. FACES OF SANT'EGIDIO

Sant'Egidio's pluralist identity is not easily handled, as seen by the multiplicity of representations it is (or has been) subjected to, as much in diplomatic activity as in that of experts of emergency activity. For specialists in diplomatic studies, the passive activity of Sant'Egidio provides a pertinent example of 'track two diplomacy' carried out by a religious order. Many expatriates we met during our investigations, who work in the humanitarian field, see a talented NGO there, specialised in conflict resolution. If it is true that Sant'Egidio has many faces, it is and remains above all a Catholic organisation, dedicated to charity on a local level in a very personal way. The community of Sant'Egidio demonstrates, in light of its evangelical culture, certain *integralism*, organising its vision of the world around a religious reference. The Catholic identity is thus a synonym for commitment in order 'to shape a world'.

(a) Geopolitics of Charity

The founding members of Sant'Egidio are accustomed to being introduced as the 'sons of Vatican II and of May 68'. The Second Vatican Council played a guiding role in the doctrine of the community. Vatican II represents a key period in the history of Catholicism at the end of the twentieth century. Sant'Egidio received the Council retroactively. At the start of the community action, only passages and ideas, and not texts, held the attention of its founders: change and reform being necessary, the Church of the poor and the primate of God's Word took their place next to the words of Jean XXIII on the verge on Vatican II: 'the Church is presented as it is and as it would like to be, as the Church of all and particularly that of the poor'. It was later that the Council was truly internalised after studying its texts, in particular, *Dei Verbum*.

As an organisation, Sant'Egidio has myths and protecting figures: St Francis of Assisi; the Mission of Paris; figures such as His Grace Affre[5] and His Grace Darboy,[6] as well as worker priests, among others, fill the unconscious collective of its founders. Jean Paul II, Bishop of Rome, was an eminent figure of the 'world of ideas' of the community and can be considered the author of its institutionalisation at the seat of the local church. Sant'Egidio succeeded in winning the esteem and friendship of the late Pope, who travelled several times to Trastevere and from 1986 entrusted Sant'Egidio with the responsibility of organising, following his Prayer of Assisi, the inter-religious meetings of Assisi. Sant'Egidio also maintains strong relations with diverse religious organisations, demonstrated by celebrating the Wednesday before Easter at Santa Maria's Church in Trastevere in memory of those who died as martyrs throughout the year. In 1995, the Jesuit General, the Master General of the Dominicans, the Mother Superior of the Sisters of Sacré-Coeur, the Superior-General of the White Fathers and the Abbot Primate of the Benedictines addressed a letter of support and friendship to the community. Special ties were formed with the Eastern churches:

> We have very good relations with all Christian churches in the East. We have always said that Christians, and Western Catholics in particular, as well as Protestants elsewhere, are indebted to the Christian churches of the East: the debt of faith. Because Faith, the Gospel comes from there, from the East.[7]

In 1982, Sant'Egidio intervened in Lebanon in favour of lifting the siege of the village of Deir El Khamar carried out by the Druzes and became involved in the accord to protect Christians in the Shouf district. During the Iran–Iraq War, Sant'Egidio organised the rescue of Iraqi Christian populations bound for Europe, the United States and Canada:

> The work and history of the relationships between the community and the Eastern churches is the most advanced, most extensive, the longest- running, and the most historical of all sectors of international relations of the community. That is why we have woven such good relations with the Armenians and with the Eastern churches in general, and we have no problems, neither with the Russians nor with the Gregorian Armenians.[8]

[5] Denis Auguste Affre (1783–48), Archbishop of Paris, killed at the insurrection of June.

[6] Georges Darboy (1793–1848), Archbishop of Paris, was one of the first hostages shot by the Council.

[7] Interview, Rome, 2004.

[8] *Ibid.*

(b) Spirituality and Action

In the colourful language that is unique to the members of Sant'Egidio, they often symbolise the essence of their actions through what they call the 'Parable of the Good Samaritan'. This founding parable asks that,

> We do not walk down the street simply thinking of where we are going and at what time we will arrive, but with our eyes open to those we cross (...) that we see who we meet and above all those who are exhausted, sick, in difficulty, nearly dead.[9]

Among the community's identity markers, prayer is of primary importance. Characteristic of the community, members claim that action begins with prayer. It is: An invitation to convert, by ceasing to live only for oneself, and by beginning, with free-will, to be the instruments of a bigger love for everyone, men and women, and especially the most destitute'.[10]

Practising *Lectio Divina*, inaugurated in 1973, has never been interrupted. Every evening a communal prayer is held which is open to everyone. The community has its own liturgy: its prayers mix Byzantine rituals with African songs. None of its activities is exempt from referring to Scripture, whether it is a matter of helping undocumented refugees or supporting prisoners. According to Article 3 of the statutes of the association, 'the community is conscious that in them (the poor), the Lord Jesus is mysteriously present, as we learn from the teachings of St Matthew, chapter 25'.

> St Matthew, 25:35 and following:
>
> For I was hungry and you gave me food
> I was thirsty and you gave me drink
> Naked and you clothed me
> Ill and you cared for me
> In prison and you visited me
>
> And the king said to them in reply:
> Amen, I say to you
> Whatever you did for one of these least brothers of mine
> You did for me.'

Articles 2 and 3 of the statutes of the community state:

> Article 2: The first aim of the community of Sant'Egidio is evangelism, 'essential mission of the Church' (Evangeli Nuntiandi, 14). The community recognises the Word of Jesus: 'I must announce the good Word of the Kingdom of God' (Luke, 4:3) also applies to the community and adopts the teachings of Paul the Apostle: 'For though I preach the Gospel, I have nothing to glory of: for necessity is laid upon me; yea, woe is unto me, if I preach not the Gospel!' (I Cor 9:16). The

[9] *Ibid.*
[10] Extract from the community's website: www.santegidio.org.

> community lives this commitment to evangelism especially for those who are the most remote, in order to be able to form one family with them at the table of the Eucharist, in mutual charity and in the spirit of the Lord.
>
> Article 3: Another fundamental aim of the community of Sant'Egidio is helping the poor; the community, guided by Scripture, knows that God is the defender of the poor: 'To you the poor man relinquishes himself, for the orphan you are sustenance' (Ps 10:35). Through evangelism and serving the poor, the community 'wishes to be—according to the teaching of Jean XXIII—a Church for everyone, especially for the poor'.
>
> 'There is no map, even if the adhesion of Sant'Egidio symbolises something very concrete because it means commitment to helping the poor, prayer, moments shared with the community which has a long history. One enters but does not leave the same. There is a border, even if it is still very large and not well established'.[11]

However, it is possible to extract an ideal triptych that is typical of Sant'Egidio's adherence:

1. Sharing Christian values in Catholic readings accenting charity and solidarity.
2. Sharing common objectives such as evangelism and serving the poor.
3. The willingness to share one's existence with others in a fraternal way.

(c) A New Mission for Africa: A Mozambican Illustration

Mozambique holds a special place in the history of Sant'Egidio: it is the first African country in which the community found something to open up to. It must have been the first time in the Community's history that it was confronted with the problem of peacemaking and diplomacy. But before that episode, Mozambique was an opportunity for the 'missionary ethos' of the organisation to develop. Since then, various local communities have emerged, and particularly in Africa. If we choose to describe and present the 'Maputo side', it is because of its 'historical weight', but the same dynamics are at work in Burundi.

It was in 1988, before getting involved into the peace process, that Andrea Riccardi and Matteo Zuppi, during one of the numerous humanitarian aids orchestrated for Mozambique in Rome, met young people from Maputo. Here the Sant'Egidio community is made up of an astonishing number of young people, many of whom are students, and boasts between 300 and 400 members.[12] While the Roman centre remains a model and source of inspiration for action, the 'Parable of the Good Samaritan' rests in

[11] Interview, Rome, 2004.

[12] Approximately 4000 members of Sant'Egidio can be counted throughout Mozambique into roughly 20 communities. The three most important are Maputo, Pemba and Beira.

opposition of reality on the local level. The distribution of food is organised by the neighbourhood every Thursday evening. The community has neither offices nor archives. Prayer gatherings and various meetings held in the home of one of the officers rapidly became too cramped. The community is also called to take care of children. The 'Schools of Peace' ('*Escola da Paz*') are open both to children who are not sent to school and those who receive an official education. The first group is taught to read, count and write: each year the community attempts to educate the largest number of children possible. The second group benefits from tutoring sessions. The *Polana Canicio*[13] school is not much to look at, consisting of four blue walls with water damage, a sheet metal roof, a few benches and tables as well as an old blackboard. About 30 children do their homework, study and sing there and the older students help the younger ones.

The community also has a mixed variety of ceremonies. Therefore, after the weekly ceremonies, each departure or arrival of an 'international volunteer' that occurs in Sant'Egidio is an occasion for farewell or welcome songs. Sant'Egidio is also a place for socialising and meeting: couples develop and families grow there. Today, members of Sant'Egidio are accustomed to gathering for the Saturday prayer session in one of the annexes of a convent, on Julius Nierere Avenue, tucked between the 'shopping centre' and the 'Wedding Palace'; non-initiates do not easily find the well-hidden entrance. The icon of Christ, shared by all the communities, rests on the small platform where ceremonies are held, to the left of the lectern. The reading of the Gospels gives way to a homily and is concluded by the Lord's Prayer. Maccario is the head of the community in Maputo. Of the six original pioneers, he is the only one remaining. Game controller, and father of four young boys, he is roughly 40 years old. He does not know exactly how many communities there are throughout the country, but counts at least 19, many of which are new and bound for the villages:[14]

> 1988 ... Andrea and Matteo came here with boats filled with different supplies to help Mozambique. It was during the war. In June 1988, they asked to see the young people. After a mass at the church, they explained what the Sant'Egidio community was. I was there. They invited people to become friends with them. I accepted. During this time, they helped us, taught us the importance of prayer and of helping others—the goals of the community. I think what brought us together was compassion. We all have families but the community is also one large family. Mediation from Rome during the peace process was very important! We are not a political organisation, but a Catholic one. We believe that all problems can be resolved by discussion. Our peace is the fruit of the Community. The Community's involvement was very important. It is neutral. The Community believes that ending the war is possible. The best thing to do is to sit down and realise that we are

[13] The district of *Polana Canicio* is one of the ghettoes surrounding Maputo.
[14] Interview, Maputo, 2004.

> losing friends, development has receded and the infrastructures are broken down. Negotiations for peace lasted two and a half years. The conflicts must end once and for all. Today we still have problems, but never again will we have war. We have problems with crime, but that is true in every country.
>
> Frequent contact with Rome is maintained, whether by post or telephone. Sometimes they come here or we go there. When we want to do something we take a collection and when it is not enough we ask Rome or other communities. Likewise, if Pemba needs something and we can help, we do. With the children, as well as the school, we have created a real friendship. We never consider them as students, we think of them more like little brothers. We must help them. We know their names, their families, where they live, with whom, their histories ... We also go to visit them. We maintain a rapport with the child and his/her family. Sometimes we travel with them for three or four days. It is our responsibility. At the start, this was very hard. The parents resisted. With time, they understood that this was good for them. They trusted us. Some of the children had never left the city or even taken the train!!! At Christmas, we organise a big dinner. Some children do not have families and live on the streets. If we do nothing, they cannot be happy. Instead of buying beer, I buy pens. It is always possible to help others. It comes from the heart. If you want to do something, you can. I understood the importance of going to church. It is easier to understand problems and learn good ways of doing things. Practicing what the Bible says in concrete terms. The average Christian is just going to church. In the community...When Jesus said 'love each other', I see what that does concretely. It's a complement to your Christianity. In Sant'Egidio, I understood how to put it into practice. Helping people is a way of finding peace. Changing mentalities, that is a way of working toward peace. We teach the children to refuse violence. We play with them, we dance. Little by little we tell them: do not fight. You know, children understand! They grow up with this mentality. It's our contribution to peace. We don't teach catechism, at least not directly. They have a family. It's up to the family whether or not to bring the child to the school. Adults, they will choose. Generally speaking, we teach them manners and how to live with others.

The community is known for its concrete methods of action in favour of the poor. Discussing 'the connection' or the 'synergist culture' accompanies a genuine group effort. The ability to build a web of connections, and collaboration with those involved in actions with the community, is a characteristic element of Sant'Egidio's attitude towards its involvement. Its members view this collaborative link with the exterior as a necessity, but as well, and especially, as the directive value of their actions and their connection to others. None of its members sees the community as an institution or a social service aid for the most destitute. They consider the community as a 'home' where 'the door is always open' to those in need. Supporter of the Third World but non-Marxist, Sant'Egidio was heavily influenced by Vatican II and the Theology of Liberation. But it saw also the situation of the French Church in the 1970s as a source of inspiration. Through the numerous links between the different communities around the world (and especially in Africa) and by the multiplicity of it's activities,[15] Sant'Egidio illustrates a missionary's Utopia (the revival of the Church of the poorest of the first Christian communities) and bridges the gap between the militancy of the 1970s and the missionaries dynamics of the former century.

II. GOVERNMENTALITY AND 'PARALLEL DIPLOMACY': THE TRANSNATIONAL SPACE OF PEACEMAKING

In this part, I shall examine the 'global ecology' in which the activities of Sant'Egidio in favour of peace found a place to develop. If Sant'Egidio's rise as a 'peace broker' coincides with the emergence of the notion of 'citizen diplomacy', we must nevertheless asks what is at stake with the phenomenon of 'parallel diplomacy' and its consequences concerning the place and the role of the state.

(a) The Privatisation of Diplomacy

'Newness' and 'decline': here are the two prominent terms emerging in the literature on recent developments of diplomacy (Hocking, 1997). Some scholars have identified some significant changes, both in the context and practice of diplomacy. The decline or crisis of diplomacy has become 'a well rehearsed proposition'. Diplomacy is sometimes suggested as a candidate for endangered species list (Cooper, 1997: 174) and Zbigniew Brzezinski's quip in 1970 to the effect that if foreign ministries and embassies 'did not already exist, they surely would have not been invented' is frequently quoted (James, 1980: 933; Hamilton and Langhorne, 1995: 232; Hocking, 1999: 23). On the other hand, there are voices questioning the amount of change and emphasising instead the continuity of diplomatic practices (James, 1980: 932). The increasing number and types of international actors, along with the expanding diplomatic agenda, are usually identified as significant changes in the international order. Not only has the number of states more than tripled since 1945, but new types of actors have come to participate in international relations. Diplomacy no longer seems limited to relations between states and has to take account of wider relationships and dialogues, involving such entities as regional and international organisations, multinational firms, sub-national actors, advocacy networks and influential individuals. In May 1997, the announcement of a signing of a ceasefire agreement between the government of Pierre Buyoya and Léonard

[15] Sant'Egidio gave birth to various worldwide movements of solidarity, ranging, for instance, from the fight against the death penalty to the support of refugees.

Nyangoma, chief of the Hutu rebellion in Burundi, revealed the notion of 'parallel diplomacy'. The originality of this phenomenon was not only the signing of the agreement, but, and above all, the key role played by a private actor: the Roman Catholic lay community of Sant'Egidio. Should we then conclude that transnational actors and other 'skillful individuals' thanks to globalisation, bypass states? We don't think so.

Globalisation has now become a buzzword in academic and political discussion. The fact that such phenomenon of growing internationalisation and integration exists is virtually the most accepted point. How new this phenomenon is, and what its consequences are, are issues of much discussion. If diplomacy is no longer limited to relations between states, should we conclude the state has lost its central and exclusive role? Proponents of global studies assume that we are now witnessing a unique period in which three overlapping tendencies coincide. According to them, we are experiencing, first, a new acceleration of globalisation while secondly, at the same time being confronted with the effect of a deliberate and ideologically motivated policy of liberalisation, deregulation and exclusion of the state from economic life. Thirdly, we are confronted with a profound transformation of the productive structure, partly caused by technological innovations and by the transition from an industrial economy to a service-oriented economy in industrialised states (Coolsaet, 1997). Hence, it seems that the state has been 'sentenced to death' more than once (Bayart, 2004). First, the state has been forced to retreat in front of the diffusion of power in a global economy (Strange, 1996). Then, the state would have lost its sovereignty in conjunction with a new regionalisation of the international system. Finally, the multiplication of 'new wars', instead of contributing to state formation according to the classical teaching of historical sociology (Weber, 1991; Foucault, 1997; Giddens, 1987; Tilly, 1990) or international relations theory (Shaw, 2000) illustrate its crisis and its destruction (Holsti, 1996; Kaldor, 1999; van Creveld, 1991). But nothing proves that globalisation and the development of economic and cultural transnational relations are synonymous of the retreat of the state (Rueschemeyer and Skocpol, 1985).

(b) Turbulences in Sovereignty?

As we have seen, proponents of global studies underline the devolution of state authority, so central, for instance, to the work of the late Suzan Strange. Nevertheless, we would like to overcome the ongoing debate about whether or not globalisation undermines state power and authority. Globalisation allows the emergence of new forms of governance and new patterns of interaction between states and private (non-state) actors. Following the seminal work of Max Weber and the reading by Jean François Bayart of the foucaldian concepts of 'power' and 'governmentality'[16] (Bayart, 2004; Foucault, 1976, 1994, 1997) Béatrice Hibou (1999) has shown how the 'privatization of the State', in matters of national defence, security, taxes or diplomacy is the equivalent of a procedure of 'leasing'. Through this mechanism, the public power gives to private agencies the execution of a few chosen tasks; and these tasks produce sovereignty and coercion. According to Max Weber (1991), the 'leasing' ('*Verpachtung*' or '*Uberweisung*') was the leading mode of government in contexts characterised by a weak bureaucratisation. But this does not imply that there was no state or no government! Through a leasing characterised by the use of private means, this process of privatisation today generates one of the leading forms of governmentality in the south, where the 'formation' of privatisation has an ascendant on its 'construction' (Berman and Lonsdale, 1992).

Then, talking about the privatisation of the state implies that we should try to seize the accompanying diffusion's processes of private intermediaries in relation with functions previously belonging to the state and the redeployment of this one. 'Leasing' and 'privatisation' are not synonymous of retreat or renunciation of the state. Besides the growing role allowed to so-called private actors, a continuous bargaining is emerging between the leading actors (private or public). We witness a never ending reformulation of the boundaries between the public and private spheres. We can also notice the continuous ascendancy of politics and power relations in general. Then, the state's delegation of some of its prerogatives does not mean a loss of sovereignty or a democratic shortage. Public institutions allow this transfer of place of decision. This trend illustrates this kind of more and more privatised indirect rule. In industrialised countries, the indepth reforms of state management systems, echoing a 'governance of management', systematised the use of indirect action. Here also, the privatisation of the state is less a desegregation of the state than a transformation of power relationships.[17]

[16] Governmentality ('*gouvernementalité*') is 'une configuration ou une séquence historique donnée—par exemple la cité évergétique étudiée par Paul Veyne ou l'Europe libérale traitée par Polanyi—dont on entend analyser le "gouvernement" comme mode de structuration du champ d'action des individus ou des groupes' (Bayart, 1998). This notion brings the historicity of the state back in and also underlines the wide range of relations between the social and the politics. The concept of 'governmentality' allows us to understand the current developments of privatisation as a change in the modes of government.

[17] This approach is not without difficulties. Some may argue the 'conceptual stretching' of the notions, the fragility of the distinction between 'private' and 'public' and the confusion between state, power and elites. Following Hibou (1999) we can briefly justify our position in four points. In order to understand the state, the analysis of concrete situations teaches us that it is impossible to make a clear distinction between state and power, between state and the ruling class. Understanding the state means understanding the people who rule it: we need to understand their strategies and their historical practices. This mutual dependence shapes the form of the state: once again, it is impossible to make a clear distinction between politics and economics, between public and private interests. In order to understand the current transformations, we have to make a distinction between the different attributes and functions

This transformation of power relations gave birth to new technologies which, in a discretionary way, aim at incorporating and involving social actors according to their own recognized utility (Rouban, 1998). The privatisation of authority in embedded in given historical situations. The privatisation of coercion and its diplomatic counterpart appears to be a modality of the state's activities reinvention and should be linked to the 'new theory' of the contemporary 'liberal moment' (Bayart, 2004). This reinvention of the state's activities got the support of multilateral development institutions and international organisations. And peace goes the same as war: the activities of the community of Sant'Egidio and its involvement in African civil wars, in conjunction with the Farnesina, the Curia and different foreign ministries, is a topical example of this state's redeployment.[18]

(c) Peace as Transnational Space

Following political independence and development, violence and the possibility of its eradication constitute a new challenge for Africa. The Sahel Club leaves rural development and drought for conflict analysis. The military cooperations of occidental countries transform themselves into peacekeeping's support initiatives. New transnational actors, specialising in conflict resolution (like, for instance, International Crisis Group) or mediation are flourishing on the international stage. More than their 'newness' (think about the Quakers or the Mennonites) it is their growing visibility that strikes the observer. This 'work for peace', this constellation of activities—from 'grassroots resolution' to 'mediation' through 'humanitarian help',

of the state. More specifically, we have to distinguish state power from sovereignty. We need to be able to make a difference, for instance, between the use of power by the state and its capacity to master a regulative authority. The redefinition of the relationship between private and public and the modification of 'governmentality' constitute the two faces of a same process. Roland Marchall and Achille Membe have shown, for instance, how the development of violence (war, riots, lootings) in junction with economics goals gave birth to a renegotiation between public and private spaces and, *in fine*, contributed to state's formation. This analysis of the 'privatisation of the state' does not aim at giving a global and uniform reading of this phenomenon. Instead, it pays attention to the peculiar configurations of the new arrangements between values, norms and principles of action. The phenomenon of leasing and the never ending bargaining have to be thought in the *longue durée*. They are an important element of the historical trajectories of these political entities. Because of the normative representation of the state, the process of leasing seems new. But we have to keep in mind that this phenomenon is a very old one. The 'privatisation of the state' proceeds both from globalisation and from local history.

[18] The European Union and the USAID funded projects of mediation and conflict resolution in the Great Lake region. The Scandinavian, Japanese, German and Dutch governments were among the most important contributors of these programmes. The mediation process initiated by the community of Sant'Egidio in Burundi was funded by the government of Norway and by an American foundation with the support of the Italian foreign ministry.

'socio-economic development' and 'political reforms'—became progressively a claimed attribute for a wide range of actors. A large number of important NGOs is claiming new skills or formalising old ones (like, for instance, Caritas, CARE, Oxfam, Mercy Corps and World Vision International). Other NGOs, such as Search for Common Ground, Conflict Management Group or International Alert, are ad hoc creations. Some religious NGOs take this 'work for peace' explicitly into account in relation with their own development, like, for instance, World Relief or Catholic Relief Service.

Interest for theses 'new' activities is illustrated by the creation of specific programmes and services in the public administration of several industrialised countries (Canada, United States of America, Great Britain, Sweden, Norway and Holland) as in some international institutions, for instance the PNUD (1995) or the World Bank (1997). This trend, coupled with a substantialist reading of a 'new wave of conflicts', in conjunction with the promotion of 'new' conceptions of international relations ('human security'), along with the consequences of a harsh competition for funding enlarge the growing visibility of this kind of intervention. At the *avant garde* of theses new practices, some big foundations have directed their peace researches to this new field of intervention (Carnegie Corporation, Council of Foreign Relations, US Institute of Peace, Winston Foundation).

(d) A Burundian Illustration

Considered by the international community as a laboratory for conflict resolution, Burundi has been the object of heavy diplomatic bargaining (Chrétien, 2000). Since 1994, this little country has attracted a disproportionate volume of international actors' activities specifically involved in conflict resolution, compared with its relative strategic interest. Burundi is perceived as acting as guinea pig for conflict resolution. De facto, the responsibility of an international response to these crises was first assumed by private humanitarian organisations, following the reappearance of death and genocide on television screens. In the Great Lake region, transnational actors played quasi-governmental roles, facilitating dialogue between belligerents, sitting as partners on the negotiations table and having easy access to important resources as to international medias. Some private actors, such as Sant'Egidio, initiated a political process of parallel negotiation.

Nevertheless, we must notice that the management of the different regional conflicts allowed different private diplomatic actors great latitude for action. Globally, these actors, thanks to their weight, their involvement and skills had a 'cognitive' function in the different governmental projects at work (Harra, 1997). In Washington, for instance, a political forum institutionalised the exchange of information and analyses between the State

Department and the NGOs. In many cases, the phenomenon of 'parallel diplomacy' followed official mediations. The various private actors involved in Burundi, thanks to their flexibility and their skills, attracted the representatives of international organisations and initiated unprecedented logics of straddling. The special envoy of the UN general secretary in Burundi, Amedhou-Abdallah, managed a significant part of the mediation activities of the NGOs and organised the diplomatic work in correlation with its own strategy. During his mandate, from 1993 to 1995, an empirical method of cooperation and delegation between private and public spheres was at work.[19] The Great Lake crisis shed light on the rise of a 'market of peace and mediation' as show in the following table:

Organisation	*Type of Organisation*	*Project*
Sant'Egidio	Catholic NGO, Roma, Italia	Mediation
African Dialogue Center for Prevention, Management and Resolution of Conflicts	NGO, Arusha, Tanzania	Support to Nyerere's mediation
Carter Center	NGO, Atlanta, USA	Organisation of the summits of the regional heads of Sates (Cairo, Tunis)
Catholic Relief Service	Humanitarian agency from the US Catholic Bishop Conference, USA	Humanitarian help, reconciliation project in cooperation with Burundian bishops.
International Alert	NGO, London	Mediation and conflict resolution techniques, mediation

(*Continued*)

[19] Since the coup of 1993, the international reading of the Burundian crisis gave birth to two paradigms. First, top priority was given to 'moderate' forces versus Hutu extremists and Tutsi militia. Secondly, in 1995, another diagnosis emerges: the 'terrorists' should be included in the negotiation process (Chrétien, 2000). In the Great Lake region, a dozen special official envoys and private mediators were active. Regarding the different relationships of clientelism between the region's countries and the great powers—and especially the war of influence between France and the United States—the official mediators were all accused of partiality. In Burundi, the multiplicity of definitions and analyses was the illustration of the fragmentation and of the lack of consistency of the international community. And Burundians politico-military actors played on this confusion in order to consolidate their legitimacy. Excluded by Nyerere's regional mediation, Lenonard Nyangoma had, through the involvement of the community of Sant'Egidio, the opportunity to become a credible interlocutor.

Organisation	*Type of Organisation*	*Project*
International Center for Conflict Resolution	NGO, Capetown, South Africa	Mediation
Mennonites Central Committe	Pennsylvania, USA	Reconciliation
Search for Common Ground	NGO, Washington	Organisation of the Burundian Policy Forum
Swedish Agency for International Development Cooperation	Governmental agency, Stockholm, Sweden	Training, mediation
Synergie Africa	NGO, Geneva	Support to official mediations, dialogue initiatives

Source: Barnett RR (1998) (ed), *Cases and Strategies for Preventive Action* (New York, The Twentieth Century Fund).

The NGOs involved in 'pacification' contribute to the building of a new legitimate space for intervention, a new 'window for action', for themselves but also for their networks, for international organisations, for international financial institutions, for local organisations, for private firms and for universities (Lefranc, 2006). This space allows a revision of the practices and traditional forms in matters of humanitarian help and development. The autonomisation of this space gave birth to the new figure of 'expert'—between 'believer' and 'missionary of the universal' (Dezalay, 2004). This 'transnational space of peace', together with a redeployment of the state and with 'humanitarian' readings of actual conflicts, is also sensitive to evergetical logics (Veyne and Brown, 2001).

III. FROM THE ROMAN SUBURBS TO UNESCO: ACQUISITION AND DEVELOPMENT OF SYMBOLIC CAPITAL

As we have seen, the rise of the community as a legitimate peace broker is partially due to the mutation of the transnational space of peacemaking and the emergence of new forms of governmentality. But, as we will see in this third part, the rise of the community has been made possible by the specific form of social capital of its founders. Thus, we will shift from a global and structural standpoint to a local and social one. Using Pierre Bourdieu's work, we will try to apprehend how the community nurtured a specific form of symbolic capital and, by using it, how it came to represent a major peace broker. As was shown above, the rise of Sant'Egidio as a peace broker cannot be fully understand through the lenses of the 'new diplomacy' paradigm, particularly with regard to the religious aspect of this actor; and moreover with regard to the symbolic legitimacy it acquired in a few years within the transnational space of peace building. Accordingly, Sant'Egidio emerged as a central and legitimate peace broker because it owned a strong symbolic capital based on its religious foundations as well as the 'interest in disinterest' of its members.

(a) About 'Natural Peace Brokers': Legitimate Competence or Capital?

Before dealing with symbolic capital and symbolic goods, it is first necessary to clarify the concept of 'symbolic capital' which Bourdieu conceptualised in his seminal work, *The Logic of Practice* (1990). According to him, the 'symbolic capital' is a cultural form of *credit*, in the broadest sense; it is a set of resources available to a social agent, or a group of agents, on the basis of prestige and recognition. It is a cognitive-based capital which depends on a shared belief, knowledge and acknowledgement. It is not a universal form of capital; it is highly historical and deeply entrenched in socio-cultural practices. It depends on social principles of vision and division according to which social agents agree (to a certain extent) on the value and the meaning of symbols. That is why symbolic capital is always defined by the social system in which it is valued. To sum up briefly: first, economic and symbolic economies proceed from a different rationality; secondly, every field has its own interest which is for a major part irreducible and non-exportable to other fields; and thirdly, some fields are promoting an interest in material disinterest, thus the economy of symbolic goods constitutes a major part of social relationships among them.

One of the main aspects of symbolic capital is that it is largely unrecognised as *capital* and recognised as *legitimate competence*. In doing so, symbolic capital allows a form of authority which exerts an effect of misrecognition: symbolic capital is never taken for what it is—a socially constituted form of recognition—but is rather taken as an unexplained (not to say 'natural') property of some social agents. Whereas this kind of capital could be perceived as *given* or *taken for granted*, it is highly mobile and, as every economic good, it could be valued or devalued depending on social contexts. Symbolic capital changes, mutates, as well as social hierarchies and orders. Even if it rarely changes overnight, even during revolutionary times, symbolic capital evolves precisely because it obeys a historical process. In each and every society, symbolic capital is constantly evolving because of the social practices of agents exchanging, using (and abusing), losing or acquiring this special form of social capital. As a religious NGO, Sant'Egidio owns a particular form of symbolic capital. The following section will seek to demonstrate how the community accumulated this specific form of capital and how it used it to achieve its goals.

(b) The Question of 'Interests': Hidden Agenda versus Disinterested Actions

Analysing Sant'Egidio's actions automatically raises the question of *interests*, or, more precisely, the question of the finality of the community's action: why is Sant'Egidio involved in several peace processes? What is the community's interest in peacemaking? What is materially and symbolically at stake? As Bourdieu outlined many times, every social space—every *field*—has its own hierarchy, stake, logic and interests. Even if the boundaries between those fields are permeable, and even if many authors demonstrated the existence of interstitial spaces (and actors) acting like links (or gates) between social universes (like the field of 'security' between the political and the academic), one of the most important aspects of a field is precisely the nurture of a specific symbolic capital within. Basically, the kind of ongoing symbolic capital among the traders of Wall Street is not exactly the same as among the Amish community. In other words, every field produces its own form of interests (both material and symbolic) and within every field the economies of material and symbolic goods don't share the same logic. They are interrelated, but they need to be distinguished to be better understood. (Bourdieu (1990: 120) wrote about the necessity of a comprehensive balance sheet of symbolic profits without forgetting the interrelation with material losses or gains to grasp the economic rationality of an agent's conduct.)

As a specific form of *capital*, symbolic capital is submitted to a very specific kind of economy, which Bourdieu used to refer as an 'economy of symbolic goods'. And here we have to outline the differences between the economy of material goods and the peculiarities of an economy of symbolic goods. These economies don't share the same rationality. Even if both economies could be described as based on the logic of cost and benefit, something symbolically beneficial could be considered as economically costly (or irrational). On the contrary, the very fact of doing an economic activity, eg, being a merchant and earning money, could be considered as symbolically counterproductive in some social spaces (like for aristocrats in Europe or in Ancient China, and in every social space where money is symbolically depreciated, like in literature, or in arts generally). So, as Bourdieu outlined in *The Logic of Practice*, you can find a symbolic interest in being economically disinterested. This is why we need to study the structures of the field to understand the very nature of capital within; and thereafter we will be able to study the logic of practices in this social sphere. But this explains, too, why an act which could within a particular field amount, symbolically, to payment in full might be seen as irrational or disinterested from an external point of view (from where you can not grasp the logic and the outcome of this act).

The question might be asked because of the logical tendency to think that the more disinterested action in appearance could have an agenda. The more disinterested action could be expected to obey to another form of interest: for a Buddhist monk for example, ascetic behaviour could ensure a free meal, and then, you can reverse the logic of action by saying that he *ought to* be ascetic *in order to* ensure a free meal. This kind of radical doubt or suspicion has been too easily drawn from Bourdieu's writings. To the question of whether or not an act can be disinterested he answered: 'yes' without a doubt; not because of the purity of someone's soul, but because it exists in some social universes where you can have an explicit disinterest in material interests (Bourdieu, 1990). And this is particularly true among the social universes of religions. Here we have one of the most important particularities of these worlds: the interest in disinterest. Therefore, the question of virtue and ascetic behaviour is highly dependent on the existence of social universes where lasting and sustainable arrangements can be made to ensure this 'interest in disinterest'. So it requires a historical foundation during which this kind of sustainable disposition has been gradually implemented in order to ensure the principles of regular virtuous behaviour, as in Sant'Egidio.

(c) Social Capital of the Community Founders

The founding members of Sant'Egidio are accustomed to being introduced, as we have said in the first part, as the 'sons of Vatican II and May 68'. The community of Sant'Egidio began in Rome in 1968, at the initiative of Andrea Riccardi, a young man who was then less than twenty. He gathered a group of high school students, like himself, from Virgil High School, to listen to and to put the Gospel into practice. These founding members still constitute the core of the community. The small group began going to the outskirts of Rome visiting the slums and where they started an afternoon school ('*Scuola Popolare*'—'People's School'—nowadays 'schools of peace') for poor children. They originally disagreed with the traditional order of the Catholic Church and stayed at the margins of the Church. They were deeply influenced by both the Gospel and Marxism. As a founding member, Matteo Zuppi explains: 'Marxism is something that the founders of Sant'Egidio experienced together. Personally I experienced it at the end of the 60s at school; it was thinking about the practice of Marxism. (...) Our goal was to unify the social and spiritual dimension of action.[20] Here lies one of the most important peculiarities of the community's founders' beliefs: the Marxist influence reintegrated in the matrix of religious dogma.

[20] Morier-Genoud (2003).

As a religious community, Sant'Egidio combines and nurtures piety and dedication. On these bases, the community demonstrates reliability and economic disinterest. But alongside this very strong religious dimension, the founders share another specificity: they own a very distinctive form of social and cultural capital. Both laymen and priests are highly educated and come from wealthy families. Andrea Riccardi's father was a successful banker. He was born and raised in a wealthy social environment which allowed him to dedicate himself to studies and religious activities. He has a PhD in history and specialised in Christian history and became one of the youngest professors in Italy. He now teaches at the University of Sapienza in Roma and is a worldwide well-known intellectual figure (he is also Doctor *Honoris Causa* of several universities). In 1997, *Time* magazine declared that he was one of the '10th most influential Italians'; he declined several times to run for mayor of Rome and has a very influential social network in the city and beyond. He was also very close to Pope Jean-Paul II and is a close friend of Walter Veltroni, a former mayor of Rome, who was ran for prime minister). Matteo Zuppi is a priest and now vicar of the Church of Santa Maria in Trastevere. He was born and raised in a religious family close to the Holy See: his father was a journalist, he has been leading the *Osservatore della Dominica*, which is the Vatican's weekly journal and he is the nephew of Cardinal Carlo Confalonieri. He studied literature and theology at the University of Sapienza and dedicated himself to the problems of justice and development in Africa. Like Riccardi, he has a very powerful social network and, as a priest, he stands as a figure of religious dedication and virtuous commitment. Mario Giro is, with Zuppi and Riccardi, one of the historical founders. He defines himself as Catholic, but, according to him '*in a very ordinary way*'.[21] He is a trade unionist at the International Confederation of Free Unions (ICFU) and is involved in the diplomatic relations of the community. His social networks are running from through the unionist and political fields through to the diplomatic area.[22]

(d) The Influence of Social Networking

So as we can see at a quick glance, all the founders and the contemporary members are sharing the same socio-cultural profile: they are Christian,

[21] Interview, Romea, 2004.

[22] Along with these historical figures of the community, there are members such as Canelli, historian and scholar at the University of Bari; Vincento Paglia, a former priest who is now a bishop and Andrea Bartoli—a former member of the community—who was in charge of relations with the United Nations during the Mozambican peace process and is the founder and director of the Center for International Conflict Resolution at Columbia University.

highly educated males, with high positions in their respectiveng fields, all tied in a powerful social network. In terms of social capital, they all combine a strong socio-cultural capital (education and family background) with economic wealth. In terms of symbolic capital, the priests are easily granted virtuousness, and the laymen—like Riccardi—combine both the symbolic capital of scholars (in terms of knowledge, rationality and expertise) and of religious agents (righteousness and dedication). The combination of both aspects (symbolic capital coming from a religious activity and social capital coming from high social position) constitutes the sociological specificity of the community founders. The economic reliability of the members (scholars, unionists, journalists or priests) allows them to discharge themselves from economic contingencies. As Bourdieu pointed out, you cannot base a long-lasting virtuous behaviour upon a free will commitment: it requires a favourable social network and environment. In other words, there is no doubt that the solidarity among the members of the community rests on Catholic values and a shared commitment to 'helping the poor'. But the core of the community (the founders) is based on a narrow group of individuals who share the same socio-cultural capital, the same social network and the same educational background. Sant'Egidio's commitment to helping the poor and implementing peace is obviously rooted in religious belief, but the very possibility of expressing, materialising and putting into practice these beliefs is deeply related to (not to say dependent on) the socio-cultural capital of its historical founders.

The very existence of the community has been made possible by the social capital of its promoters. As the sociology of the networks clearly showed, the social network of an individual constitutes a specific form of social resource. Translated into Bourdieu's framework, this clearly outlines that a set of effective or potential acquaintances helps in producing and reproducing specific forms of social capital. The social relation can be seen as a conscious (or unconscious) form of social investment directed towards the production and reproduction of available (and potentially useful) social relations. In the case of Sant'Egidio, the (socially) inherited social network has been gradually implemented by a strategic expansion of this network; as Mario Giro told us:

> As the journalists use to say, we have a lot of 'addresses in our notebook' (laughs). How did this happen? By sedimentation I guess (laughs). Yes it's because ... hu ... the activity of the Community, either international or local with the poor, brings us to contact a lot of people and to promote our activity, so ... Sometimes, you find again people you know in other situation, a completely different situation. I mean officials, diplomats or civil servants. And so, one of our characteristic is never losing track, never breaking the link with the people we know. If you want an example, if we have met an Ambassador of France or Italy, with whom we worked for something, and then a few years later the guy has been transferred to another state department or an other Embassy, we always keep the track, keep the

link between us. Anyway one day or another, we meet again, and so ... this has been gradually implemented, yes, I guess we can say by sedimentation![23]

The effective social networking of the members helped in constituting the symbolic capital of the community. If Sant'Egidio has been well known for its dedication to the poor and the effectiveness of its charity work in the suburbs, the publicity around its actions has been made possible—and has been tremendously successful—by the fact that the founders had a strong know-how of social networking. So the symbolic capital of the community is primarily based on a religious form of dedication that seems to be the raison d'être of the community. The very 'interest in disinterest' that nurtures the symbolic and material aspects of the members' dedication has been made socially possible by the fact that they are either priests or occupying a social position which is seemingly consistent with their commitment (none of them is a CEO for a big corporation, or international businessman; even if Sant'Egidio doesn't exclude them as potential resources). And this specific form of social capital (wealthy environment, highly educated people with a strong religious background) favoured a high-potential networking that helped considerably in implementing the symbolic capital of Sant'Egidio.

(e) Social Legitimacy and Religious Dedication: The Rise of a New Peace Broker

The Mozambican context provided Sant'Egidio with an optimal environment (local, regional and international) favouring the maximisation of its work through networks, the fruit of a long and solid history between mediators, the Catholic Church and FRELIMO: its connections, coupled with the charisma of mediators, paved the most secure path towards negotiating the issue between the combatants[24] (Anouilh, 2005: 11–40). It was also able to increase its repertoire of activity in favour of working towards peace resonating directly with its evangelical culture. From then on, Sant'Egidio was widely considered as a 'new kind of peace broker' and its legitimacy was draw from its 'Mozambican experience'.

In terms of symbolic capital, the community's legitimacy increased in a spectacular way. However, it is still not quite clear how Sant'Egidio became a preferred and successful negotiator in the first place.[25] Theoretically,

[23] Interview, Rome, 2004.

[24] About the nature and dynamics of the Mozambican civil war, see Geffray (1990), Cahen (1988, 1994). Concerning the mediation process, see Morozzo Della Rocca (1997) and Moïses and Chan (1998).

[25] This history has still to be written. There were various and heterogeneous candidates fort the negotiation. A profound teleological reading of the events marks the vast majority of the literature on this subject: Sant'Egidio appears as the 'natural peace broker' for Mozambique.

my hypothesis is that there is some homology between the 'Mozambican civil war field' and the 'religious charity field' (and more broadly the European/international 'left-wing solidarity', especially in Italy, in favour of Mozambique before and since the country gained its independence) in which Sant'Egidio was working before becoming politically involved in Mozambique.

Sant'Egidio was a religious community whose leaders were mixing both religious probity with academic knowledge (rationality). Using their social networks and interacting with a growing number of people interested in the community's actions, Sant'Egidio's leaders took the change to gain advantage from a huge amount of symbolic capital within 10 years, and this specific form of capital allowed them to extend their prerogatives. At a symbolic level, the community's capital was largely built on the number of prizes they received and through the sales of their books. In 1994, the community received the 'Colombe d'Oro per la Pace' prize, conferred by the *Archivio Disarmo* in recognition for its work for peace; in 1997, the World Methodist Council conferred the 'World Methodist Peace Award' on the community; in 1999, Andrea Riccardi and Vincenzo Paglia were awarded Unesco's 'Gandhi Medal' for their commitment to a culture of peace; in 2000, the community received UNESCO's 'Félix Houphouët-Boigny Peace Prize'; and in the same year, New York City Council honoured the community with a public recognition for its commitment to defend human rights; in 2001, Notre Dame University conferred the 'Notre Dame International Award' to Andrea Riccardi; and in 2002, the Italian Parliament nominated the community of Sant'Egidio for the Nobel Peace Prize. Since then, Riccardi has published several best sellers;[26] he was conferred the honour of Doctor *Honoris Causa* of several universities (like St John's) and has been honoured by prestigious universities like Georgetown. He is now a prominent figure in the transnational space of peace building and holds a tremendous amount of symbolic capital in this area.

At a material level, the community has always been financed by two kinds of support: quests and the donations. It worth saying that it is very difficult to find any documents relating to the community's finances, and the leaders are rather vague or remain silent on the question of money. This is partly due to the fact that the symbolic capital of the community is based on economic disinterest and the publicity of the (sometime huge) numbers of donations could appear contradictory to the community's image of

[26] Riccardi has written or edited several books, including *French Catholicism, Neo-Gallicanism and Bourgeois Catholicism*; *Rome From the Conciliation to the Sturzo Operation*; *The Roman Party after World War II*; *The Power of the Pope from Pius XII to John Paul II*; *The Mediterranean of the 20th Century*; *The Mediterranean: Christianity and Islam Between Cohabitation and Conflict*; and *A Century of Blood and Faith: Christians in the 20th Century*. His latest books are entitled *Preemptive Peace* and *Living Together*.

religious dedication. Moreover, in the case of Sant'Egidio, economic wealth is symbolically expensive. Even if, in rather practical terms, the community needs financial support to achieve its goals, economic wealth is something it cannot praise (or show) without interfering with its symbolic capital. In other words, showing signs of economic wealth could be symbolically expensive. This is a peculiar paradox of Sant'Egidio today: its social network and the results of its work attracted financial support and rewards, but in the meantime, these economic forms of reward must not be shown in order to preserve the symbolic capital of the community.

Thus, the quests, like those following the pray for peace, rise by between €50,000 to €75,000 per year. The donations made by institutions (like the STET or Italian Telecom) annually support the community by up to €110,000. In addition, those two enterprises, together with the Bank of Roma granted the community €1 million in 1996. The annual budget of the community can be estimated at €2,500,000. Two-thirds is dedicated to charity work (meals, healthcare, teaching and help to prisoners) and the other third is dedicated to the inter-religious meetings and to peacemaking. The Italian government, and also the Norwegian government, the municipality of Rome and the Latium region finance two-thirds of the annual budget (about €1,500,000 only for the city of Roma and the Latium State). Moreover, the European Commission finances some of Sant'Egidio work in Guinea, Bosnia and Albania. To some extent, the community benefits from logistical support granted by Fiat or Mercedes that allow the members to use their cars, or by some famous hotels in Rome that rent their rooms for free. In terms of symbolic capital, this kind of deal clearly shows how the sacerdotal and non-economic aspects of the community attract economic entrepreneurs who provide them with material goods in order to be remunerated in a symbolic way: 'We Mercedes-Benz support the work of Sant'Egidio'. But in the meantime, both Riccardi and Zuppi are well aware of their symbolic legitimacy and they clearly use it to achieve their goals. Symbolic capital gives symbolic power, and symbolic power can be a useful asset, whether or not you are a dedicated Christian peace broker.

In under 15 years, Sant'Egidio has become one of the most celebrated and trusted peace brokers on the international stage. As we have seen in this chapter, this is partly because of its success in Mozambique; but it also has to do with the social capital of its founders, their intensive networking as well as the opening of a transnational space for their actions. Whereas their initiatives aren't always successful, as in Burundi, the image of the community—its symbolic capital—remains quiet strong. The community appears to be upright and righteous, honest and disinterested, operating only for peace and the common good of humanity. But as we see, this was made possible by the social capital of its founders and their social capabilities in economic disinterest and religious investment. Moreover, this has been made possible by the implementation of their (already powerful) social networks.

IV. CONCLUSION

The rise of Sant'Egidio as a legitimate peace broker is based on a two-level legitimising process: on the international scale, the growth of a transnational space favoured the emergence of private actors specialised in conflict resolution and mediation. At a local level, the social properties of the community founders, as well as their active social networking, has enabled them to build a strong symbolic legitimacy that allows them to get involve in peacemaking. Although Sant'Egidio has become institutionalised on a fully-expanding 'market of peace' while offering its presence and services to certain conflict zones (like, for instance, Algeria, Angola, Burundi or Casamance), the community has never yet reproduced the success seen in Mozambique. During a conference at the Catholic Institute of Paris in December 2001, Andrea Riccardi said that the future of the community was not his problem. The community's members in charge of the peacemaking activities are the founders of the community: in time, they will all be replaced and so it is highly likely that the community will return to its original work with the poor in the years to come. For now, Sant'Egidio is still a legitimate peace broker on the international stage. The symbolic capital accumulated during its Mozambican experience allows its members to appear as legitimate peace brokers. Moreover, the religious dimension of the community has a tremendous impact on its legitimacy. In terms of symbolic capital, the interest in disinterest displayed by the community members plays a central part in their worldwide reputation. But, as we have seen, the community's authoritative embodiment of Christian values, dedication and economic disinterest has been made possible by the social properties of the community founders. In other words, the success of the community (in spite of its Mozambican experience) relies on a specific form of symbolic capital (its religious aspect and its dedication—its interest in disinterest). Nowadays, the symbolic capital of the community is reproduced by various and numerous presentations of its work.[27] The implementation of this form of capital is currently favoured by the sibylline presentations (in the press or on several websites) that allow hagiographic discourses about the 'destiny', the 'dedication' and the 'commitment' of the founders. Consequently, Sant'Egidio epitomises a universal commitment to peace and progress. As has been shown in this chapter, this specific form of symbolic capital grew out of a very specific socio-cultural background. In other words, beyond the representations displayed by the symbolic capital of the community, the emergence of Sant'Egidio as a legitimate peace broker has been the product of a two-stage process: the historical emergence of a transnational peace

[27] See, for instance, the portrait of Andrea Riccardi on the website of Georgetown University.

brokering (and the state's redeployment accompanying this trend)—the first stage of the process—allowed a religious community made up social actors and endowed with a strong socio-cultural capital (as well as a powerful social network) to become a world renowned peace broker—the second stage of the process.

REFERENCES

Anouilh, P (2005) 'Des pauvres à la paix. Aspects de l'action pacificatrice de Sant'Egidio au Mozambique' 17 *Le FaitMissionaire. Social Sciences and Missions* 11–40.

Barnett, RR (ed) (1998) *Cases and Strategies for Preventive Action* (New York, The Twentieth Century Fund).

Bayart, J-F (1998) 'Fait missionnaire et politique du ventre: une analyse Foucaldienne' 6 *Le FaitMissionaire. Social Sciences and Missions.*

—— (2004) *Le Gouvernement du Monde. Une Critique Politique de la Globalisation* (Paris, Fayard).

Berman, B, and Lonsdale, J (1992) *Unhappy Valley: Conflict in Kenya and Africa* (London, James Curney).

Bourdieu, P (1990) *The Logic of Practice* (Stanford, Stanford University Press).

Braudel, F (1949) *La Méditerranée et le Monde Méditerranéen à l'Epoque de Philippe II* (Paris, Armand Colin).

Cahen, M (1988) 'La crise du nationalisme' 29 *Politique Africaine.*

—— (1994) *Les Bandits: un Historien au Mozambique* (Paris, Centre Culturel Calouste Gulbenkian).

Chrétien, J-P (2000) 'Le Burundi après la signature de l'accord d'Arusha'80 *Politique Africaine.*

Creveld van, M (1991) *The Transformation of War* (New York, Free Press).

Coolsaet, R (1997) 'Pouvoir et mondialisation' in *Memento Défense-Désarmement 1997* (Brussels, Grip).

Cooper, AF (1997) 'Beyond Representation' 53 *International Journal* 174.

Dezalay, Y (2004) 'Les courtiers de l'international' *Actes de la Recherche en Sciences Sociales* 151–52.

Foucault, M (1976) *La Volonté de Savoir* (Paris, Gallimard).

—— (1994) *Dits et Ecrits.1954–1988* (Paris, Gallimard).

—— (1997) 'Il faut défendre la société' in *Cours au Collège de France, 1976* (Paris, Gallimard et Le Seuil).

Geffray, C (1990) *La Cause des Armes au Mozambique: Anthropologie d'une Guerre Civile* (Paris, Karthala).

Giddens, A (1987) *The Nation-State and Violence* (Berkeley, University of California Press).

Harra, F (1997) 'La diplomatie parallèle ou la politique de la non indifférence: le cas du Burundi' 68 *Politique Africaine.*

Hamilton, K and Langhorn, R (1995) *The Practice of Diplomacy: Its evolution, Theory and Administration* (London, Routledge).

Hibou, Béatrice (1999) *La privatisation des Etats* (Paris, Kathala).

Hocking, B (1997) 'The End(s) of Diplomacy' 53 (1) *International Journal* 169–72.
—— (1999) 'Catalytic Diplomacy: Beyond 'Newness' and 'Decline' in J Melissen (ed), *Innovation in Diplomatic Pratices* (London, MacMillan and New-York, St Martin's Press).
Lefranc, S (2006) 'Pacifier, scientifiquement' in M Le Papre, J Siméant and C Vidal (eds), *Crises Extrêmes. Face aux massacres, aux guerres civiles et aux genocides* (Paris, La Découverte).
Holsti, K (1996) *The State, War and the State of War* (Cambridge, Cambridge University Press).
James, A (1980) 'Diplomacy and International Society' 6 *International Relations.*
Kaldor, M (1999) *New and Old Wars: Organized Warfare in the Global Era* (Cambridge, Polity Press).
Morozzo Della Rocca, R (1997) *Mozambique, de la guerre à la paix: histoire d'une médiation insolite* (Paris, l' Harmattan).
Morier-Genoud, E (2003) 'Sant'Egidio et la paix. Interview de Matteo Zuppi et Riccardo Cannelli' 13 *Le FaitMissionaire. Social Sciences and Missions.*
Rouban, L (1998) 'Les Etats occidentaux d'une gouvernementalité à l'autre' 1 *Critique Internationale.*
Ryfman, P (2004) *Les ONG* (Paris, La Découverte).
Rueschemeyer, D and Skocpol, T (1985) *Bringing the State Back In* (Cambridge, Cambridge University Press).
Shaw, M (2000) *Theory of the Global State. Globality as an Unfinished Revolution* (Cambridge, Cambridge University Press).
Strange, S (1996) *The Retreat of the State: Diffusion of Power in World Economy* (Cambridge, Cambridge University Press).
Tilly, C (1990) *Coercion, Capital and European States AD 990–1990* (Oxford, Blackwell).
Venancio, M and Chan, S (1998) 'Roman Talks' in S Chan and M Venancio (eds), *War and Peace in Mozambique* (Basingstoke, Macmillan).
Veyne, P and Brown, P (2001) *Genèse de l'Antiquité tardive* (Paris, Gallimard).
Weber, M (1991) *Histoire économique. Esquisse d'une histoire universelle de l'économie et de la société* (Paris, Gallimard-NRF).
—— (1995) *Economie et Société* (Paris, Pocket).

6

*The Catholic Church as Mediator in the Chiapas Conflict**

PILAR GIL TÉBAR

SOCIAL CONFLICT, AT times clearly discerned, while others openly declared, has always been present in the historic discourse of Chiapas. Since the Colony up to our day, the indigenous peoples have used the institutional channels within their reach to express their discontent at the abuses to which they have been victim:the imposition of excessive taxes, labour exploitation bordering on slavery, the banning of practicing their rites and beliefs, etc. But with repressions as the response—be it from the oligarchy or from the government in power at the time—or due to the sluggishiness of the institutions when it came to finding solutions, all this led to no few rebellious uprisings, some of which are important landmarks in the history of Chiapas. We shall take a brief look at some of these rebellions, the most emblematic, in this journey through time, bringing us up to the present marked by the Zapatista uprising of 1994, considered the first revolution of the twenty-first century; a conflict characterised, furthermore, unlike previous ones, by the ongoing protagonism of the Roman Catholic Church, and more specifically, by the Diocese of San Cristóbal de las Casas, as mediator and driving force behind the peacemaking process.

All the indigenous uprisings that have sprinkled the history of Chiapas ended with the overwhelming victory of one of the parties—in some cases, it was the representatives of the colonial powers, while in others it was the white and *mestizo* (hybrid) powers of the independent era—who would nullify and humiliate their counterpart, the indigenous population. This nullification stemmed from the enormous difference in prerogatives and social abilities between both groups, which would allow one of the two to impose their absolute dominion over the other. With this, therefore, any initiative involving dialogue was stamped out between the conflicting parties and, in turn, any mediatory process was hindered in order to reach a commonly agreed solution: from the dominating position, the notion of a consensus of opinion with the conquered group was out of the question.

* Translated from Spanish by Ian Emmett.

Nevertheless, from the 1970s onwards, but more especially, since the 1980s, a new actor appeared on the scene which was to change the model for the distribution of forces: the Catholic Church. During the bishopric of Samuel Ruiz García, the Catholic pastoral was to undergo important about-turns in its approach, doctrine and application. This was due to the influence of various factors such as, among others, the new breath of air coming from the second Vatican Council, the Theology of Liberation—born in Latin America—and its subsequent *incultured* version, the Indian Theology of Liberation (the Mayan Theology of Liberation, in the case of Mexico).[1] The previous balance of forces was broken: the Church was not longer allied to the oligarchic, political and economic powers, as it took on the task of accompanying the poorest, most underprivileged social groups which, in the case of Chiapas, was largely made up of the indigenous population. The next period, covering over thirty years in which the Church explicitly backed standing up for the human, political and economic rights of this population, was to lead to the indigenous Zapata supporters calling for the establishment of a figure of a mediator in the conflict, as well as demanding that such a mediatory task be carried out by Bishop Ruiz García, as representative of the San Cristóbal de las Casas Diocese.

With this contribution, I set out to provide a series of guidelines to explain why this ecclesiastical institution was given the approval of all to take on, almost on its own, the task of mediating in the Chiapas conflict.

I. THE INDIGENOUS REBELLIONS DURING THE COLONIAL PERIODAND IN THE ERA OF THE INDEPENDENCE

Since the outset of the Conquest, the indigenous peoples of Chiapas resisted the Spanish troops, although due to the disputes among themselves that confronted the different ethnic groups, they failed to set up a common front. The colonial situation involved labour abuses (*labour distribution*, providing free and compulsory services, producing surplus and tax excess); abandonment of their settlements and relocating in *reducciones*;[2] coercion and abuses perpetrated by their own traditional authorities; a ban on maintaining their cosmic view and religious practices replacing them with the acceptance, by coercion, of the new Christian codes.

[1] Following the consolidation of the Theology of Liberation (1980s) the theologians themselves began to refer to the need to give value to indigenous cultures and to incarnate the Catholic religion in them. This incarnation involved accetping the rituals, ceremonies and even indigenous beliefs, and incorporating them into the Catholic doctrine and practice. This process was termed the 'inculturisation of the faith'.

[2] These are newly-created areas where the settlers and missioners relocated the indigenous people in order to keep them under control more efficiently.

In view of the variations on dominion exerted by colonist land controllers, administrators and the clergy, the indigenous people also adopted various forms to mobilise their resistance and protest. The reiterated use of legal mechanism to table their complaints before the Crown, the flight to the mountains in order to escape from taxation and providing services, the option of suicide and the refusal to give birth, the clandestine practice of their customs and original religious beliefs, are just some examples of non-violent resistance.

But this resistance also turned into open rebellion. The first uprisings took on native and revivalist orientated hues since, in the belief that they were living in an idealised Golden Age, they were desperately seeking to restore the previous cosmos and their damaged tradition. The most emblematic example of indigenous resistance was the indigenous rebellion of the Zendales of 1712. As from the *appearance* of Our Lady of the Rosary, who tells them of her intention to save them from Spanish dominion, from the Tzeltal town of Cancun, the cry of rebellion sounded out against the colonialists. Now with the rebels joined in an army of 'soldiers of Our Lady', they confronted the Spanish troops who, under the protection of Our Lady of Charity, were to overcome the army of Our Lady of the Rosary. The conquered towns were cruelly razed to the ground and burnt, their settlers suffering from starvation and epidemics.

It should be noted that the breakdown of the mechanisms serving as intermediaries between the Spanish and indigenous *republics*—on the one part, the Indian authorities imposed by the Spaniards lost credibility with their towns and, on the other, in their socialising function, the monks proved to be incapable of calming the rebellious feelings—together with other factors (abuses in payment of civil and ecclesiastical taxes, cycles of poor crops and large scale famines), accelerated the upsurge of feelings of social discontent and of the expansion of the rebellious current. Our Lady of the Rosary became transfigured, therefore, in the consciousness that led them to rise up against the exploiting regime, which had them confined to the most extreme level of subordination.

Mexico being an independent nation, Chiapas was controlled by Creole and mixed race oligarchies. Regal power disappeared, meaning the end of the legal protection of the rights of the indigenous population. Scorn towards this population is expressed in crude terms through the new laws governing political, social and economic life. The new agricultural legislation repealed the communal ownership of the land, owned by the indigenous communities, making it susceptible to purchase-sale.[3] This unleashed the hoarding of lands by the landowners who, by means of legal subterfuges or using expeditious methods, would snatch the land from their original

[3] Inter alia, the Federal Law of Wastelands (1826) and the Lerdo Law (1856).

owners. In order for the original owners to be able to subsist, they were forced to work on the estates under terrible conditions of overexploitation and suffering.

The system of recruiting and the work conditions of the indigenous labourers involved a slavery previously unheard of; this gave rise to the figures of the *baldío*[4] and the *mozo* Indian. There was a need to rely on a large and cheap workforce on the extensive agricultural exporting plantations and on the timber exploitations, linked to the traditional oligarchy, set in the town of San Cristóbal, with the capitalist stamp of the low lands. The former kept control over the indigenous population; the latter needed this population for its lucrative economic activities. The elite of San Cristóbal converted this transfer of *their* work effort to the companies, along the coast, in the valleys and jungle, into the most fruitful of their businesses. Resorting to deceit or to force, they would recruit those who were to work on the estates.

Within this context, a new indigenous movement sprang up, its epicentre being a village in the Tzotzil community of San Juan Chamula. In 1867, after finding some speaking stones, a young indigenous girl became 'Mother of God' by giving birth to some clay figures. In the village, converted into a religious centre of pilgrimage, a market was set up that would attract an increasing number of converts. This market slightly weakened the power of the mixed bloods who controlled the trade exchanges among the indigenous communities and the market in the town of San Cristóbal. Due to the complaints from the mixed bloods, a detachment ransacked the church and seized the leaders of the movement. At this point, Ignacio Fernández de Galindo, a mixed blood hailing from Mexico City who, according to the more conservative-minded chronicles, became the new head of the movement. He brought weapons together and gave the indigenous people military training, convincing them that they had to attack San Cristóbal. But, however, other versions take the view that Galindo, far from arming and convincing the indigenous people to launch the attack, did in fact take on the role of mediator, sensing the difficult outcome of events (Rus, 1995). The rebels were captured and executed by the San Cristóbal troops and the insurrection was harshly quelled.

In this movement, known as the 'Caste War'—a war of indigenous people against mixed bloods—such a description is refuted on the grounds of three facts. The first was the acceptance of a mixed blood joining the movement

[4] The *baldío* Indians were the indigenous people whose lands had been included in the surrounding large estates and who could continue to work a plot of land for subsistence. In exchange, they were forced to offer the landowner their labour free of charge (three or four days per week on the land and one full week per month in the large estate owner's house). The *mozo* Indians had no plot of land for subsistence and were linked to the estate owner by means of an efficient debt based system. This ensured manpower in reserve since such debts could only be paid off with free labour.

and acting as mediator between the conflicting parties. The second is that the indigenous people's complaints were not levelled at all the mixed blood population, but rather at the representatives of authority and of economic power. The third is that the Indian population showed no unanimous attitude towards the rebels' cause: many communities kept a neutral stance while others were loyal to the mixed blood power.

II. THE TWENTIETH CENTURY. CHIAPAS, WHERE THE REVOLUTION FAILED TO REACH

Following the harsh repression of the last rebellion, the indigenous population headed no further events, until the so-called *Guerra del Pajarito*, a war taking place at the turn of the twentieth century. It was the socially ostracised mixed blood elite—located in the region of Los Altos—who were to launch the most important social mobilisation by defining the position of the different oligarchic groups in the social power scale. This ostracised elite did not want to take part in the modernisation applied under the government of Porfirio Díaz, nor in its state version known as 'illuminated despotism'. On the contrary, the trading and business elite of the Central Valleys and the Coast turned out to benefit from backing Porfirio and, later, the politics of Madero and Obregón.

With the victory in the Chiapas government of the liberal over the conservative tendency, the San Cristóbal elite noticed the loss of their economic and political power. So in 1911, the San Cristóbal oligarchy recruited thousands of Tzotzil indigenous people to fight against the state government. This took in another indigenous battalion, but of Zoque origin. The first Indian and mixed blood troops managed to seize control of the entire Los Altos region. Near the capital, the indigenous Tzotzil people killed the notorious mixed bloods, which led the mixed bloods who headed them to question their loyalty, and opened the way for the Tzotzil people to decide to rebel against their authority.Relying on an absolute power over the area, the Tzotzil troops, commanded by an indigenous leader named Pajarito, settled some scores and avenged themselves against the mixed bloods. The fear that this attitude would give rise to a new 'caste war', led both elites to sign a peace treaty and submit the indigenous people to 'ear-cutting as the most efficacious way for the Chamulas to learn how to respect the authorities and society' (García de León, 1984: 30).

III. HOW THE REVOLUTION WAS INSTITUTIONALISED

In Chiapas, following the revolution, the hegemony of the oligarchy was bolstered over the peasant and indigenous population, which did not avoid reactions arising against the government authorities. One of the first reactions was the constitution, in 1920, of the Chiapas Socialist Party (PSCH) which, through the Workers' and Peasants' Union of Soconusco, made several achievements in its negotiations with the farmers, especially with the end of the debts system that chained down the indigenous labourer and his descendants to working on the estate for as long as the landowner wanted (Benjamín, 1995).

As far as agricultural reform was concerned—imposed by the federal government—the farmers in the Central Valleys set up private armies to prevent the lands being shared out and to intimidate the indigenous populations surrounding their estates. Nevertheless, the worst quality lands were granted to the indigenous cooperatives, lands that were not even suitable for self-subsistence. In Los Altos, agricultural reform had no effect whatsoever since the oligarchs also prevented any governmental intervention that might have been to the advantage of the communities. The same occurred with the large coffee plantations in El Soconusco.

At a later date, the Cardenism of the 1940s applied agricultural reform in certain untouchable areas and included in the governmental apparatus the entire working class and agricultural protests. With Cárdenas, the state brought together the social forces, changing them into cooperatives and keeping a pact with each of them separately. Horizontal relations broke up and there was a tendency towards dependency on the government apparatus. Cárdenas organised the social basis into three different sectors: the workers, the peasants and the population related to the armed forces. It was possible to identify the visible heads of these three sectors with the state and class consciousness became weakened.

In Chiapas, the indigenist politics of this period drew together the inclusion of the Indian into national life protected by his traditions and social organisation. Despite the progress made (improvements in working conditions, educational, health and housing services), its application promoted the consolidation of the modern indigenous local political bosses who, as government civil servants, acted as intermediaries between it and the population and secured considerable economic and political benefits. This group's monopoly over the management of the resources and the decision making was to end up by worsening the internal conflict in the communities and in the corporate farms.

IV. THE INDIGENOUS CONGRESS OF SAN CRISTÓBAL DE LAS CASAS (1974)

Until the 1970s, there was a certain degree of calm in the rural and indigenous area, due to two mechanisms that managed to delay sharing out the land. The first was the opening of the agricultural border at Selva Lacandona. With the stimulus given by the federal government, thousands of Tzotzil, Tzeltal and Ch'ol peasants colonised the jungle area and prepared it for agricultural and livestock use. Secondly, with international funding, the government applied improvement projects to the living conditions of the indigenous people. Even so, a social protest movement began that was to open up new, self-managing, independent channels alien to the official channels imposed.

In 1974, at the initiative of the Chiapas government and with the request for the collaboration of the Catholic Church, the First Indigenous Congress was held in San Cristóbal, to commemorate the fifth centenary of the birth of Brother Bartolomé de las Casas. For one year more, meetings and assemblies were held that brought the communities together to debate the issues to be dealt with at the Congress. This organisational task was carried out by a corporation made up of a general coordinator, several regional coordinators, a group of translators and two priests. The discussion in the communities gradually left aside the official indigenist turns, taking on the inevitable political hues. Such a change acted as a wake-up call for the government authorities, leading to considerable friction between the state government and the Catholic Church, since the latter 'always advocated the Congress being indigenous, favouring protests with no pressure and freedom of expression' (González Esponda, 1992: 170).

In reply to this, the state government not only reiterated its support of the meeting, but repressed the representatives and over three hundred communities of all ethnic groups, which changed the congress into a forum in which to express reports of violations inflicted on them by the government and its civil servants, traders and landowners. Free of official control, the indigenous people pushed the Church into defining its position more radically. Thus, two positions were established: the more conservative ecclesiastical sector kept up its support of government demands, expressing its rejection of the *politicisation* of the congress inasmuch as those leaning more towards the indigenous people accepted the challenge put forward by them.

With the new organisation, the problems discussed in the communities fell into four categories: land, business, health and education. In the course of the Congress, each ethnic group outlined its specific problems in each of these categories and, via the Congress, set some common objectives: to arouse awareness of unity, as an independent organisation; to take on an economic and political fight to change the social system. As a result, the foundations were laid for communication among the ethnic groups and the communities went beyond their limitations and became aware of the problems of others who, although geographically distant, were near in terms of the similarities in their living conditions. Despite governmental repression, the peasant organisations arising from the Congress were maintained and developed in the 1980es (Benjamín, 1995; Collier, 1994). Such was the case in the more conflict-ridden areas such as Selva Lacandona. With their colonisation, settlements were founded, farm land was gained, the large scale farmers were confronted with who wanted to take these lands away from them and they stood up against the Presidential Decree of 1972.[5] When they refused to be relocated, they were harshly repressed in the form of eviction from their living accommodation, their crops and houses were burnt and they were continually harassed by the Mexican army.

As a result of this discontent, the settlements in the jungle joined together into three large cooperative farmer unions assessed by delegates who took part in the Congress, by catechists and priests, as well as by young activists from the north of Mexico. These unions were: *Kiptic Ta Lecubtesel* (United in our Strength), *Tierra y Libertad* (Land and Freedom) and *Lucha Campesina* (Peasant Struggle). In the 1980s, these groups joined together with others to form the *Unión de Uniones Ejidales* (Union of Cooperative Farmer Unions) and *Grupos Campesinos Solidarios de Chiapas* (Chiapas Solidarity Peasant Groups). The new *Unión de Uniones* (UU) kept up a negotiating attitude with the state in order to achieve its objectives. As a result of differences arising in terms of administrative matters, *Kiptic Ta Lecubtesel* and *Tierra y Libertad* broke away from the grouping and, in 1988, joined the *Asociación Rural de Interés Colectivo* (Rural Association of Collective Interest, ARIC).

In 1978, the *Central Independiente de Obreros Agrícolas y Campesinos* (Independent Centre of Agricultural and Peasant Workers, CIOAC) arrived in Chiapas, which under the influence of the Communist Party, was interested in signing up all the agricultural workers in the union. The CIOAC decided to negotiate with the government and, unlike the *Unión de Uniones*, it considered it appropriate to intervene in electoral processes. The third independent peasant movement was the *Organización Campesina Emiliano Zapata* (Emiliano Zapata Peasant Organization, OCEZ), whose maxim was to maintain complete political and economic independence. Also, since there were strong adversaries among the landowners in the Central Valleys, the OCEZ left an image of a fighting organisation, considered to be the most radical.

Together with the heavy-handedness of the state government, federal policies were applied to alleviate poverty in the more depressed Indian areas. This application came up against the filter put in place by the state, regional and municipal powers which decided, depending on certain interests, who to benefit. One of the effects of these policies has been the consolidation of an elite cultured indigenous people (especially developers

[5] With this Decree, the government handed over more than 600,000 hectares (almost half the jungle) to 40 Lacandona families, a territory where thousands of Tzeltals and Ch'oles lived who were considered as invaders in their own lands.

and bilingual schoolteachers) who, far from being modernising agents, have become a local power (Pineda, 1995).

The effects of this system of local bosses were felt when followers of the Theology of Liberation and Protestants in various indigenous settlements were expelled. But these expulsions, perpetrated with extreme violence, conceal political and economic causes: the system of local bosses, maintaining the burdensome system of civic-religious commissions, control over transport of goods and people, control of trading with alcohol, fizzy drinks, rockets or candles of compulsory use in rituals. As they themselves expressed it:

> The so-called local bosses are the greatest agents of destruction, without the slightest respect for humanity or for living beings, forgetting that being hit or mistreated hurts us all. These evil deeds are (sic) the result of the education given by teachers, indigenist authorities and the plan to integrate us into the most savage, brutal, disgusting society of the capitalist system. (Oriach, sf)

V. IN THE 1990S, THE UPRISING HID ITS FACE

In the 1990s, the conflict increased: organisations spread, branched out, divided up and caused other new ones to appear; a permanent repression running inevitably alongside the official development programmes. With modernising airs, economic neoliberalism penetrated and worsened the crisis of life. So the federal government, despite having channelled more resources into Chiapas than into any other state, failed to cope with the economic excesses affecting the impoverished populace. Added to this was the fact that the application of such programmes was in the hands of the local boss set up of the local and regional authorities.

The clearest exponents of economic neoliberalism in Chiapas are the reforms, put in place in 1992, of Article 27 of the Constitution and of the Agricultural Law, as well as the signing of the Free Trade Treaty (TLC) with the United States and Canada, in 1994.

The TLC reordered the trade relations established between Mexico, the United States and Canada. Signing of this treaty implicitly involved an effect that was to collapse the subsistence economy in regions such as Chiapas. Such is the case of growing basic grain produce since it was cheaper for Mexico to import corn from the United States than to produce it on their own lands. The first to be affected were the small producers and peasants and indigenous people growing it for self-consumption since, as a result of the withdrawal of governmental subsidies, they would have to purchase what, until then, they themselves had been producing.

The reforms of Article 27 of the Constitution and the Agricultural Law pursued several objectives. One of these was to change the legal status of 'social property' (cooperative farms and communities) to change them into private property,[6] and to repeal the legal guarantees that protected this type of communal property. Another goal was to suspend the state's obligation to give lands to the cooperative farmers and communities applying for an extension, thus drawing to a close the share-out of agricultural land.

The imposition of this neoliberal policy has opened a new stage in social mobilisation in Chiapas. The policy has not only led to an inevitable crisis of subsistence among the more underprivileged part of the population, but to the corresponding political instability. The clearest example is the insurrection led by the Zapata Army of National Liberation (EZLN), in January 1994, with the coming into force of the Free Trade Treaty.

This insurrection arose in the midst of a scenario characterised by a fragmented, disperse social mobilisation. Surprising the groups of economic and political power, Zapatismo managed to secure the widespread backing of independent social organisations and of those who were not militantly active in any party. The insurrection also relied on the support of the main political group in the opposition, the Democratic Revolution Party (PRD). The Zapatista demands, made explicit in the 'First Declaration of the Lacandona Jungle', summed up the expectations and interests of the vast majority of such associations. These demands were synthesised into eleven points: work, land, roof, food, health, education, independence, freedom, democracy, justice and peace.

It was to be precisely the support from the civil population and their demands that was to put a stop to confrontations which, after two weeks of attacks, managed to achieve a unilateral ceasefire from the government and the rebel group. Also, the pressure exerted by the population led to the commencement of dialogue between the adversaries. The Zapatistas asked for a meeting to be held, under the supervision of the bishop of the Diocese of San Cristóbal de las Casa, Samuel Ruiz García. Once he was acknowledged by both parties, the Dialogue began in the cathedral of San Cristóbal.

The negotiating agent for the government—the Commissionaire for Peace, Manuel Camacho Solís—proved to be open to the demonstrations made by the Zapatista delegates, to such a point that he declared:

> When the causes of the conflict and rightness of many of their claims are known more deeply, the long term ways of solutions, that the country needs, will be seen so much more clearly. When this is done by peaceful means, nothing legitimate should be left untried.
>
> (Diálogo de San Cristóbal, 1995)

[6] The cooperative farms arose from a share-out of private properties occurring throughout the whole process of agricultural reform and with the regularisation of waste lands. In the communities, ownership of land harks back to the times of the Colony.

The peace agreements seemed to be imminent, but the assassination of the PRI presidential candidate in the elections due to be held in August 1994 cast a shadow over such expectations. The reconciliatory attitude shown by the candidate towards the Chiapas conflict was not to the liking of the more reactionary wing of the party. This hypothesis was also echoed by the resignation of the Commissioner in view of the pressures brought to bear from within the party, due to his tolerant stance in the Dialogue of San Cristóbal. Such internal differences over relations with the Zapatistas are noted in the government's last report presented by the outgoing president, Carlos Salinas de Gortari, who always referred to the rebels as 'delinquents' or 'terrorists'.

Alongside, the social mobilisation reached boiling point. Throughout the country, Zapatista supporting committees were set up and numerous demonstrations expressing support were called. In Chiapas, there was an escalation of marches, road blockades, occupation of waste lands and estates and, above all, storming the town halls. Dozens of town halls were occupied by Zapatista supporters and by those who, in times past, had reported abuse of power and corruption in the use of public funds. In many of these demonstrations, there was violence since they were stifled with the use of force, both from government and private armies (white guards) from the estate owners.

Meanwhile, the need arose to confirm a figure able to articulate and coordinate all the groupings to create a common front to give a unified strategy; thus the State Council of Indigenous and Peasant Organizations (CEOIC) was founded. This State Council joined the Democratic Revolution Party (PRD), the Movement for a Civil Society (MOSOCI) and the State Convention of Chiapas Women to establish the State Democratic Assembly of the Chiapas People (AEDPCH). This Assembly, as a unifying body of all the critical forces, was the main support in setting up the 'Transitional Government in Default'. The last rung in this coordinating process was reached with the establishment of the National Democratic Convention (CND) grounded on the 'Second Declaration of the Lacandona Jungle'.

Meanwhile, the Dialogue between the federal government and the Zapatista army was broken. The resignation of the Commissioner for Peace, and the non-acceptance by the presidency of Bishop Ruiz as mediator, severely heightened the tension.

Following the elections, with the victory of the PRI, the escalation of tension became unsustainable. This tension was added to with an escalation from 'civil resistance' to 'civil insurgency' by supporters of Zapatismo. The response was a slight increase in state militarisation. This escalation of the military offensive—and given the probability of a new military outcome—led Bishop Ruiz to keep up a prolonged fast as a way of attracting the attention to both contenders over the need for thought, so that they would realise the consequences of 'the calamities to which they were going to condemn the poor people in the communities'.[7]

With Zapatismo, internal dissension grew deeper. The phenomenon of expelling on the grounds of beliefs—although with political undercurrents—was repeated in a substantial part of the communities. Now the reason was not so much for being Protestant or liberationist Catholic, but rather for being in those religious currents identified with belonging to the PRD (the opposition party) or for being Zapatista. And now, the problem of internal rebellion was no longer solved by expulsion, but rather by reporting to the authorities or to the army, disappearance, torture or even by death.

Another disastrous consequence for the population has been the periods of famine that the communities have suffered following the military offensives. Especially in the Lacandona Jungle, the strict monitoring by the federal army, out of fear or because of prohibition, led to the settlers not moving away to their plots of land to sow them. On the other hand, the government adopted the strategy of sending them 'pantries'[8] channelled through the military garrisons; pantries which, as a general rule, were rejected by the peasants. Added to this, there came a long dry period lasting for months during the rainy season which, coupled with malnutrition and by the subsequent lack of hygiene, led to epidemics of cholera or mountain leprosy.

A further painful effect was that of internal movements. Tens of thousands fled from the military operations in the interior of the jungle. Before the conflict, these settlements knew how to survive by overcoming their differences, but the increased tension led them to a complete break up. The sector of the population that remained close to the government chose to take refuge in the towns and cities, whereas the population with EZLN sympathies chose to venture deeper into the jungle.

In April 1995, the meeting that had been broken between the Zapatista army and the government was held anew, sparking off the 'Dialogue of San Andrés'. In this Dialogue, unlike the previous one, the government was no longer to be represented by a single individual, but rather by an

[7] When the media referred to fasting as a hunger strike, the bishop stated that he was not taking a political attitude, but rather one of reflection and purification. As in the Bible, he resorted to fasting in order to clear up any doubts and to be able to put forward solutions in such an extreme situation as Chiapas was facing. Despite his fasting, the bishop continued despatching matters to do with his function as mediator (chairman of the National Intermediation Commission (CONAI) and as a church leader. One of these tasks was the daily homilies in the Cathedral of San Cristóbal. These homilies informed the believers of how the process was developing whereby he endeavoured to return to the dialogue that had broken down. In one of these homilies that turned out to be especially emotive, since the bishop, in view of the lack of results, broke down into bitter tears, he begged the adversaries to sit down and reflect on the terrible consequences of war, for a people already stricken by hunger, misery and fear. He drew special attention to the women and children since, as he claimed, they are always the ones who suffer most in these cases because evil takes it out on them.

[8] Basic food products.

associated body comprising senators and Members of Parliament from the majority political groups: the Concord and Pacification Commission (COCOPA). The EZLN proved reticent to accept the COCOPA because it understood the Commission to be a government strategy to substitute the National Intermediation Commission (CONAI) in its mediating task. The latter Commission was set up on the grounds of a call made by Bishop Ruiz to several independent citizens from different Mexican states, to help him in the task of mediation. The COCOPA refused to supplant the task of CONAI, but rather to complete it by collaborating with it and converging in the search for a negotiated solution to the conflict.

At the same time, throughout 1995, the EZLN bolstered its national identity, as it left clear in the 'Third Declaration of the Lacandona Jungle'. From their point of view, the situation of the Indian native would not change as long as there were no changes to the power structure throughout the Republic. So, the EZLN put to the civil Mexican society the setting up of a National Liberation Movement (MLN), which drew together all the social and political entities which had anything to do with recriminating the power structure currently in force. To achieve this, they proposed a nationwide consultation, which resulted in calling on the EZLN to change from an armed group to a civil group in order to continue to represent all the similar social forces. In January 1996, the EZLN in its 'Fourth Declaration of the Lacandona Jungle' expressed its wish to become a social and political force, changing from 'Army' to 'Front' to become the National Zapatista Liberation Front.

VI. CONCLUSION: WHY THE CATHOLIC CHURCH AS MEDIATOR?

This look at the convulsed history of Chiapas allows us to see how the relationships between the antagonising social groups have been marked by a high, constant burden of conflict. This ongoing presence leads one to think that, never when hostility has broken out between the indigenous people and the Spaniards, between the indigenous and the mixed blood people with the institutions in power, be they civil or ecclesiastical, has a solution been found that has been satisfactory to the parties concerned, been able to heal the wounds and help to build a social model based on mature living together in a satisfactory manner for all concerned.

Both during the colonial period and the independent era, all manifestations of indigenous social discontent—which always formed a part of the ultimate expression of pent up frustrations—were harshly and violently repressed by the groups which, in turn, held power. Such repression involved arms, harassment, relocating villages or shows of public humiliation such as whipping or cutting off ears; the revolts were considered as finished but the problems that they caused continued.

In none of the uprisings—not only in the overt ones, which were the most significant—was there allowed to be a mediatory figure in the conflict: the social blocks were perfectly defined, their reciprocal interests were irreconcilable and self-excluding and their positions were clear in the hierarchy of power and respective loyalties. Only in the case of the erroneously named 'Caste War' did such a figure appear, represented by Fernández de Galindo. This person was a mixed blood coming from Mexico City and was, therefore, alien to the hostilities between both social groups. It is interesting to see how the chronicles written by those forming part of the San Cristóbal elite portray the image of this character hailing from the capital as an instigator of uprising, a trickster of the Indians and ambitious for power. Nevertheless, judging from some researchers, nothing was further from Galindo's intention, this being—knowing how the revolt would end—to attempt to mediate between both groups in order to avoid repression of the indigenous people. The breakdown in mediation could indicate that the Chiapas society was still not ready to accept the presence of a figure—a mediator—who was attempting to reconcile the irreconcilable.

It was not until the twentieth century that the mediatory function was to return in this secular conflict afflicting the society of Chiapas. And this function was taken on board by the Catholic Church. Looking back to the past once again, the Church had always been an ally of the political and economic powers, being a power in itself, especially during the time of the Colony. In the twentieth century, however, the scenario was to change. And this change is to be found in the about-turn experienced as from the papacy of John XXIII, with the celebration of the Vatican II (1962–65) and its subsequent echoes in Latin America. Linked to this change of outlook was the onset of the 'Theology of Liberation' and the changes it brought in its wake with regard to the way of understanding pastoral policy, both by the hierarchy and by the grassroots.

Neither Bishop Ruiz—having arrived in San Cristóbal in the 1960s—nor the priesthood and members of the diocese, could escape such liberationist influences. It was to be the colonisation of the Lacandona Jungle, led by the indigenous people, that would be the first test in which this change was to be put into practice. Moving deeper into the jungle to gain land for crops and founding new settlements is remembered by the indigenous people as a long stage of suffering, pain and effort. In the course of venturing into the jungle, they were accompanied by some Catholic priests who directly experienced the hardships of colonising and helped in the birth of new communities, with new social and cultural values. Also, the bishop, far from sitting comfortably on his episcopal seat, decided to make pastoral tours in order to gain first-hand knowledge of the peasant population within the diocesan territory or, as he himself had declared on more than one occasion, he stopped having chocolate with the ladies to have pozole stew with the indigenous people.[9]

Equally important is the role played by the Church in developing the First Indigenous Congress, held in San Cristóbal in 1974. This event was certainly an important landmark in the recent history of Chiapas since, for the first time, the ethnic groups of the region were able to have an open area for making known their complaints, opinions and proposals. And this forum was able to open up with the explicit backing of the bishop and pastoral agents (priests, monks and nuns) with similar interests. A backing which meant a considerable displeasure and deception for the oligarchy and the state government, putting it down to an act of treason on the part of the Catholic Church. From that moment, great differences rose to the surface that were to separate them from each other.

Both events gave rise to the bishop and many priests arriving in Chiapas abandoning any conservative positions previously held. One of the most visible consequences was how Bishop Ruiz became a key figure in standing up for the indigenous people, in the various episcopal encounters held in Latin America.[10] Thus, what was to become known as the 'preferential option of the poor', the grassroots of liberationist postulates, in Chiapas ended up by being the 'preferential option of the indigenous people'. In this manner, the so-called 'Indigenist Pastoral' was launched, its main objective being to attempt to draw nearer to the culture of the various different ethnic groups in order to find points of convergence with Catholic beliefs and practices. In this pastoral, however, although the indigenist was protagonist, a position as receiver of the message still continued. It was not till the 1980s, but more so in the 1990s, when this indigenist pastoral was to become an indigenous pastoral. The great novelty here was that the indigenous person was now to take up an active role in designing the same.

A product of this pastoral has been the creation of a body of indigenous catechists and deacons who took on a significant responsibility in pastoral work. Likewise, both types of pastoral agent, along with the unquestionable authority that it enjoyed in the communities, through a critical reading of the Bible illuminated by an ethic of the universal dignity of the human being, and following their custom of holding assemblies, the indigenous Catholics have managed to develop and consolidate the awareness that they too are depositaries of this human dignity. Likewise, in these community

[9] On his arrival in San Cristóbal, the bishop was invited to lunch with the families of the local elite. With his trips out to the communities, he substituted this custom with that of sharing pozole—a stew made of cooked corn and water—which the indigenous people would offer him to alleviate the heat of the road.

[10] Out of these, particular mention is made of the Episcopal Conferences of Medellín (Columbia, 1968); Puebla (Mexico, 1979) and Santo Domingo (Dominican Republic, 1992).

meetings, they have gradually built up a considerable capacity of analysis of their daily, political, economic and social surroundings. In order to make this dense pastoral task more effective, a complex network organised into levels has been joined together which puts all the indigenous pastoral agents in contact, no matter what their respective ethnic region may be. The crowning glory of this dense structure is the so-called 'Believing Nation', a conference in which all those involved—indigenous and non-indigenous people—take part to consider the problems besetting the people or the Church as well as to put forward possible solutions.

Catechists and deacons have also taken on a deeper function in their communities: that of mediating in the internal conflicts of these settlements. Places of worship are not just places for prayer, but are discussion forums, places for tabling problems, for expressing concern. The pastoral agents listen, with the moral authority granted to them, and put forward suggestions for solving the problems facing the members of a family, the hostilities between neighbours, dissatisfaction with the schoolteacher or with the representative of government power, or the delegate of the peasant organisation in the area. All this is understood when it is known that these pastoral agents, before being put forward as such by the dioceses, should be elected by their own community, on a compulsory basis. And, as a general rule, they should be men and women who stand out for their reconciliatory nature, their patience and be eloquent and thoughtful.

A further element entailing the involvement of the Diocese of San Cristóbal in the lives of its faithful, has been the foundation, by the bishop, of the Fray Bartolomé de las Casas Centre of Human Rights. In the 1980s, on several occasions the indigenous people were persecuted, harassed, tortured and even killed, by the Chiapas government and the oligarchs using their private armies; and along with the indigenous people, the priests, monks and nuns that went along with them. In this regard, the incarceration of the parish priest of the Tzotzil place of Simojovel became a symbol. He was imprisoned for supporting the demonstrations of the farm labourers claiming improvements in their working conditions. The bishop reported such practices to the federal government, as well as the lack of democracy and justice in various towns of the diocese. In exchange, he was accused of fostering instability in the state, to which the prelate replied,

> if stability means robbing the indigenous people, killing them with impunity and stripping them of all that they have, and if destabilizing means that the indigenous people, through the Gospels, realize that they should unite and, in line with their analysis, organize themselves and defend their rights, then the dioceses certainly is a destabilizing element. (Rojas, 1995: 74)

But the dioceses, via the Centre of Human Rights, not only stand up for the Catholic indigenous people. The task carried out with the Protestants is well known since they were violently expelled from the communities of origin. So much so that when during the Zapatist uprising, the Protestants in the north of Mexico launched an attack on the bishop and the diocese, the evangelicals in Chiapas came out in their defence, alleging that both the bishop and the Catholic Church were the only ones to have offered them help and shelter in the most difficult times. This inter-confessional collaboration has been dramatised, on more than one occasion, in the ecumenical ceremonies held jointly at the cathedral by the bishop and the evangelical pastors. Another settlement given the same treatment were the Guatemalan refugees who, in their terrible flight from Guatemala, settled on the border between Chiapas and their country. Since their arrival, the Church has been the only institution to have drawn near to them in order to find out their needs and offer them the right answers.[11] With this purpose, the Christian Solidarity Committee was set up, committed to looking out for the integrity and safety of refugees. This fact led to the prelate being subject to renewed criticism from the oligarchy and government, although he was given the support of the Chiapas peasants and indigenous people.

The year 1994 heralded the Zapatista uprising. This event highlighted the intense institutional crisis affecting Mexican political life in general, and the Chiapas political life in particular, while underlining the definite threat of resorting to violence as the only way of solving the conflicts. In this case, the upsurge of direct violence became patent, if not circumstantial—the violence perpetrated by the Zapatista army—in response to the structural and even institutionalised violence that had set in, over time, as a naturalised process of subjecting one social group to another.

Knowing the pastoral career followed by the diocese, it is not surprising, therefore, that the rebels should elect the bishop as the only person able to take on the function of mediator in the conflict that had just come to the fore, although it had welled up from deeper undercurrents. It is surprising, on the other hand, that at no point did any other social force rise to the occasion, such as the parties in opposition, the trade unions or the peasant and indigenous people's organisations themselves. The Church, unlike all these other forces, had demonstrated and represented a sturdy, ongoing moral base, which it had patiently built up over the years. A morality in line with its religious as well as its political actions. This has meant that not only the Zapatistas, but the vast majority of the Mexican population, disenchanted with its political, social and union representatives, considered that the San Cristóbal Diocese could play an important role in strengthening people's awareness and encourage dialogue and negotiation.

[11] Later ACNUR and COMAR (the Mexican Commission for Help to the Refugee) were to follow suit.

In this regard, one of the great difficulties facing the task of mediation is the constant effort that must be made, on the one hand, to keep itself apart from the conflicting parties and, on the other, to make it clear that its task is to represent neither the Zapata supporters nor the government. Furthermore, apart from this effort to achieve a neutrality despite the difficulties, the great responsibility of the mediator involves—in the words of the bishop—'finding a way to translate what they are trying to say to each other' (Santiago, 1999: 51), ie, the mediator—the Bishop and the CONAI—must be a translator, not only in the linguistic sense, but also, more particularly, in the cultural sense, since they have to make intelligible such widely different logics, by means of a work in cultural interpretation. This capacity of linguistic and cultural translation is what the Catholic Church has been developing through its pastoral work in the indigenous communities, a task that has allowed them to learn, first hand, in situ, about the harsh way of living in the rural areas.

But in this task, by achieving peace in Chiapas through dialogue, the Church did not act as intermediary to achieve it at any price. It should be, as the bishop himself and the pastoral agents stated, a peace perfectly combined with justice. To achieve this, it is understood, it was essential to overcome all levels of discrimination and exclusion, taking on attitudes of repentance and pardon. As far as the pastoral agents were concerned—from priests to catechists,

> [I]t means a task to be carried out well inside the communities, to help heal the wounds, to overcome mistrust, to get over all hate and all resentment. It means that all the pastoral agents have a deep-sounding work to build, without becoming disheartened, involving unity within a healthy pluralism that respects those different as being different ... at national level, it means the civil society's commitment to put in place the conditions of democracy ... able to guarantee, for all, the basic human rights that correspond to each and every one through justice. (VV.AA., 1995: 47)

It was precisely this conjunction of the values of peace and justice that convinced Bishop Ruiz to accept the assignment to mediate in the conflict. The pastoral implemented during his mandate considers that the main objective of evangelisation is to announce justice among men, since it is only once it has been applied can there be true peace. From this point of view, 'mediation is an important element on which we have reflected in the light of our Christian faith and in the context of the building of the Kingdom of God in our specific situation' (Santiago, 1999: 54). Thus, mediation is not just the task of a single person—the bishop— but of the entire diocese, and even of the civil society as a whole. It was the latter reason that moved Bishop Ruiz to set up the National Intermediation Commission (CONAI) to represent this civil society.

However, since the diocese considered that mediation cannot simply be restricted to achieving dialogue between the Zapata supporters and the government,[12] but rather that it should aspire to a more profound task of reconciliation within the indigenous communities themselves; communities divided by tensions from the past that have been brought back to life by external factors, such as the arrival of new religions (diverse Pentecostal versions) or by the Zapatista uprising itself. In fact, this reconciliation process ended up becoming one of the main cores of the diocesan pastoral.

In view of the increasing, worsening conflicts within the peasant and indigenous communities following the Zapatista uprising, the Diocese of San Cristóbal along with the CONAI (National Intermediation Commission), Civic Alliance and the Civil Bodies Network 'All rights for all', decided to create, in 1996, the Commission for the Support of Community Reconciliation and Unity (CORECO). In view of the breakdown of dialogue between the government and the rebel group, this Commission, since it was founded and up to the present, considers that its priority objective is the need to identify mechanisms able to encourage intra and inter-community dialogue in order to overcome the differences and disputes present in certain settlements.

Without losing sight of the structural nature of the conflict and violence in Chiapas, CORECO opted for finding solutions at local level, going about this task following an approach involving various strategies. On some occasions, attention is given to communities which, *motu proprio*, apply for aid in order to hold meetings between the parties affected by the problem, so that they themselves design the ways to solve it. They also accompany them to the settlements and/or conflicting organisations so that they intervene in the process of changing the conflicts. Also, CORECO carries out an increasing effort in training, as shown in the training of local commissions of peace and reconciliation promoters and in setting up a diploma course and workshops in the positive change of conflicts and another on 'Strengthening the Heart'.

This civil organisation with Catholic roots—although now it keeps itself independent from the current diocesan curia—inasmuch as it has inherited the alignments marked by the previous pastoral group, is nowadays the backbone in Chiapas in terms of looking for peace, not only in abstract terms, but, and more importantly, at the small scale of the local level and in day to day human relations. To paraphrase their declarations:

> Peace is not a dream, but rather a place in this world: it is not sufficient to wish for 'another world' that is fairer and more equitable, for this to become a reality. Peace (...) is built up by creating areas for peace and social, economic, community and peaceful religious alternatives, covering the reality of the poor and the alienated. Peace grows where we respect our dignity and the dignity of the other; it grows when we listen to the word coming from our brother and sister and when we talk to one another honestly, simply and in truth. (CORECO, sf)

[12] This dialogue was broken off in 1998 due to the government's failure to comply with the agreements reached and taken on by both parties. The CONAI was disolved that same year as an expression of its rejection of such non-compliance.

Meanwhile, the dialogue between the Mexican government and the Zapatista rebels continues to be in deadlock. In view of the executive's indifference and its strategies entailing the *peaceful* dissolution of any social discontent—be it through the application of controversial governmental funding to improve education or health; through the militarisation of the state, using arguments to do with drug-trafficking—the rebel movement keeps some bastions of resistance, with the backing of certain NGOs. It is now the NGOs that, in order to avoid the isolation to which the Zapatista communities are subject by the Mexican government, have taken on the function of intermediaries with the outside world.

REFERENCES

Benjamín, T (1995) *Chiapas. Tierra rica, pueblo pobre* (México, Grijalvo).

Collier, G (1994) Basta! Tierra y rebelión zapatista en Chiapas (Food First Books).

CORECO (sf) *Folleto informativo* (Mimeo).

'Diálogos de San Cristóbal' (febrero de 1995) *Proceso* 956 (México).

Fazio, C (1994) *Samuel Ruiz. El Caminante* (México, Espasa Calpe).

Garcia de León, A (1984) *Resistencia y utopía* (México, Era).

González Esponda, J (1992) 'El Congreso Indígena de 1974: contexto y consecuencias' in *Memorias del Primer Congreso de Mayistas* (México, UNAM).

Oriach (sf), *Cristóbal Colón y sus crímenes* (San Cristóbal de las Casas Folleto divulgativo).

Pineda, LO (1995) 'Maestros bilingües y poder político en Los Altos de Chiapas' in JP Viqueira and MH Ruz (eds), *Chiapas, los rumbos de otra historia.* (México, UNAM).

Rojas, R (1995) *Chiapas. La paz violenta* (México, La Jornada).

Rus, J (1995) 'Guerra de castas según quién? Indios y ladinos en los sucesos de 1869' in JP Viqueira and MH Ruz (eds), *Chiapas, los rumbos de otra historia* (México, UNAM).

VV.AA. (1995) 'En búsqueda de la paz' in C Bravo(ed), *Chiapas: el evangelio de los pobres* (México, Temas de Hoy).

Santiago, J (1999) *Seeking Freedom. Bishop Samuel Ruiz. On Time and History,*
Prophecy, Faith, Politics, and Peace (Toronto, Toronto Council of the Canadian Catholic Organization for Development and Peace).

Part III

Mediation Programmes in Europe and Africa

7

Management of Violence and Mediation Practices at Urban Interfaces in Northern Ireland

ELISE FÉRON

IN NORTHERN IRELAND, in spite of a relatively efficient peace process implemented at the institutional and political levels, recurrent episodes of physical and symbolic violence still happen at urban interfaces between Protestant/Unionist and Catholic/nationalist neighbourhoods, which are one of the few places where the working-class members of the two communities can meet. It is very difficult to assess the exact number and impact of these episodes of violence, as the media coverage of these events, even as far as the local newspapers are concerned, has been particularly poor.[1] Evidence from the fieldwork,[2] however, points to the sustained impact on local populations of such violence and insecurity, as many people still fear crossing the boundaries of their own community's 'territory', have themselves experienced physical or symbolic violence and have the feeling of being under continuing threat from members of the 'other' community. All registered trends and reports also point to the fact that spatial segregation (especially as far as housing is concerned) has been

[1] Among the numerous reasons that can account for such a trend, one can mention the so-called 'good news lobby', which means avoiding putting the stress on further episodes of violence focusing instead on 'success' (reconciliation) stories. There has also been a tendency among media circles to adopt unquestioningly the official discourse held by British authorities about 'criminal' and 'anti-social' elements among the Northern Irish population, thus pinning down the most radical elements of each community as genuine criminals and delinquents who deserve no media attention, and should be put in jail.

[2] This chapter is based on research and observation carried out at various interfaces in several Northern Irish cities, especially Belfast and (London)Derry since the beginning of 2006. Approximately 20 interviews have also been carried out with local community workers, as well as with representatives of public and private organisations specifically dealing with issues related to interfaces.

continuously increasing these last years, even following the signing of the 1998 Agreements.[3]

However, according to many observers 2008 has been the quietest year for a long time, and on average there appears to have been a lot less violence at the interfaces over the last years. Many factors can account for this decrease in the number of violent incidents, especially the implementation of a peace process at the regional level. Other explanations can also be put forward, such as the patient and progressive development of negotiation schemes at the local level (Féron, 2008) and, since 1995, a general increase in local capacity to manage violence, which however did not always succeed in avoiding outbursts of violence such as happened in Belfast in 2001–02. With this perspective, after a brief history of interfaces in Northern Ireland, this chapter aims to identify the various modes of management of inter-community violence in Northern Ireland, by looking specifically at violence happening at interface areas and during parades, and by contrasting the cases of the two main cities of Northern Ireland: Belfast and (London)Derry.

I. HISTORY AND DESCRIPTION OF INTERFACE AREAS IN NORTHERN IRELAND

In Northern Ireland, segregation between Protestant/unionist and Catholic/nationalist communities has existed since the seventeenth century, especially within urban areas which are thus often divided between residential areas mostly inhabited by one or other community. Segregation, common in ethnic conflicts, meets several needs of the local populations. Boal, Murray and Pool (1976) have for instance identified four main purposes of residential segregation:

- First, defensive functions, as segregation enables organisation and defence of the area.
- Second, avoidance functions, in that each community is thus allowed to stay 'within itself'.
- Third, preservative functions, as segregation allows the preservation of a specific cultural, linguistic, religious, social, etc, heritage.
- Fourth, attack functions, as segregation provides safe areas for organising and supporting guerrilla warfare.

[3] There are various ways to refer to the peace agreements signed in April 1998. While many nationalists refer to them as the 'Good Friday Agreement', Unionists tend to describe them as the 'Belfast Agreement'. I use here the expression '1998 Agreements' which is more neutral and whose plural refers to the fact that several agreements were in fact signed at the same time. In the same manner, I use the phrasing (London)Derry in order to avoid the Londonderry (mainly used by Unionists) and Derry (mainly used by nationalists) debate.

Research has shown that an increased segregation and polarisation occurs after periods of intimidation and trouble, during which people decide to secure a position within a 'safe' religious heartland (Darby, 1996). The constitution of mono-confessional areas, as well as low levels of contact between communities, in turn reinforces the perception of an exterior threat and besiegement.

Interface areas between these mostly mono-confessional zones can be traced back to the nineteenth century and the Industrial Revolution. Since that period, interfaces mark the boundaries between predominantly Protestant/unionist areas and predominantly Catholic/nationalist ones. There can be different types of interfaces, but the three most common are:

— A split, which can be embodied by a wall, a fence or any kind of other clear boundary separating two communities.
— An enclave, where a community is totally surrounded by areas inhabited by the 'other' community.
— A buffer zone, inhabited by people from both communities, but which is usually unstable and tends ultimately to fall within the 'territory' of one community.

(Belfast Interface Project, 2004: 5)

The first official 'peace line' was built in 1920 in the Short Strand area of East Belfast, in order to separate a Catholic/nationalist enclave from its Protestant/unionist surroundings, and since then their number has gradually increased. Nowadays, according to figures released by the Secretary of State Peter Hain in April 2007,[4] there are around 60 'peace lines' dividing Protestant and Catholic communities in Northern Ireland, of which 46 are walls or fences and 11 are gates. The majority of these are located in North and West Belfast and the rest in other northern Irish cities like Portadown and (London)Derry. On the whole, over the last years and in spite of the signature of the 1998 Agreements, segregation seems to have increased, but there are strong variations across places and cities, with an increase in tensions in some areas, while others have remained relatively trouble free (Shirlow and Murtagh, 2006).

New 'peace lines' are constantly erected. Among the most recent ones is a 25-foot fence at Hazelwood Integrated Primary School in North Belfast whose plan was drawn in May 2007 after a series of arson attacks in 2005 and 2006, and which has cost £250,000. Most of these 'peace lines' are meant to be temporary, but most of them become permanent. In addition, these barriers do not seem to have provoked a significant decrease in the number and intensity of incidents occurring between members of rival communities, and some of them even seem to have become magnets for violence

[4] Sam Lister, 'Divided by 57 Peace Lines' *Belfast Telegraph* (26 April 2007).

and trouble. Interface areas face many problems, among them socio-economic ones. In these interface areas it is not unusual to forego employment as well as social services if this means going through or spending time in an area dominated by the 'other' community. Unemployment affects more than 24 per cent of the active population living in interface areas, over twice the Belfast average of 9.8 per cent (Belfast Interface Project, 2004: 9). But the most obvious problem faced by those living in these areas is the one of violence. It should be noted that interfaces are the sites, rather than the sources of violence. Most 'peace lines', and generally speaking, residential segregation, are the result and not the cause of violence. They have been erected precisely in order to avoid confrontation and to protect communities from the attacks of the 'other'. Very often, perpetrators of violence come from within heartlands and not from interface areas themselves, and use interfaces as frontlines of defence. People living at interfaces are thus very often more the victims of violence than their perpetrators.

Violence at interfaces, and more particularly riots, are as old as urban segregation itself, and can be traced back to the nineteenth century. Early riots were usually related to major political issues as well as to annual festivals and parades. However, since 'the Troubles' erupted in Northern Ireland in 1968, incidents have become more closely related to the evolution of the conflict in general, as well as to a growing wish to enforce complete separation between the two communities. Mixed areas are on the whole losing ground, and members of the 'other' community which inhabit a heartland are very often victims of intimidation and even of direct physical violence, and thus often quit the area, as explains Siobhán McEvoy (2000: 89):

> At the beginning of the current phase of the conflict (1968–1969), street disturbances, sectarian intimidation, and killings promoted long-lasting bipolar divisions into Catholic and Protestant enclaves, particularly in the larger urban centers. In cohering against external danger, these besieged populations collaborated to discourage internal dissent. In this way, localised violence contributed to the minimization of intragroup diversity, the rise of identity politics, and the creation of wider psychological communities beyond the core group of conflict participants.

Of the approximately 1612 politically motivated deaths that have occurred in Belfast between 1966 and 2003, more than two-thirds have occurred within 500 metres of an interface (Belfast Interface Project, 2004: 11). Clearly, interfaces are areas within which politically motivated deaths are most likely to occur. However, patterns of violence are diverse, and there are a number of forms through which violence can manifest itself at interfaces (Belfast Interface Project, 2004: 20):

— 'Recreational' or youth-led violence, mainly due to young people who are looking for an area where there are not constantly under adult control. For young people, riots provide excitement and an adrenaline rush (Hall, 2005). They therefore fulfil a dual function of recreational activity and defending one's community.

— Orchestrated and premeditated violence, organised under the auspices of paramilitary groups. By far the most dangerous and life-threatening form of interface violence, it involves petrol bombings, crowd attacks, pipe bombings but also shootings. It is globally on the decrease as some paramilitary groups (mainly the Irish Republican Army on the nationalist side and the Loyalist Volunteer Force on the loyalist side) have decommissioned their weapons, and the others are officially on ceasefire. But there is evidence that some paramilitary groups still orchestrate episodes of violence whenever it fits their purposes. This is what happened for instance in Bangor on 1 August 2007, when the loyalist paramilitary group UDA organised a riot after police searches. The riot involved around 200 people hurling petrol bombs, stones and fireworks at police lines. UDA gunmen were also accused of having fired shots at police landrovers. Here the disturbances were directly linked to feelings of hostility towards police forces and methods, rather than to inter-community clashes.

— Event-linked violence, and especially troubles linked to parades (see for instance Jarman in Hargie and Dickson, 2004). The parading season (July and August) in particular is a period during which tensions are exceptionally high. Many other events can trigger violence, like cultural or sporting events such as a football match (clashes between rival groups of supporters). It should also be noted that demographic change, and more specifically the growth in size of the Catholic/nationalist community, in a context of housing scarcity, has also contributed to violence. Demographic changes indeed mean that many Orange parading routes that used to pass through mainly Protestant/unionist areas now have to go through Catholic/nationalist dominated areas, thus generating clashes. Similarly, the Catholic/nationalist communities' needs for housing mean that they tend to put pressure on previously Protestant/unionist dominated territories, which then tend to feel besieged and threatened in their own existence.

— 'Casual proximity-related violence (...) typically perpetrated by people passing the interface on their way home after a night out, or after an "old firm" match or similar' (Belfast Interface Project, 2004: 11). In these instances, local populations are simply observers, or victims, of violence perpetrated by 'outside' elements in the name of the defence of the whole community. Needless to say, these episodes greatly reinforce hostility and fear between the two sides of the 'peace lines', even if the direct responsibility for the violence does not lie with the inhabitants of the area.

On the whole, there has been a seasonal variation of sectarianism, with the worse incidents occurring during the marching season, and contacts between rival areas almost non-existent during that period. Community workers stress that they spend most of the following months trying to make up for the ground lost during the summer. Work for peace is thus seen as more efficient during the winter, while spring already sees discussions and heated debates around forthcoming parades.

Many causes of interface violence can thus be identified, sometimes local and regional, historical, social, cultural and obviously political. Interfaces embody a set of interlocked problems and issues which seem to feed each other in a kind of vicious circle. As summarised by Chris O'Halloran, the director of the Belfast Interface project:[5]

> [I]nterfaces display three main kinds of specific problems: violence and legacy of violence (psychological, material, symbolic, etc. legacy); social and economic disadvantage; limited access to services and reduced mobility of local populations.

Each of these problems in turn generates frustration, resentment and then violence in a vicious circle that both local community workers and politicians find hard to break.

II. GENERAL RESPONSES TO VIOLENCE AT INTERFACES

Initiatives designed to reduce and suppress violence at interfaces or during parades are obviously not new (Birrell, 1994). Running parallel with 'tough' options—police and military operations organised since the end of the 1960s—'softer' options, including negotiation processes between local political, paramilitary or religious actors, have been attempted when the first riots erupted. Because of the level of violence which bred mistrust and hostility, most of these 'soft' processes have been limited to management of violence functions, rather than to reconciliation processes. 'Soft' options have also continuously faced almost open hostility from some parts of local communities, in a context where any willingness to enter into dialogue might be seen as an act of treason. However, in the wake of the peace process initiated by the British and Irish governments during the 1990s, the range of options available for the management of violence has undoubtedly widened.

On the whole, these last two decades have seen the growing involvement of local actors in the management of interface and parade-related violence (Jarman, 2002; 2006). Local organisations dealing specifically with interface issues have blossomed—particularly in Belfast and (London)Derry—as well as local residents' groups. The Belfast Interface Project, for instance, gathers more than 40 local organisations, nationalist and unionist, working only in interface areas of Belfast. This growing awareness and involvement

[5] Interview conducted in Belfast at the Belfast Interface Project premises, 5 September 2008. Further details of the Belfast Interface Project are available at: www.belfastinterfaceproject.org.

of local actors has, among other things, been favoured by the peace programmes funded by the European Union, which have for more than a decade provided funding for local organisations working towards peace, or at least a reduction in violence. While most of these organisations focus on socio-economic issues, such as providing professional education or social help, some are also concerned with the containment and reduction of violence at interfaces and during parades. For these purposes, they have developed various tools—from the building up of cross-community contacts and programmes to conflict management procedures.

Developing and maintaining operational lines of communication between interface communities in order to fight rumour and suspicion, but also to tackle violence as soon as it appears, has been a major initiative developed by local organisations in order to manage violence at interfaces. Mobile phone networks have been one of the tools used for that purpose. One of the best examples in this respect is the development since 1996 of mobile phone networks in the Springfield area of Belfast, which since then have also been adopted in other parts of Belfast and also in (London)Derry (See, for instance, Hall, 2003; Jarman, 2005). These mobile phones are used by community workers or simply by volunteers living on each side of a given interface, who agree to contact each other in case of an emerging trouble. They can also contact other people from their own community, such as political, religious or paramilitary leaders, who can then intervene in order to appease tensions. However, according to several of my interviewees, often the community workers using them don't actually meet, they simply talk to each other on the phone. Thus, if mobile phone networks have allowed for positive evolutions, and for the containment of many outbursts of violence, they have not ushered the development of meaningful cross-community contacts, even among community workers. Needless to say, suspicion and fear are worse among 'ordinary' people. If such initiatives are on the whole positive, they cannot by themselves produce a significant decrease in violence and inter-community hostility; these need to be complemented by other measures.

Generally speaking, there has also been an overall trend leading to the decentralisation of policing and security policies as far as the management of interfaces is concerned, which can be explained by the fact that political and administrative authorities have gradually taken into account the emergence and growing involvement of local resident groups on the ground (whose development has been spectacular after they first attracted media attention in 1995 around the Drumcree parade events, a contentious parade which takes place in the city of Portadown).[6] In other words, a case

[6] This involvement of local community groups in the management of parades and interfaces issues has to be contrasted with the relatively low-key position of most civil society actors in

by case approach is increasingly being developed, allowing for the use of local know-how and resources. In the parades case, such a mode of management is logical, as each parade raises different issues according to the route it takes, the communities involved, experiences of previous years, etc. Responses to violence are also characterised by the involvement of a growing number of actors, from a great variety of backgrounds: local community groups, local elected representatives, (former) paramilitary members, representatives of churches, local community workers, local, national and international NGOs as well as governmental offices and bodies such as the Parades Commission[7] and obviously the police forces. This multilayered approach acknowledges the fact that the causes of violence are multiple and intertwined, and therefore that the actors involved in its management, as well as the solutions offered, should represent this diversity. The involvement of such a variety of actors allows for the development of various options, including the following:

— Preventive measures, whether in the long term (local development measures, economic incentives, building of infrastructures, etc) or the short term (for example, summer programmes for young people). Development measures are most favoured by local community workers, who think that social and economic problems should be tackled before political ones. For them, inter-community negotiation is useless unless the reasons (economic and social deprivation feeding despair, resentment, feeling of being despised, etc) for violence are not dealt with.
— Containment measures, mainly implemented by police forces, but also, to a certain extent, by local community leaders, in order to contain violence within certain areas (barrages, fences, curfew).
— Intervention policies, whose aim is to provoke an immediate decrease in the level of violence: local community leaders, both social and political leaders, as well as police forces are here again the main actors, though at various degrees according to the type of violence at stake (obviously, in case of violence orchestrated by paramilitary groups, the intervention of police forces is both more likely to happen and to be effective than that of local community leaders). Inter-community negotiation is the method most favoured by local politicians as well as by officials from British and Irish governments, and the European Commission. They think that violence cannot be sustainably contained unless there is a

the 'peace process' itself, namely in the political process on which media attention has been focused.

[7] Established in 1998, the Parades Commission is an independent, quasi-judicial body responsible for placing restrictions on (like a re-routing or a prohibition on music played), or banning parades it deems contentious or offensive.

genuine process of discussion and negotiation implemented both at local and regional levels.

On the whole, it should be stressed that the role of the police has been significantly reduced as a consequence of local community groups' involvement in managing local disorders (especially after first Drumcree episode in 1995). The activities of the police now seem more focused on the reduction of crime and paramilitary violence, in particular as paramilitary groups seem to have reshuffled their activities around arms, cigarettes or drug-dealing, money-laundering and other criminal activities. Police forces intervene in local disorders only as a last resort because their presence alone tends to add oil to the fire and thus increase mayhem. In addition, the attitude of the local population towards the police is changing (Moran, 2008) even in Catholic/nationalist surroundings, where the legitimacy of the police and the Army—seen as biased in favour of the Protestant/unionist community—were, until recently, not recognised.[8] When asked by local people to intervene to calm down a disorder, republican leaders, who are often former paramilitary (IRA) activists, now increasingly ask them to call the police instead. This important shift can be explained by the fact that Sinn Féin, the main republican political party, has now accepted the legitimacy of the reformed policing institution; but another crucial factor is that ever since the IRA declared that its war was over, and subsequently destroyed its arsenal in July 2005, republican leaders no longer have the weapons which had given them an almost uncontested authority in republican strongholds, and thus on youths who are often at the origin of the riots and clashes. Without this threatening power, they can no longer act as the administrators of police and of justice in their constituencies, and have to accept that security problems are now policing problems. What remains to be seen is whether this trend actually proves to be positive in terms of levels of violence as there is still defiance and suspicion towards the police in nationalist communities, and in the absence of a general acceptance of the police forces, coupled with a retreat by the republican leadership, there is a high risk that the number of incidents within republican areas could rise. And indeed, these last years (since the beginning of 2008) have seen a steady rise in the number of paramilitary punishment beatings, which can seemingly be attributed to dissident republican groups eager to take hold of previous IRA strongholds.[9]

[8] It should be stressed that Sinn Féin, the main nationalist political party, agreed to back the new policing forces in January 2007, but not without internal opposition.

[9] According to the figures published by the Northern Irish Police in August 2008, paramilitary beatings and shootings have trebled in a year; the number between April and June during this year rose to 11 compared with just four assaults and no shootings carried out between April and the end of June 2007. Source: *Belfast Telegraph* (18 August 2008).

III. CONTRASTING THE CASES OF BELFAST AND (LONDON)DERRY

Before focusing on the contrasted cases of Belfast and (London)Derry, it must be stressed that, as described by Brendan Murtagh (Hargie and Dickson, 2004: 210), almost all kinds of situations can be found on the ground, from mixed and relatively trouble-free areas (usually middle and upper-class), to complete division, conflict and hostility between mono-confessional areas (usually working-class) and unstable situations where violence erupts from time to time and where gradual rapprochement or estrangement can both happen. Situations also vary a lot according to the city under scrutiny. For instance, one could also have considered the contrasted cases of Coleraine and Portadown: Coleraine with a greater social mix and a location further away from other zones of violence; Portadown being more segregated and also more affected by violence happening in Belfast. However, because Belfast and (London)Derry are the largest cities in Northern Ireland, and because their histories of interface violence seem to differ significantly, contrasting these two cases brings about interesting lessons about local mediation practices.

(a) Belfast

In the 2001 census, the population within the city limits (the Belfast Urban Area) was 276,459, while 579,554 people lived in the wider Belfast Metropolitan Area. Among these, 49 per cent were Protestant and 47 per cent Catholic. According to Doherty and Poole (1995) since the seventeenth century segregation in Belfast has increased in a series of spasmodic jumps, each time rioting broke out. The 'Troubles' during the years 1969–72 in particular led to a large-scale residential relocation, and nowadays it is estimated that more than half of Belfast's population lives in highly segregated wards. The highest level of segregation is in Belfast West, while the lowest levels are found in middle-class areas in the south and city centre. Belfast has seen some of the most violent episodes of the conflict between the two communities, especially during the 1970s when bombing and street violence were almost an everyday feature. Territoriality is an important source of conflict, as it relates to concerns over available housing, demographic changes, fears of ethnic cleansing and of course parading routes. As elsewhere in Northern Ireland, interface rioting is generally more common and more intense during the parading season.

While the general level of violence and the number of casualties have steadily decreased since the mid-1990s, there are still episodes of strident inter-community violence, like for instance during the year 2001–02, which saw riots at interfaces sometimes stretching over weeks (Byrne, 2005).

The dispute over Holy Cross School in June 2001, in particular, generated serious abuse and scenes of extreme violence directed at young Catholic schoolgirls. Colm Heatley (2004: 15) thus summarises the episode:

> Protestants from Glenbryn insisted the schoolgirls would not be able to walk past their estate to get to school because, they claimed, the IRA was gathering intelligence in this way. The Catholic parents were equally adamant that their girls should be allowed to get to school in the quickest way possible, comparing the protesters to the white supremacists of 1950s Alabama. While an alternative route was available, many Catholic parents refused to use it, asking why should they have to 'use the back door', which to them symbolised second-class citizenship.

Clearly, mistrust, negative stereotypes and memories of past confrontations and injustice account for the tense atmosphere, but the intermingling of territories, by making some inter-community contacts unavoidable, explain the recurrent outbursts of violence.

There have been many initiatives by civil society groups, community workers, local non-governmental organisations, as well as by governmental offices set up in order to deal with these issues, and to try to appease tensions, but so far the trend towards increased segregation has not been reversed; fear and hostility remain very high in several parts of the city and more particularly in the north which can be seen as a mosaic of mono-confessional areas and enclaves. Thanks to security measures and to the compromises found by the Parades Commission or by local residents' groups and marching orders themselves, summer 2008 saw the quietest Belfast marching season in years, but the spectrum of renewed dissident republican paramilitary activity, coupled with the current difficulties in which the power-sharing institutions seem stuck, is generating fears of new waves of inter-community violence.

(b) (London)Derry

(London)Derry is a mainly Catholic/nationalist city, with nearly 80 per cent of its population of 83,652 inhabitants (2001 census) having a Catholic background. There are nevertheless some interfaces and enclaves, like for instance the nationalist fenced-off Fountain Estate. However, prior to the 1960s and the outburst of 'the Troubles', the political cleavage was rather mitigated with very few riots. Desmond Bell (1990: 143–44) wrote as follows:

> The mid-1960s had seen a considerable improvement in inter-communal relations in Derry. The IRA campaign waged from 1956–9 had been a dismal failure and the Nationalist Party, to which the majority of the Catholic population gave their political allegiance, was being incorporated into political life at Stormont.

> Militant Republicanism seemed an anachronism. Moreover, Unionism under the leadership of O'Neill was promising modernizing change if not actual reform.

The eruption of politics on the streets at the end of the 1960s was, however, to usher a dramatic change in the nature of inter-community relations. Some events, like 'Bloody Sunday' or the 'Battle of the Bogside'[10] which happened in (London)Derry, contributed to the strengthening of splits, and even to a growing hostility between the two communities. However, violence decreased significantly at the end of the 1980s and at the beginning of the 1990s. Some analysts even claim that the republican movement had already negotiated a de facto ceasefire in the city as early as 1991, a decision which might explain the fact that (London)Derry witnessed less violence than other Northern Irish cities, and more particularly Belfast, since the beginning of the 1990s. As a consequence, the same period saw an overall easing of the parading situation in (London)Derry and in 1994 the Apprentice Boys paraded a section of the city walls for the first time since 1969. The subsequent years were, however, not trouble-free, as conflict re-erupted around parades in 1995, but over the last years local community groups have looked for a solution together, sometimes with the help of local politicians such as John Hume or the mayor who has often acted as an intermediary between both sides when these were refusing to talk to each other. They have also chosen neutral places for negotiation, away from media presence and scrutiny. Debates have involved all sections of civil society, and many shared the belief that a solution was within reach, even if difficult to achieve.

As a consequence, since the beginning of the 2000 decade, parades held in (London)Derry have usually passed off peacefully, as for instance the Black Parade, organised by the Royal Black Institution, which was held on 30 August 2008, and which generated little trouble and opposition, despite the fact that it involved 4000 marchers in (London)Derry city centre. It was held after a series of talks between marching orders, politicians, businessmen and local resident groups. Earlier that month, the largest parades in (London)Derry, during the annual Apprentice Boys Relief of Derry celebrations, gathering up to 20,000 people, had passed off relatively peacefully too, with only minor skirmishes and public order offences. The climate is, however, not always so quiet, as there have been disturbances in situations other than parades, such as serious incidents at the interface of the Fountain Estate in March 2007, and during the same month a cross-community football

[10] The Battle of the Bogside involved intense rioting from 12 August to 14 August 1969, between Catholic/nationalist residents of the Bogside area, who were protesting against a loyalist parade, and the police forces of the Royal Ulster Constabulary. As the police failed to enter the Bogside area, and therefore to restore order, the British Army was deployed, a move which generated widespread violence in the whole region.

match, arranged over the internet by young people themselves, turned into a riot during which several people were seriously injured.

IV. SIMILAR MEDIATION POLICIES, DIFFERENT LOCAL SETTINGS

At a general level, and despite the continuing occurrence of local incidents (London)Derry almost looks like a success story, especially when compared with Belfast, where interface problems and contested parades give rise to dozens of riots each year, each with its lot of casualties, destruction and social, psychological and economic costs. What accounts for such a difference? Research suggests that differences between these two cases are rather linked to local settings and to local histories than to diverging management policies. Indeed, similar methods of management have been used in the past, mainly the usual interventions of police and the Army whenever a riot erupted, and the building up of 'peace lines', walls and fences between warring communities. Dialogue and reconciliation were left for the regional political leaders to develop, and local and multi-level approaches, at least until the mid-1990s, were grossly neglected.

Four main characteristics of local settings and histories can be identified to account for the differences between the two cases. The first is the history of inter-community relations in both cities. As has been seen, up until the end of the 1960s in (London)Derry the relations between the two communities were, if not good, at least mostly peaceful. The two communities had learned to live side by side, and to tolerate each other, even if the situation of the Catholic/nationalist community was far from satisfactory as the eruption of 'the Troubles' proved. By contrast, the history of Belfast has been constantly marked by recurrent clashes and riots between the two communities. After the toughest phase of 'the Troubles', actors on the ground in (London)Derry tried to re-initiate previously established channels of communication and negotiation, whereas in Belfast most of these channels had to be created from scratch.

The second element accounting for differences is demographic factors: in Belfast, important demographic shifts have taken place over the past decades. With the growth in the size of the Catholic/nationalist population in Belfast, areas which were previously occupied by Protestants/unionists have gradually been 'taken over'. As a consequence, traditional parading routes, which used to pass mainly through Protestant/unionist areas, now generate clashes as they enter areas now occupied by Catholics/nationalists. (London)Derry is, by contrast, an old Catholic/nationalist city, where demography has evolved more smoothly and has therefore generated less dramatic changes on the ground. Demography is also linked to the housing issue, which has been a constant source of conflict in Belfast: housing scarcity has weighed particularly heavily on the Catholic/nationalist community which is growing. The problem is particularly strident for Catholics/nationalists living in enclaves surrounded by the 'other' community, but it is also significant for those living close to an interface barrier, which sets in stone previously invisible boundaries. Protestants/unionists in turn see this 'Catholic expansion' as a direct threat, leading to 'ethnic cleansing' processes, against which some are willing to use violence. In (London)Derry, housing is a slightly less contentious issue, as Catholic/nationalist neighbourhoods usually have the possibility to extend beyond their current boundaries.

A third significant factor is urban geography. Obviously, it is easier to manage interfaces when the two groups are clearly separated, than if contacts and negotiations have to be managed street by street. In the case of (London)Derry, and with the exception of the Fountain Estate, the two communities are clearly separated by the River Foyle, with at its north a mainly Catholic/nationalist area, and at its south a mainly mixed or Protestant/unionist area. When there are enclaves and 'patchwork' communities, as is the case in Belfast, the situation is deemed to be a lot more complicated and dangerous. Urban geography also plays an additional role related to parade routes: in (London)Derry, there is only one particularly contested parade (the one which passes by the city walls, at the top of the Bogside area inhabited by a mainly Catholic/nationalist population) and a lot less interfaces than in Belfast. Because the communities are more clearly segregated, parades are less likely to go through the territory of the 'other' community. By contrast, in Belfast, there is a whole range of contested parades, such as the Workman Parade, the Tour of the North, etc. This can be explained by the fact that urban geography is much more complex in Belfast (and thus parades are more likely to pass through contested routes). Over the years, there has been a lot of negotiation around these parades, but progress has been slow and can always be questioned in subsequent years. In addition, the fact that there are a lot of interfaces in Belfast means not only that there are more opportunities for clashes, but that it is difficult to negotiate an approach to a parade or a specific local issue without impacting on other interfaces or enclaves. It must finally be stressed that in the case of Belfast there is a contagion effect at play between interface areas, which explains that riots and clashes seem to spread very quickly, whereas in (London)Derry this contagion effect is limited because of the scarce number of interfaces. In addition, (London)Derry is located further away from other sites of violence, whereas Belfast is surrounded by areas, such as Portadown, where contentious events regularly occur.

Finally, one has to stress the role of local leadership and especially the role of paramilitary groups. In (London)Derry, there has been a happy conjunction of two main conflict-decreasing factors: first, the presence of a non-violent and very popular and influential nationalist leader (John Hume), ready to take part in negotiations on the ground; in Belfast, Sinn

Féin, and its military branch, the IRA, were stronger, and less likely to compromise; and secondly, the relative weakness of republican paramilitary groups in (London)Derry, with a very low level of activity since the end of the 1980s. In Belfast, support for militant republicanism has been higher, and the leadership of the IRA waited until 1994 to announce a ceasefire. This element is obviously crucial when one recalls that paramilitary groups have been an important source of inter-community incidents, even if not the only one.

It therefore seems that policies and political skills are not the main factors accounting for differences observed on the ground. If policies and political initiatives can indeed make a difference, as clearly shown by the impact of the current peace process, it seems that many local issues and settings have also to be taken into account. While there has undoubtedly been a growing awareness of these issues among political and policy circles, there is so far no significant and encompassing initiative dedicated to the reduction of interface violence, as if it was the problem of local actors only. Most, however, lack the necessary political, economic and financial leeway. In relation to parades, though, some interesting initiatives have recently been set up. For example, Paddy Ashdown—together with well-known republican and loyalist leaders, as well as parading institutions and local residents' groups—has been preparing a 'Strategic Review of Parading in Northern Ireland'.[11] A draft report of their findings has already been produced, but the report itself initially due in early 2009, is still pending. It is hoped that it will help to sensibly appease these highly contentious issues.

REFERENCES

Belfast Interface Project (2004) *A Policy Agenda for the Interface* (Belfast, Belfast Interface Project).

Bell, D (1990) *Acts of Union, Youth Culture and Sectarianism in Northern Ireland* (London, Macmillan).

Birrell, D (1994) 'Social Policy Responses to Urban Violence in Northern Ireland' in S Dunn (ed), *Managing Divided Cities* (Keele, Ryburn Publishing).

Boal, F, Murray, C and Poole, M (1976) 'Belfast: The Urban Encapsulation of a National Conflict' in S Clark and J Obler (eds), *Urban Ethnic Conflict: A Comparative Perspective* (Chapel Hill, University of North Carolina).

Byrne, J (2005) *Interface Violence in East Belfast during 2002. The Impact on Residents of Short Strand and Inner East Belfast* (Belfast, Institute for Conflict Research).

Darby, J (1996) *Intimidation and the Control of the Conflict in Northern Ireland* (Syracuse, Syracuse University Press).

[11] See the website: www.srpb.org.uk/index.cfm.

Doherty, P and Poole, M (1995) *Ethnic Residential Segregation in Belfast* (Coleraine, Centre for the Study of Conflict).

Féron, E (2008) 'Restaurer la confiance en Irlande du Nord? La négociation aux interfaces urbaines' 1 *Négociations* 41.

Hall, M (ed) (2003) '"It's Good to Talk". Springfield Mobile Phone Network' Newtownabbey 51 *Island Pamphlets.*

—— (2005) 'Finding Common Ground, An Exploration by Young People from Both Sides of the East Belfast Interface' Newtownabbey 69 *Island Pamphlets.*

Hargie, O and Dickson, D (eds) (2004) *Researching the Troubles, Social Science Perspectives on the Northern Ireland Conflict* (Edinburgh, Mainstream Publishing).

Heatley, C (2004) *Interface. Flashpoints in Northern Ireland* (Belfast, Lagan Books Publishing).

Jarman, N (2002) *Managing Disorder—Responding to Interface Violence in North Belfast* (Belfast, OFMDFM Research Branch Report).

—— (2005) 'Managing Conflicts by Phone. The Mobile Phones Network in Northern Ireland' in P Van Tongeren, M Brenk, M Hellema and J Verhoeven (eds), *People Building Peace II: Successful Stories of Civil Society* (Boulder, Lynne Rienner).

—— (2006) *Working at the Interface. Good Practice in Reducing Tension and Violence* (Belfast, Institute for Conflict Research).

McEvoy, S (2000) 'Communities and Peace: Catholic Youth in Northern Ireland' 37(1) *Journal of Peace Research* 87.

Moran, J (2008) *Policing the Peace in Northern Ireland. Politics, Crime and Security after the Belfast Agreement* (Manchester, Manchester University Press).

Shirlow, P and Murtagh, B (2006) *Belfast, Segregation, Violence and the City* (London, Pluto Press).

8

A Bridge to Lasting Peace: Post-Conflict Reconciliation and Mediation in Burundi and the Democratic Republic of Congo

AURÉLIEN COLSON AND ALAIN PEKAR LEMPEREUR[1]

EXACTLY ONE CENTURY ago, Georg Simmel, in his work *Sociologie* (1908; translation 1999) noted that war and peace 'are so interwoven that conditions of future wars are formed within conditions of a situation of peace, and conditions of future peace within a situation of war' (1999: 336 our translation). The insight of this sociologist—whose founding contribution to conflict analysis in international relations was recently highlighted by Frédéric Ramel in particular (2006)—remains very modern. It is further demonstrated in the works of Vasquez, for example, for whom 'certain types of peace have been fairly successful in avoiding a repeat of the war, while others have actually promoted a war's recurrence' (1993: 266).

Thus, in contrast to the summary definition that is given in the realist paradigm—in Bull's work for example: 'the absence of war among member-states in the international system' (1977: 7)—peace does not arise when war stops. The end of hostilities only marks the opening of a critical transitional phase in which, although fighting may have stopped and/or a formal agreement negotiated, each of the parties feels the acute fragility of the moment, and the possible return to hostilities. This transitional period should preserve a progression towards 'a great reduction in the probability that political actors will resort to violence to achieve their ends', which for Vasquez, constitutes the definition of peace (1993: 264).

[1] We would like to thank Cédric Pierard, formerly in charge of the 'Negotiators of the World' programmes at ESSEC IRÉNÉ (www.essec-irene.com).

Simmel is quite justified in emphasising that 'peace is not so directly an emanation from the conflict; the end of conflict is a specific step that does not belong to either of these categories, much as a bridge is of a completely different nature from the two river banks it connects' (1999: 337 our translation). What should draw the attention of the researcher as well as the practitioner is the way in which a conflict comes to an end, the nature of the bridge linking the conflict side to the side of peace.

Yet the architecture and construction of this bridge leading to peace is made more complicated by two factors. The first is related to the interstate or infra-state nature of a conflict. At the end of a war between two sovereign states, the belligerents can foresee their destinies in separate ways; and as can be shown for the French–German example, this does not prevent reconciliation. In contrast, civil war leaves the same wounded and divided social body: separated by hatred, communities continue to live together. This *imposed* proximity will only be sustainable if the communities in question come to *accept it*, which implies a *modus vivendi*, or even, if possible, a reconciliation. This is in part linked to the acceptance of common game rules, the restoration of confidence between actors, the capacity to overcome past suffering—which supposes acknowledgement and pardon—to better focus together on questions concerning the future. There is reconciliation once the conviction becomes widespread enough that a common future has more importance than the divided past. Researchers in conflict resolution studies therefore consider this notion as essential—as illustrated by Ramsbotham, Woodhouse and Miall (2005: 231–45).

However, this reconciliation—and this is the second complicating factor—will be made all the more difficult if the conflict has been marked by serious human rights violations, war crimes, crimes against humanity or acts of genocide, thus transgressing the *jus in bello*.[2] The recollection of atrocities, and the legitimate need for justice expressed by the victims, will not make the reconciliation process easier, however necessary it may be for the pursuit of a life as a community. Thus forms a difficult-to-resolve tension between a logic of peace and a logic of justice, as demonstrated by Colson's analysis concerning the former Yugoslavia (2000).

It is therefore in these extreme contexts—a civil war characterised by the worst atrocities—that the question of reconciliation must be considered. This is what we will do in light of data collected in two cases which demonstrate these two complicating factors: Burundi and the Democratic Republic of Congo (DRC).

But a paradox already appears. The notion of reconciliation is not found in works related to negotiation, with a few rare exceptions including a book

[2] In response to studies on the Just War Doctrine—*cf* in particular the volume by Jean Bethke Elshtain (1992)—Jacques Sémelin (2005) explores what he calls the 'black hole' of mass crimes and extreme violence, already taken up by Ervin Staub (1992).

by Thuderoz, who notices this subject's absence (2000: 102). This omission constitutes a troubling paradox as negotiation is a central tool for the end of an armed conflict, whether the belligerent parties deal directly with one another or are assisted in their negotiations by a mediator (Bercovitch and Jackson, 1997; Pekar Lempereur, Salzer and Colson, 2008). Furthermore, this absence invites a reflection on the subject, for, as early as 1737 following François de Callières' work, Antoine Pecquet, in his book which establishes the founding principles of a general theory of negotiation, wrote that negotiation 'is the instrument of reconciliation between princes'. (1737, edn 2003: 15 our translation).

Hence, the three objectives set out by this chapter: to clarify the links that exist between negotiation and reconciliation in post-conflict contexts (section 1); to present an original system of intervention in two countries having experienced serious civil war, Burundi and the DRC (section 2); and finally to analyse the nature, and the extent to which such a mechanism can contribute to different kinds of rapprochement and reconciliation (section 3).

I. NEGOTIATION: RECONCILING THE IRRECONCILABLE?

Several typologies have outlined the range of processes that allow a conflict to end, in particular those of Dupont (1982: 27). Simmel, once again a precursor, put forward his own, which we will use as our guide (1999: 339–46). He considers three 'habitual ways' of ending a dispute: *victory* of one of the protagonists, notably the defeat of the other; *compromise*, in other words, negotiation; and finally *reconciliation*, whereby the two parties choose to end their disagreement without demanding compensation. Yet, Simmel has a *distinct* approach concerning these three typologies, for at the crux is to consider their structure. It consists of exploring, the day after a victory, how a reconciliation seems possible, and even necessary, to the actors involved, and to determine the role that *negotiation* can play within this prospect.

For that purpose, a typology of the place given to the notion of reconciliation in the negotiation process is proposed. Schematically, three configurations can be discerned.

(a) Reconciliation is Unrelated to the Negotiation Process

This case seems to be the most commonly assumed, for two reasons. First, in the aftermath of an armed conflict, the agenda is dominated by immediate, concrete and obvious issues that are at the antipodes of the features that define reconciliation: the long term, the symbolic and the underlying issues.

Secondly, the parties involved, even if they are united around the negotiating table, remain in an antagonistic logic that polarises their differences, making them stand firmly in their own positions so as not to be perceived by their respective audiences as compromising the interests they represent. Negotiation in this example takes on a logic that is mainly distributive: that what can and must be divided—territories, resources, power and responsibilities. Negotiation takes place; then everyone goes their separate ways.

This example is all the more common because these negotiations take place under the auspices— and partly under the pressure of—third parties. As Simmel noted: 'compromise [in other words negotiation] is out of the question [...] in conflicts motivated by hatred or vengeance' (1999: 350 our translation). Hence, the frequent recourse to mediation in civil wars: the good offices of traditional diplomatic efforts aiming to mediate peace with local warlords. The international pressure is often so intense that chiefs feel obligated to sign peace agreements, although deep down they are not always convinced of their validity or legitimacy. They at times consider these agreements rather like truces, pauses, before taking up arms again.

These leaders are even less sure that their respective troops—for whom the 'Other' has been referred to as their sworn enemy—will see themselves in the signed clauses, weakening the fragile stability that has been obtained and increasing the risk of a split from either side: moderates tired of war on the one hand and radicals drawn to the mirage of a subsequent armed conflict, on the other. Any rapprochement with the former enemy can be perceived as treason, and as a sign of weakness from one's own side; the victors in the field and the negotiators at the table are well aware of this problem. As a result, reconciliation is kept at the sidelines of negotiation.

(b) Reconciliation Appears as an End of Negotiation, Albeit a Distant One

In this second configuration, which can entail multiple terms, reconciliation is present in the minds of the parties involved, or at least in some of them. It becomes a desirable end. If the negotiation intends to lead to a lasting peace, it must foresee mechanisms for the future that will favour reconciliation between the communities in question.

As a result, an additional and particularly sensitive variable has to be brought to the negotiating table. The process becomes all the more complex. The negotiation must lead to a decision concerning the mechanism that will be adopted to promote this reconciliation. It may include favouring the oversight of past events, or, on the contrary, investigating past events, possibly institutionalising an exchange of confession and pardon—following the example of the Truth and Reconciliation Commission chaired by Archbishop Desmond Tutu in South Africa (2000). Another model entails the resort to legal proceedings, whether they be national (as in Ethiopia when the crimes of the Mengistu regime were judged), or international (such as the criminal courts created for the former Yugoslavia and Rwanda).

Although the process has been made more complex, the hope is that in the long term the negotiation will have gained in solidity. We can speak of integrative negotiation: one negotiates and hopes that a rapprochement will follow as a result. In this configuration, reconciliation comes *after* negotiation. But Simmel also thinks that reconciliation can constitute an element *before* the negotiation: 'Reconciliation, a purely subjective mode, contrasts with the objective character that the end of combat entails through compromise. Here I have in mind reconciliation that is not the consequence of compromise, or another reason for renouncing combat, but the cause of the latter' (1999: 342 our underlining and translation). Reconciliation can result from negotiation or the end of combat; but it can also facilitate negotiation. This is in the spirit of the last configuration of our typology.

(c) The Negotiating Process itself as an Outcome of Reconciliation

If, as Simmel seems to indicate, negotiation is seldom achievable in situations marked by hatred or revenge—which are precisely the characteristics of civil wars marked by serious crimes—it is definitely reconciliation which offers an antidote to the need for revenge, and which can dissolve hatred. Reconciliation would then be a precondition to an effective approach to negotiation; a precondition, or in any case, an essential complement. In the New Caledonian conflict, for example, the Nouméa agreement of 5 May 1998 was preceded by a preamble that illustrates this approach. This text, as brief as it is elegant, acknowledges the conditions of the 'Grande Terre' colonisation, and weaves within the same framework the two communities' distinct perspectives: 'the time has come to recognise the shadows of the colonial period, even if it was not devoid of light'. The existence and content of this text were essential to achieving an agreement on fundamental questions.[3]

The conviction that efforts of rapprochement and reconciliation must be led simultaneously along with the negotiation sequence, and that the negotiation process itself must give way to these same efforts, is the basis of the post-conflict mediation mechanism that will be presented. Admittedly, this mechanism is not a negotiating process in the strictest sense—and, moreover, therein lies the very condition of its success. For it is truly on account of

[3] From an interview on 13 March 2003; this is what Aurélien Colson was told by Alain Christnacht, *Conseiller d'Etat*, former *Haut-Commissaire* in New Caledonia (1991–94), French Overseas Department Minister's cabinet director during the Matignon Agreement (1988) and advisor to the Prime Minister during the Nouméa Agreement (1998).

this unconventional process, both indirect and deeply integrative, that the rapprochement between ex-belligerents begins, and the outlines of reconciliation appear, thus favouring a conclusion on the fundamental issues.

II. A MECHANISM PUT TO THE TEST IN TWO CASES OF POST-CONFLICT: BURUNDI AND THE DEMOCRATIC REPUBLIC OF CONGO (DRC)

It is not the purpose of this chapter to describe in detail the conflicts which have torn apart Burundi and the Democratic Republic of Congo (DRC)—where, as we write, deadly clashes still continue in the eastern regions. In Burundi, a country of approximately six million inhabitants, between 1993 and 2003, 300,000 people were victims of civil war and acts of genocide; by 1972, approximately 350,000 people had already been massacred; therefore, within one generation the population has been literally *decimated*. In the DRC, civil war and the resulting sanitary conditions have killed more than four million people—the greatest toll on human life provoked by a conflict since the Second World War.

It was within these two contexts of human disaster that ESSEC IRÉNÉ[4] teams, in partnership with the Woodrow Wilson International Center for Scholars (Washington) and CMPartners (Cambridge, MA) were called on to devise and then run post-conflict intervention mechanisms. These actions, taking place since 2003 in Burundi and since January 2006 in the DRC, with a permanent local presence in both places, are respectively the Burundi Leadership Training Programme (BLTP), and the Initiative pour un leadership collaboratif et pour la cohésion de l'Etat en RDC (ILCCE—Initiative for Collaborative Leadership and State Cohesion in DRC).

Both of these post-conflict mediation processes are, in many respects, a product of the theoretical framework proposed by Burton in the field of conflict studies. First, and generally, the pluralist paradigm of international relations and political systems presented by Burton (1972) is reflected in the transversal choice of the diversity of actors involved in these processes: political representatives from every level, officials and 'rebels' of course, but also representatives from the civilian, economic and media worlds. Exiting a conflict, and a fortiori reconciliation, involves this multiplicity of non-state actors. Subsequently, the very foundations of facilitation— its non-imposing nature, the facilitators' constant concern to not take sides concerning substance, the emphasis on the process itself and on putting the actors in contact

[4] Alain Pekar Lempereur would like to thank Aziza Akhmouch, Liliane de Andrade, Eric Blanchot, Aurélien Colson, Florrie Darwin, Antoine Foucher, Thierry Gadaud, Cédric Jouniaux, Eric Le Deley, Ricardo Perez Nuckel, François Perrot, Cédric Pierard, Fahimeh Robiolle, Tina Robiolle and Astrid de Valon who gave their assistance, as well as members of ESSEC IRÉNÉ during the development of these programmes.

with one another—fit into the *conflict resolution* approach developed by Burton and his school (1990). Finally, the attention given to perception problems and the role of communication in the dynamic of conflicts refers once again to a constant characteristic of the Burtonian approach.

(a) The General Configuration of a Post-conflict Mediation Mechanism

The broad outline of this mechanism—described in detail by Lempereur (2007)—consists of regularly organising formative retreats bringing together groups of key leaders meant to work together, but having to overcome disagreements linked to past—or still current—events. The basic workshop, planned to take place over five days, consists of two distinct parts:

- A *methodological and relational part* (three days): the key leaders reinforce their skills—decision making, negotiation, dialogue and problem solving; they also learn to better know, respect and understand one another. This first part, where topics that are a cause for dispute are not yet addressed, brings together the conditions that are essential for the next phase.
- A *practical and substantial part* (two days): participants identify the most important and urgent topics for their country, choosing those on which they can exert an influence, and search together for solutions and reach commitments, for which follow-up mechanisms are put into place.

In the first part, our teams of facilitators have the goal of weaving links between former combatants *(first, the people)* and structuring methods to be applied in the next part *(then, the process)*. During the second part where key questions are examined *(finally, and only then, the problems)* and solutions are sought out, the facilitators are mediators who have made the choice of limiting their input as to how the process is conducted. The distinction between *mediator-facilitator* (focusing on the process) and *mediator-advisor* (proposing solutions) in this instance appears as fundamental to us. It is the former that describes the methodological approach which prevails in these workshops. The participants remain in control of the content. In no way do the facilitators intervene to say to the participants: 'here are your problems, their causes and solutions, thus here are the recommendations and commitments that you should make'. The citizens from Burundi or the DRC, who are in their own environment, are the ones to develop the content. The prevalent idea is that the participants learn from one another.

In this spirit, the BLTP brought together almost 8000 national and local highest level leaders in workshops destined for political decision makers (from the executive and legislative branches), for executives from security sectors (army and the police), for civilians, for the press as well as for training of trainers (in Paris, Washington and in Burundi). A midway assessment of this process is the subject of a report by Wolpe, Lempereur, et al (2004). In the same vein, in the DRC, through ILCCE, more than 800 national and provincial leaders from the political and security sectors, and civilians have participated in workshops that have already been held at national and local levels. The local dynamic has been focused on the Kivu region, which was very hard hit by the war.

(b) The Mechanism's Three Inherent Principles appear as Driving Forces for Reconciliation

The first principle necessitates the appropriation or ownership of the mechanism by local actors; the second principle requires its fitting into the local and long-term scheme; the third demands the integration of the most radical actors.

(i) Reconciliation cannot be Imposed by External Forces. It is Constructed from the Inside by the Actors Involved

In Burundi as in the DRC, the starting point for the mechanism is the agreement—or at least the non-opposition—of all the state's highest level figures, the signatories to the peace agreement (and if possible including the agreement of those who could not participate for various reasons). It is not simply a matter of convincing top leaders of the need to hold workshops or conferences taking place here or there, bringing together the country's key actors. The workshops must take place with their 'will'; the project must be nationalised, the initiative must be 'Burundised' or 'Congolised' even before it has even begun.

Although foreign personalities may facilitate the process, the country's citizens are the ones who guide the project, and give it content. Leaders, who at times have the feeling of having been pressured by exterior forces during the agreement's negotiation and signature, welcome the idea that the dialogue that will subsequently take place with key leaders is indeed a national one. They must be guaranteed that the facilitation is limited to a smooth method that allows for the process to progress towards fundamental issues.

This first principle is in itself a factor of rapprochement, a premise of reconciliation: leaders who are in fundamental disagreement, at times violent, agree on a common process. For example, the first workshops in Burundi—*the Ngozi process*—and in DRC—*the Nganda process*—brought together participants who were as representative as possible of the national leadership. These heterogeneous groups were comprised of figures from the political world and highly-placed civilians. This intermingling was the best way to 'take the temperature' of a society divided and weakened by war. These *unlikely encounters* were also opportunities to prove to the seminars' participants that they could even be together, work together, and then recognise each other. Once the election results were known in Burundi, the president-elect Pierre Nkurunziza, the two vice presidents and the ministers attended a government retreat that took place in September 2006. This team-building experience at the highest level allowed the members of the cabinet to better know one another and reflect on methods of action for the executive branch.

(ii) Consequent upon the Previous Principle, the Undertaking of Reconciliation must be Developed within the Local Frame of Reference and this for the Long-term

This continuation takes place in Burundi and the DRC in training retreats, on a monthly basis when possible. Either a basic workshop for a new group is organised, or a follow-up workshop is given every three months, briefly convening participants from a previous basic workshop. A network of personalities is thus built and cultivated among those who are weaving links of trust, as the commitments made together are put to work. Of course, there are ebbs and flows. But over time, this follow-up and the consequent embedding in time are, in themselves, factors narrowing the gaps between formerly divided groups.

This duration is made possible by the constantly renewed support of numerous international partners. In Burundi, the project was launched thanks to the World Bank's Post-Conflict Fund, and then continued by the European Commission, as well as the British Department for International Development (DFID) and USAID (Office for Transition Initiatives). As for the DRC, a trust fund from the United Nations Development Programme (UNDP) received contributions from the European Commission, as well as American, British, Canadian, Norwegian and Swedish support.

The duration of this process is also the fruit of permanent local units' efforts. The direction of the local branches was entrusted to local personalities who, despite the country's great liabilities, were able to maintain the confidence of all the local and international actors.

In Burundi, national representatives who were consulted often mentioned two names: Fabien Nsengimana, a former presidential advisor, and Eugène Nindorera, former Minister of Human Rights. These two eminent men set themselves apart by their unanimously recognised impartiality and dignity. The Burundian ethnic duality also dictated that through them the Hutu and Tutsi ethnicities would be represented. Merely mentioning these two men's names was enough to reassure potential participants. During the entire project, Fabien Nsengimana, BLTP director, and Eugène Nindorera, consultant, ensured that situations were deciphered properly, helped to prevent blunders, directed debates and made sure that the BLTP was managed by a Burundian.

In the DRC, the ILCCE turned to Michel Noureddine Kassa, former head of the local DRC office of OCHA (UN Office for the Coordination of Humanitarian Affairs). A French-Algerian hero in the Congo, he embodied, from 1994 to 2002, the spirit of impartial action in service of the population. The Congolese recognised him as one of their own, and he is regarded with great respect. To many a Congolese citizen, an ILCCE letter signed by him is an immeasurably valuable pass. The invaluable contribution of Father Martin Ekwa should also be noted. In charge of Catholic education in the DRC after its independence, he, too, opened numerous doors and guided the ILCCE's strategy through his standing as a wise man, his subtlety and his charisma.

This permanent local presence also allowed the effort to be brought to zones that are difficult to access. In the DRC, because of risks linked to events in the provinces of North and South Kivu, it was decided to set up local workshops in Goma and Bukavu, and even in towns such as Butembo, Minembwe and Uvira, areas where, over the past 15 years, confidence has been most seriously undermined. These workshops have allowed people to overcome their fear of elections before they took place, and then, once the change in power wanted by the electors occurred, to overcome their fear of the results. In these zones, 'volcanic' in every sense of the word, there remain barely extinguished fires that may at any moment rekindle into potential violence. Yet nuclei of good will have been constituted, and they fight as best as they can against these risks.

(iii) The Reconciliation Effort must Integrate Radicals.

There is no point in reconciliation among those who are already in agreement. Bring together moderates and they'll come together on an agreement and then the war will be taken up again through the extremists, who were excluded from the process from the beginning. This mechanism is about generating 'unlikely encounters': bringing together moderates and radicals from all sides, including hawks and all those who for better or worse will determine the future of their country for the next 20 years to come. Naturally, those in love with peace should be included if they exert an influence on the society in question; and if their presence is justified by the likely positive influence they may have on the others. As for those actors known for being 'hard-liners', their presence will give credibility to the initiative. Of course, the atmosphere at the beginning of the meetings is bound to be icy, but at least all of the conditions are united to bring together precisely those whom the conflict has pushed the furthest apart.

How are the participants chosen? Here is another area where national leaders and representatives from international communities intervene.

They know those who uphold the cause of peace, but also the hawks who could sabotage the peace process. The idea is to ask each representative to prepare a list of 30 people who could play key roles in shaping the country's future. When cross-referencing these leaders' lists (heads of state or prime ministers from present or past governments, presidents of national or provincial parliaments, religious authorities, academic personalities or civilians), the names of certain personalities come up several times and are thus considered as *influential leaders* by the country's highest authorities. Six criteria—presented without a hierarchal order—are suggested to enhance the representativeness of those who will attend the seminars:

1. *Men's and women's representation.* Noting the essential role that women play or could play in an appeasement process, our organisation team tries to ensure a high presence of women during the encounters. A goal of 30 per cent has been set to that end. It is sometimes difficult, indeed impossible, to achieve for some specific workshops, like for example those dedicated to the subject of security sectors.
2. *Professional representation.* Political and administrative officials, superior officers from the army and armed movements ('rebels', acknowledged or not), judges, lawyers, journalists, university professors, union leaders, heads of NGOs, etc.
3. *Geographical representation* with people from the capital as well as people from the provinces and as the case may be the diaspora.
4. *Ethnic representation* ensuring a balance between the country's different communities, in particular those who are at the conflict's epicentre.
5. *Historical representation* allowing for a balance between different eras in the history of the country. As an example, in the DRC, the presence of Lumumbist, Mobutist, and Kabilist leaders was essential.
6. *Representation of the whole range of opinions* including moderates and radicals from each side.

Here again, this approach favours bringing together personalities from different backgrounds. For example, during one DRC workshop, it was possible to bring together two vice presidents, the President of the National Assembly, a former prime minister, former provincial governors, the children of a former president of the country, advisors to the president, a bishop, etc.

We can observe that the choice of participants is in great part determined by the country's authorities, hence reinforcing the local nature of the initiative and its appropriation on a national level. Equally, ensuring the presence of key personalities guarantees that these mediations will be carried out between persons who 'recognise' one another. Even if at first they do not know precisely who will be participating, the first moments they spend together in the hall will assure them that they are with relevant persons, for better or for worse.

III. FROM RAPPROCHEMENT TO RECONCILIATION

In what way does this post-conflict mediation programme contribute to reconciling the participating parties? In order to answer this question, let us note that we share the cautious approach that calls for humility in evaluating the impact of any undertaking of post-conflict facilitation, as pointed out by Hoffman et al (2004) among others. The distinction between the two case situations should also be made. The case of Burundi offers a better retrospect, as interventions have been going on there since 2003. Programmes instructing training officers (through training of trainers) have allowed interventions to be widespread. Above all, the size of the country and its population lead us to believe that the post-conflict intervention programme has reached a critical dimension. The situation is different in the DRC: interventions are much more recent, and due to the larger scale of this country, it has not yet been possible to undertake a widespread trainer's instruction programme that would enable us to widen our approach, as in the Burundi case.

The account of this mechanism has already allowed us to illustrate in different ways emerging rapprochements and the reestablishment of contacts. In order to evaluate these results in a structured manner, we propose an analytical grid, distinguishing eight levels of impact in increasing order. Each level comprises elements favourable to a reconciliation.

(a) Immediate Personal Impact

Using first names among all the participants, coupled with the informal French '*tu*' form (second person singular) as well as forbidding the use of official titles during workshops helps to remove a great number of inhibitions and prejudices. Furthermore, individuals are put at ease through simulations, exercises and discussions. The facilitators' continuous acknowledgement and recognition that the participants are key to the success of the process triggers awareness, risk taking, indeed even confidences and commitments, leading to more constructive behaviour as the workshop takes place. The participants, who often come to these meetings with the secret wish of changing the others, have in fact changed themselves.

(b) Lasting Personal Impact

Once the participants have finished a workshop, they find themselves back in their initial professional and social surroundings. The risk of returning to old habits is great. This is why the follow-up meetings, in which the first moments are often spent exchanging experiences on changes being carried out back at home, are so important. A certain political leader from Ituri explains how he resolved, through negotiation techniques, a problem between two communities that could have got out of hand. Or, the woman senator from Burundi who, having finally been recognised by her peers for her leadership qualities has become a government minister.

(c) Impact on Relations within the Group (Networking)

These meetings, that are frosty to begin with, bring people from all political sides, ethnicities and opposing parties, face to face. Yet quite quickly, a convivial atmosphere is created among the participants. As days go by, through discussions, but also coffee breaks and lunches, or even evening gatherings, a number of interpersonal obstacles fall. Suddenly, participants catch themselves no longer seeing the others as *enemies*, but as *opponents*, or even *partners*. The thought of setting up and reinforcing a network naturally comes at the end of a basic workshop. The permanence of this network is essential. An example of its impact is seen in the fact that three ILCCE participants were successively president of the National Assembly. Each transfer of power saw the risk of institutional deadlock, or even violence. But these personalities, having learned to better know one another in part because of the workshops and their methods, had measured the benefits of a cooperative approach compared with strong-arm tactics. They were thus able to find the mechanisms for a smooth transition when the second replaced the first; it was the same for the third. The changes in power occurred smoothly.

(d) Impact on Relations with Subordinates

If the participants are well chosen, there is a strong chance that they will be able to pass on to their colleagues the methods and answers developed during the workshops. For example, in Burundi, following the workshops organised for the military command integrated into the police, the Burundian Military Academy now incorporates these workshops into the curriculum for all their officers, with the help of Burundian facilitators trained to use these methods.

(e) Impact on Relations with Hierarchical Authorities

The participants are bound to have to report the workshop results to their principals and constituents. Their positive feedback and influence is crucial. Several new workshops were created only because former participants used all their weight to demonstrate the importance of these workshops to their principals. They become more efficient national spokespersons than the facilitation team, and achieve a much higher level of impact, such a reach being in fact quite difficult to attain.

(f) Impact on Institutions

Once a critical number of representatives of an institution have worked together in a workshop, even if they do not belong to the same political movement for example, they can, within their institution, work in a non-partisan manner or approach some problems with less tension. In the DRC, the President of the National Assembly supported the organisation of a workshop for political group leaders. Having created a stronger sense of common belonging during the workshops, these leaders were able to treat unresolved legislative questions with greater facility. In Burundi, immediately following their participation in a workshop, military leaders from all sides were able to successfully end the deadlock on several key questions including the definition of a combatant, the harmonisation of ranks, and the allocation of posts, points that had been at a standstill for over three months.

(g) Impact between Institutions

This mechanism has already allowed for the prevention of a crisis in favour of a settlement. In Burundi, during the entire course of the year 2005, one of the workshop's practical working goals was the drafting of a code of electoral conduct, as well as raising party leaders' awareness to a responsible approach during the electoral process. Since February 2007, still in Burundi, a conflict between the executive and legislative branches had put the institutions in deadlock. At the request of the President of the Republic, a workshop was organised by the BLTP in September 2007 to bring together key personalities. Burundi's four former living presidents participated in the workshop, along with the Interior Minister, the Chief of Staff of the Armed Forces, the national police commissioner and the principal leaders of all the political parties. In the wake of this unprecedented seminar, three former heads of state—a first in Burundi's history—together mentioned the settlement of the crisis during the Isanganiro radio broadcast. A few weeks later the crisis was resolved.

(h) Impact on Society

Knowing whether these post-conflict mediation initiatives change a society, even marginally, depends on the capacity of key leaders to expand the methods and content to a large scale. Workshop participants are invited to contribute to the expansion of this process. In the DRC, the agenda of a follow-up workshop was upset due to events which followed first round presidential election results. All attention was turned towards the two second round candidates: President Kabila and Vice-President Bemba. Just at the moment when their respective troops were confronting one another in Kinshasa, the workshop participants—from all backgrounds and various geographical origins ranging from the Congo's east to west—contributed to the organisation of quiet encounters between key personalities. These participants—close to one side or the other, or some to neither—were all concerned about the fragile national cohesion that could shatter at any moment. Together they wrote and delivered an address calling for peace in the country's four national languages. The address was named 'Plea from Nguma'. During several days, the plea was broadcast on numerous Congolese television and radio stations. On other occasions, the participants have held press conferences or prompted interviews with journalists. Public exchanges between students and professors, such as those at the Bukavu Catholic University, also took place.

From the youngest school children to university students and adults in continuing education, such a high level of impact requires the largest possible integration of messages of peace, reconciliation and national cohesion, along with negotiation methods which in practice give these messages their substance. It remains that barely one Burundian inhabitant out of 1000 has participated in workshops and not more than one inhabitant out of 100,000 in the DRC, which has a population of 60 million. Even if the voices of key leaders participating in the workshops often have greater reach than those of 'common mortals', we are still far from being able to claim any long-term societal impact resulting from these types of initiatives.

IV. CONCLUSION

The post-conflict mediation mechanism described here seems to contribute to reconciliation of the parties in question through the following: organising 'unlikely encounters' between enemies or radically opposed parties; allowing opposing sides to speak, promoting mutual exchange—but especially listening; stirring a keen awareness of the other, and the interdependence that connects everyone in each social system; bringing about a new, shared experienced among former enemies—a shared reference point for the future; bringing cognitive bias that impedes reconciliation into the light in order to better cast prejudices aside; facilitate agreements on new, tangible and productive processes; creating symbols and helping spread them to a national audience; favouring the resolution of fundamental issues and concrete problems; in short, inviting participants to *plan together* for the future, and plan for a *future together*.

Now the question is whether this process can be transposed to other post-conflict situations. As long as the presiding principles proposed in our evaluation grid exist, it seems that the mechanism can be applied elsewhere. The interest in transposing this mechanism is both practical—a concrete contribution of end of conflict mechanisms—and scientific—an opportunity to observe the constants as well as the adaptations needed in function with the actual 'in the field' variables. From this standpoint, the experience in the DRC constitutes a first attempt at transposition of the mechanism launched in Burundi.

The situation remains unstable in both these countries and it is illusory to deny the risks of a return to violence. At times, an accident or a crime followed by a rumour is enough to set in motion the escalation of tragic events. With this risk in mind, it would nevertheless be cynical to not guarantee the possibility of mediation where it is needed the most, always involving persons of influence in the process.

Reconciliation needs time. There still hasn't been enough time to evaluate the impact of this mechanism and its capacity to encourage an effective reconciliation between stakeholders. It has to be constructed on the right scale, that is, in this instance, the Great Lakes sub-region. Taking into account the constant interactions between the neighbouring countries, a provincial approach in the DRC's Kivus regions has shown its limits. When the time is right, a reflection on the necessity of having an inter-institutional workshop that regroups the heads of state and politicians from the four countries that constitute the quadripartite commission (Burundi, DRC, Uganda and Rwanda) cannot be avoided.

Reconciliation is not an *explicit* aim—there is no doubt it would be counterproductive to label it that way. As Uri Savir, one of the main Israeli negotiators with the Palestinians during the Oslo peace accords, noted in another context but with the same relevance: 'in reconciliation, some will see an opportunity for salvation, others for capitulation' (1998: 37 our translation). The declared goal is to reinforce the role of the leaders in 'unity', 'cohesion' or the 'consolidation of the State'. But reconciliation is a part of the hoped-for result.

'If only this retreat had taken place before the Arusha Accords, everything would have been much easier', remarked one of the first participants in a seminar organised in Burundi, thus confirming the approach explained above: the reconciliation effort must be constructed inside the negotiation sequence itself, at the end of the conflict. It cannot be a subsequent prospect for it is intrinsically related to the process, and as we have seen, it has an impact on the process itself in numerous ways. This effort is indeed a constructive element of a bridge towards peace, each of its pillars having to be steadfastly built.

REFERENCES

Bercovitch, J and Jackson, R (1997) *International Conflict. A Chronological Encyclopedia of Conflicts and their Management, 1945–1995* (Washington, DC, Congressional Quarterly).

Bull, H (1977) *The Anarchical Society* (London, Macmillan).

Burton, JW (1969) *Conflict and Communication: The Use of Controlled Communication in International Relations* (London, Macmillan).

—— (1972) *World Society* (Cambridge, Cambridge University Press).

—— (1990) *The Conflict Series* (London, Macmillan).

Colson, A (2000) 'The Logic of Peace and the Logic of Justice' 1 *International Relations* 51, 62.

—— (2008) 'Le *Discours sur l'art de négocier* d'Antoine Pecquet' in A Lempereur and A Colson (eds), *Négociations européennes* (Paris, A2C Médias).

Dupont, C (1982) *La Négociation. Conduite, théorie, applications* (Paris, Dalloz).

Elshtain, JB (ed) (1992) *The Just War Theory* (Oxford, Blackwell).

Hoffman, M (2004) 'Peace and Conflict Impact Assessment Methodology' in A Austin et al (eds), *Transforming Ethnopolitical Conflict: the Berghof Handbook* (Berlin, VS Verlag für Sozialwissenschaften) 171, 191.

Lempereur, A (2007) 'De la médiation politique à la médiation post-conflit, ou la reconstruction nationale d'un leadership cohésif' in A Lempereur and S Bensimon (eds), *Médiation. Modes d'emploi* (Paris, A2C Médias).

Lempereur, A, Salzer, J and Colson, A (2008) *Méthode de médiation* (Paris, Dunod).

Mani, R (2002) *Beyond Retribution. Seeking Justice in the Shadows of War* (Cambridge, Polity Press).

Pecquet, A (1737) *Discours sur l'art de négocier* (Paris, Nyon Fils; reed. by A Lempereur, Paris-Cergy: ESSEC IRÉNÉ, 2003).

Ramel, F (2006) *Les fondateurs oubliés. Durkheim, Simmel, Weber, Mauss et les relations internationales* (Paris, PUF).

Ramsbotham, S, Woodhouse, T and Miall, H (2005) *Contemporary Conflict Resolution* 2nd edn (Cambridge, Polity Press).

Savir, U (1998) *Les 1100 jours qui ont changé le Moyen-Orient* (Paris, Odile Jacob).

Simmel, G (1908) *Sociologie. Etudes sur les formes de la socialisation* (Paris, Presses Universitaires de France, 1999).

Sémelin, J (2005) *Purifier et détruire, Usages politiques des massacres et génocides* (Paris, Seuil).

Staub, E (1992) *The Roots of Evil: the Origins of Genocide and Other Group Violence* (Cambridge, Cambridge University Press).

Thuderoz, C (2000) *Négociations. Essai de sociologie du lien social* (Paris, Presses Universitaires de France, coll. « Le sociologue »).

Tutu, D (2000) 'Reconciliation in Post-Apartheid South Africa' in *The Art of Peace. Nobel Peace Laureates Discuss Human Rights, Conflict and Resolution* (Ithaca, NY, Snow Lion Publications).

Vasquez, JA (1993) 'The War Puzzle' 27 *Cambridge Studies in International Relations* (Cambridge, Cambridge University Press).

Wolpe, H, Lempereur, A et al (2004) 'Rebuilding Peace and State Capacity in War-torn Burundi' 93 *The Round Table* 375, 457, 467.

9

Traditional Approaches and their Relevance to Coping with Contemporary Conflicts: Experiences from a Border Region in Africa

MONIKA M SOMMER

THIS CHAPTER IS based on fieldwork that I conducted in Gambella, Ethiopia between 2005 and 2008. Gambella is a regional state of Ethiopia that borders Southern Sudan and has become infamous for its complex and protracted conflicts that gained momentum throughout the last decades. Actors, who belong to different ethnic groups (ie, the local Anywaa,[1] Nuer, Opo, Komo and Majangir, and the 'highlanders' with numerous ethnic backgrounds) and traditions, play diverse roles in society and in the political framework of ethnic federalism in Ethiopia. In addition to these rather traditional actors, new players have entered the scene, namely local and foreign investors, and international NGOs often aiming at building peace.

The tensions between Anywaa and the highlander community came to the attention of a wider public when they erupted and culminated in the massacre of hundreds of Anywaa men in Gambella town on 13 December 2003[2] with the alleged participation of the army. Recent conflicts are among the Anywaa and the highlanders, and between different Nuer clans, mainly based on disputes over access to grazing land, to jobs and education, political power and participation. These disputes then may spiral into cycles of vengeance and retaliation.

[1] The spelling of the group's name differs in literature, ie Anuak, Anyak; I follow Sato Kurimoto and other anthropologists, which seems closest to the way the Anywaa call themselves.

[2] See HRW, 'Targeting the Anuak' (March 2005); and the comment on this paper by local observers 'to whom it may concern', available with WFP, Sub-delegation Gambella.

With this contribution I pose the question whether or not conflict resolution systems that are identified by different groups as 'traditional' are able to cope with the complexity of contemporary conflicts. Similarities and differences between existing procedures are examined and their preparedness for dealing with conflicts that have disrupted civil life in the region will be discussed. How far can traditional approaches really contribute to the process of conflict management? And what does an external mediator need to know about these traditions?

I. THE CONTEXT OF PEACEMAKING IN AFRICA

In recent years traditional conflict resolution systems—specifically in Africa—have experienced a certain renaissance. There is a growing literature on the subject.[3] One reason for this revival seems to be a certain 'desperation' among academicians and practitioners: Foreign and Western interventions in African conflicts have been, more often than not, doomed to fail. Peace agreements were not worth the paper they were written on, and were violated after a short period of time, whenever it seemed politically feasible to the local players. Moreover, this revival—at least in the literature produced outside Africa—of 'traditional conflict resolution' may be seen as part of a postmodern discourse, in search of a less formalised and more self-determined strategy towards conflict transformation. It is generally held to be the case by mediators that the expectations and perceptions of the parties in conflict need to be the starting point of any process. In an African context, this means acknowledging the specific perceptions and collective traditions of the groups we are working and interacting with.

Mediation in complex situations requires a thorough analysis of each individual case. This means understanding who is involved (the actors), why they are involved (the root causes) and what are the expectations held by the different stakeholders (the belief System). Labelling a conflict as 'ethnic' falls short of reality. Conflicts in Africa are complex and multilayered as anywhere. Some of the layers are local, others less: they span worldwide interests in resources, distribution of wealth in a globalised world and local concern for access to power and self-determination.

It follows that any conflict management work needs to appreciate how conflict is understood and processed in the specific social and cultural environment, and how the interests at stake are validated in the particular group. It is 'culture' that frames the context in which conflict occurs, by indicating what sorts of resources are subjects for competition or objects of dispute. Culture stipulates the rules, the specific procedures a society uses for dealing with

[3] See list of references at the end of this chapter, specifically.

conflict, how to begin and when and how to end them. Moreover, culture provides the cognitive, symbolic and affective frameworks for interpreting the behaviour and motives of the 'Other' and the 'Self' (Avruch, 2002: 78).

In concluding this section I underline that it is worthwhile having a close look at the ways different groups in a divided society—such as Gambella—deal with conflict. This will avoid unhelpful generalisations, inspired by more or less nostalgic ideas about the 'noble savage', assumingly less greedy, wiser and more value oriented then contemporary westernised people. A clearer picture will be achieved by analysing some of the conflict handling procedures that are practised by different ethnic groups in a specific African region, in Gambella, Ethiopia.

II. A BRIEF INTRODUCTION TO THE REGION, THE PEOPLE AND THEIR MAIN CONFLICTS

This part gives the minimum of background information that allows the reader to understand the kind of conflict we are dealing with. The Ethiopian Regional State of Gambella is one of the smallest and least developed regions in Ethiopia, situated in the western lowlands of Ethiopia. It borders with Southern Sudan towards the north, west and south. This physical setting as quasi-peninsula within Southern Sudan partly explains its socio-economic marginality and strategic (that is, political) sensitivity. The area on both sides of the border suffered from the long civil war in Sudan. Besides, the border does not reflect the settlement patterns of the local population. Therefore, it has been always a porous border, characterised by intense relations of kinship beyond the border.

Following the latest population census (which was not undisputed) the population of Gambella grew to 306,916 inhabitants in 2007, when the census was conducted. With an annual growth rate of 4.1 per cent Gambella displays the fastest population growth in the country (Population Census Commission, Federal Republic of Ethiopia, 2008: 11, 100).

The indigenous[4] population, as such recognised in the national and regional constitutions, consists of five main ethno-linguistic groups: the

[4] 'Indigenous' is defined by the ILO—Indigenous and Tribal Peoples Convention, No 169: Art 1.1.

(a) tribal peoples in independent countries whose social, cultural and economic conditions distinguish them from other sections of the national community, and whose status is regulated wholly or partially by their own customs or traditions or by special laws or regulations;

(b) peoples in independent countries who are regarded as indigenous on account of their descent from the populations which inhabited the country, or a geographical region to which the country belongs, at the time of conquest or colonisation or the establishment of present state boundaries and who, irrespective of their legal status, retain some or all of their own social, economic, cultural and political institutions.

Anywaa, the Nuer, the Majangir, the Opo and the Komo. With a 46.65 per cent of the population, the Nuer form the biggest ethnic group, followed by the Anywaa with 21.17 per cent of the populace. In particular the Nuer, but also the Anywaa, entertain intense relations to kinship in Southern Sudan. As Nilotic groups these groups share a history of marginalisation within the Ethiopian state throughout history.

Those inhabitants of Gambella who originate from different—usually less peripheral—regions of Ethiopia are commonly summarised as 'highlanders'. The term combines diverse ethnic identities, such as the Oromo, Kambatta, Amhara and Tigrayans. Following the census of 2007 they form about 26 per cent of the population. The appearance of the first 'highlanders' was closely related to the expansion of imperial Ethiopia under Menelik II. During the 1980s though, the (forced) resettlement of large farmers' communities from precarious and drought prone areas of the country has clearly enlarged the group and changed its character. While the early migrants from the highlands were predominantly traders or government officials—often of Amhara or Oromo origin—the 'latecomers' were farmers from diverse regions and ethnic backgrounds, such as Tigrayans from the very north and Kambatta and Haddiya from the south of the country (Meckelburg, 2008: 176). They are united both by their lighter skin complexion, and by the fact that their traditions and current relations are directed towards the centre of the country, rather than towards neighbouring Sudan. This is also reflected in religious terms, as they adhere predominantly to the Ethiopian Orthodox Church or to Islam. In contrast, the indigenous population follows either traditional religions, or different (mainly evangelical) Christian churches—thereby sharing cultural heritage with their direct Sudanese neighbours across the border.

Since Gambella entered the focus of attention of the imperial state in the late nineteenth century, the region has experienced its share of violence and conflict. Since 1991—when the central socialist government was overthrown—the area has seen a remarkable escalation in violence. Much of this seems to be due to the fact that with the new constitutional set-up, ethnicity became a criterion for access to power, participation, material resources and education in an unprecedented way. 'Ethnic Federalism', as the new state form came to be known, aimed at empowering marginalised communities. In effect though, as a reaction to the outbreaks of the new—mostly violent—conflicts on the ground, the central government, most prominently the federal police forces, came in as active players (Chan Gatkuoth, 2007: 165). Rather than re-establishing peace by political and constitutional means in the aftermath of the Itang incident in 2003, for instance—and then after December 2003 (mentioned above), the federal government reacted with arrests, military presence and force. The continuous state of emergency that was associated with these events, turned out to be in favour of the centralised structures—not towards the pluralism and self governance proclaimed in the Constitution. This was true in military and political terms. Central structures also dominate in the process of political reorganisation (Sommer, 2010).

The political set-up remains explosive. According to the federal and regional Constitution, the concept of ethnic group rights leads to quota for indigenous people and the phenomenon that only members of indigenous groups enjoy their full active and passive citizen rights. This leads to the somehow absurd situation that the 'highlanders' are not represented in formal political terms in the region, yet hold a good part of the military and economical power—including access to the federal political power. Indigenous groups, however, hold political offices in the region and enjoy affirmative action, but lack access to the informal networks of mainstream Ethiopia. This situation bears a tremendous potential for conflicts, which have always been dealt with in violent ways in the past (for details see Sommer, 2010; Dereje Feyissa: 2005). But the political focus on ethnicity is not only associated with violent conflict, but supports a tendency to revitalise local traditions. These traditions are not static though, not cast in stone, but change in the process of being adapted to the needs of contemporary people living in a highly volatile and unstable environment.

III. TRADITIONAL PRACTICES: CONFLICT MANAGEMENT OF THE MAIN ETHNIC GROUPS

(a) Methodology and Approach

Due to its immanent limitations, this chapter highlights the conflict resolution mechanisms of some major ethnic groups residing in Gambella. These are the two main indigenous groups—Anywaa and Nuer—and the group of 'highlanders', who are not composed of a specific tribe, but represent around 25 per cent of the population. All these groups share the experience of severe forms of violence in the past, a fact that expressed itself by the very reaction of all interview partners to general questions about traditional mechanisms of conflict resolution; they all jumped directly into the subject of how to deal with homicide and capital crimes. Mechanisms that deal with questions addressing everyday conflicts, often did not attract the full interest of my interview partners.

In this chapter I analyse traditional methods of conflict resolution of indigenous people and 'highlanders' alike. The rationale of this approach is based on the observation that many of the latter groups are de facto permanently settled in Gambella. Without being fully recognised in political terms, they constitute a part of the regional society and play their respective role in its conflicts. Albeit their elders—and the elaborate system of conflict resolution—might not be present in Gambella, as this is the case in the place of origin, people still expressed respect and understanding for the mechanisms and often referred to them. These procedures seemed to be internalised to an extent that they legitimise solutions that will be accepted and readily implemented.

As to my research methodology, I conducted interviews with people from different ethnicities living in Gambella, who were selected as a convenience sample. The interviews capture information on the following characteristics of the traditional systems: the way of initiation of conflict resolution, the process itself, the sealing or final ceremony; whether there are prevention mechanisms in place. In addition, literature on traditional conflict management systems was drawn upon.

(b) Conflict Resolution among the Nuer

Among the Nuer—an ethnic group that is still known among anthropologists as one of the best documented groups in Africa (which is largely due to the work of the British anthropologist Evans-Prichard)—the use of traditional means in cases of conflict is still vital. People from all layers of society, who played very different roles in the process, spontaneously recalled many events, where conflictual situations were addressed by the elders and brought to an acceptable outcome. This ranks from the extremely self-confident voice of a powerful traditional spiritual leader, who did not display any doubt that he was able to settle any conflict (if he wanted), to voices of women and young people, who remember having observed the ceremonies since childhood. It needs to be mentioned that the Nuer are predominantly pastoralists, social life somehow evolves around the cattle.

(i) The Initiation of Conflict Resolution

The conflict resolution process among the Nuer is initiated by elders[5], who discuss an issue that has become a problem for the community. They first gather among themselves, decide to work as a group and take the initial steps. There is a specific procedure for cases when people died in conflicts between groups, or families, otherwise they open a general discussion between the families or groups concerned. The specific procedure for homicide is apparently connected with the idea of a mysterious blood tie existing between slayer and slain that might pollute the slayer, his families and cattle. The connected blood curse is considered highly infectious and could affect other kin. The killer therefore has to be cleansed—and with him his kin (details in Falge, 2006).

[5] Like in all other ethnic groups that are presented here, 'elders' are male *per definitionem*. The idea of female elders still is widely unknown and not acceptable. Women therefore are not active or visible participants in processes of conflict resolution.

(ii) The Process

Parties to the process are families or clans, never individuals. The specific procedure starts with visiting the family of the victim, who are asked whether or not they agree to the intervention of the elders. If the family agrees, immediate retaliation will not take place—under condition that the process is successful. At this stage they define the amount of compensation that they expect the side of the perpetrator to pay. The compensation is payable in cattle; I was told that the average was 35 cows for a male person killed, and that during wars this amount might be reduced to 25 cows).[6] The elders then visit the family of the killer. They might need to go far. As the narrative of Dobuol indicates:

> In 1987 someone from our village had killed a person from another Nuer clan. When the elders ventilated (sic) the availability of the others to reconcile, they agreed. They came to us in the next step. (...) At that time, before peace could be agreed, our clan even moved out of the village, and we migrated for about six month, eager not to meet anyone from that clan.
>
> (Interview September 2005, Gambella, language English)

During the discussions of the killing, other issues between the two families or clan might be discussed less formally and settled, simultaneously. The overall aim is to reach a sustainable peace agreement between the parties.

Nuers' sense of justice is very much identified with cattle—it is a complex system to restore justice. The negotiation that leads to the settlement is done only between men, as head of households, families, husbands and fathers. Women's interests are (at best, indirectly) represented by their husbands, brothers or fathers, in marriage cases by the latter.

It needs to be stated that a considerable amount of threat is applied by the elders, especially by the spiritual leaders. Duol Korion, one of the more powerful of these leaders refers to the power of the spirit, when he states, 'I shall create peace. When I tell them to stop fighting, they will obey!' (Duol, Carrier of the Spirit of the Thiang-Nuer, interview September 2005 in Lare, language Nuer, interpretor Chuol Gew).

(iii) The Ceremony

The centrepiece of the ceremony is the sacrificial killing of oxen. Within the ceremony a distorted relationship between men and God is restored. First the animal is consecrated by ashes or grasses, an act in which the sacrificer both identifies with the animal and loads all evil onto it; the animal takes the function of a scapegoat. The sacrificer further identifies himself with the animal during the invocation. While invoking God and the clan's

[6] As comparison: an average bride price is 25 cows.

spear-name, the animal is killed by a spear. The ox, which is tied to a pole, will jump up and, pulled down by the rope, fall on the ground. The way the ox falls will determine the fate of the sacrificers concerned. The sacrifice is understood as an expression of an inner mental disposition towards God by projecting the self into the victim (Evans-Pritchard: 1956: 272; Falge, 2006). The tip of the spear that has killed the animal will be blunted and bent as a symbol that it will not be used for killings between these people any more. The head hair of the cow from between the horns will be pulled out. This hair symbolises peace (interview September 2005, Gambella, language English).

The sacrificer plays a specific ceremonial role in the sense that he—being the carrier of the clan's spear-spirit—within the ceremony curses anyone who will break the agreement once reached in the reconciliation process. The person who possesses the spirit called Gok (plural Gook) serves a multitude of spiritual functions in Nuer society, and people fear his verdict. His spirit derives directly from Kir, the forefather of all Nuer. The spirit itself is regarded as a prime power and inherited in one family from father to sons: 'Even the Christians believe in this spirit. They are Christians simply by name. They listen to the spirit. The pastor inside is empty' (interview September 2005, Gambella, language English).

The ceremonial sacrifice is followed by a joint feast.

(iv) Prevention

People I talked to saw the best prevention as the settlement agreement arrived at in the ceremony described above. From the Thiang clan it was reported that an agreement sealed by this ceremony has not been broken for the last 20 years. This may be based on the assumed spiritual power of some of their leaders, already mentioned above. Recently there are more sceptical voices dominant, like the following statement of a Presbyterian priest:

> Traditionally the elders talk about the damage done. When there is wrong doing, a cow is killed. With talking the problems go to the cow. The perpetrator will kill the cow and follow the cow when she falls. If the perpetrator does not obey, he will be cursed. But now there are just too many killings.
>
> (Interview May 2005, Gambella, language English)

(c) **Conflict Resolution among the Anywaa**

The Anywaa have the longest history in the region. Following mainly oral history, the Anywaa came to Gambella in the fifteenth century. They migrated along the river (Blue Nile) from an area that would be situated in today's Uganda, where they trace a common history with the Luo of today's

Kenya.[7] They are mainly agriculturalists and fishermen. Their social order is dominated by a rather unique type of kingdom, respective headmanship. It is extensively described by Conradin Perner, who had the chance to study them in the 1970s at the court of the main king in Adong on the Sudanese side of the border. Since these days, though, the social structures of the Anywaa have experienced severe disruption, most intensively since the Dergue, the military regime that ruled Ethiopia from 1974 to 1991. Kurimoto is one of the authors who describes the process of modernity entering Anywaa daily life and social structures. The people I have met since 2005 were coping with this immanent tension, shifting between nostalgia and expectation towards a new world. Since the killings of Anywaa during the events of December 2003, another factor has come to the surface—the fear of collective extinction. It leads—among others—to a revival of traditional practices in order to maintain identity. The following quote of a (*circa*) 90-year-old man, a former headman of a village (Abol) may illustrate this:

> At the time when we practiced our traditional procedures to solve our problems we did not have such big problems as we face now – this is not natural – they try to wipe us out from the surface of the earth.
>
> (Akwor Ochala, holder of the imperial title of Grazmach and former Kwaaro, interview October 2005, Gambella, interview language Anywaa, translated into English)

Many younger interviewees refer to traditional procedures they had heard of, but rarely experienced. There is some evidence, therefore, that the structures are not as alive any more as the actors would wish they were.

(i) The Initiation of Conflict Resolution

The traditional system of managing conflicts among the Anywaa is closely related to their leadership system. The Anywaa have two types of hereditary leaders: nyieye[8] (nobles or kings) and kwaaro (village headmen, or other leaders). According to mythology, all nyieye derive from uchuudho (Ukiro), the godlike forefather who came from the rivers. They therefore belong to a single royal clan. The tales about this forefather all imply that he was the wisest person on earth. All Anywaa are considered descendents of him, but direct descendents are the kings. All kings have to be inaugurated in Adong.

[7] I could observe a Luo man communicating in his mother tongue with the Anywaa and exchanging common myth of origin (Gambella, 2007).

[8] The style of writing differs; this article follows Sato Kurimoto, which is closest to the pronunciation of the Anywaa themselves.

The office of a kwaaro is transferred by inheritance, too. Kwaari belong to different clans. These two systems of rulership are independent, but it is said that 'Nyieye are more powerful than the kwaaro' (interview September 2005, Gambella, interview language English).

These leaders—the nyieye holding the royal emblems (Kurimoto, 1992: 43)—play a crucial role in all major affairs of Anywaa social life, and with that in conflict resolution. The procedure is basically the same, whether conducted by nyieye or kwaaro. Therefore it will be presented as done by the nyieye.

In cases of homicide, the perpetrator may seek refuge in the home of the nyieye or kwaaro. This is a safe haven for him to escape from revenge action of the victim's family. Once he enters the house of the king, any retaliation will be unjustified.

(ii) The Process

The nyieya then looks into the case. Interestingly, this does not necessarily mean asking for details of the offending act as such, but to inquire about the family history of both forefathers. This history is part of local oral tradition and knowledge. It is assumed that if there is no history of killing between two families, there is a good chance of it being solved amicably. The king then gets involved himself by sending precious demuy,[9] in cattle breeding areas also cattle, or cows to the victim's family. Once the family has accepted the gift from Otoi, the mediation procedure is accepted, too.

If the king does not get himself involved—whereby materially guaranteeing for the perpetrator at this stage—or does not grant asylum at all, the verdict is, de facto, a death sentence, as the perpetrator is left to be killed by the other family. I was told that this might happen in cases when the family feud is deep. The first meeting takes place with the elders of the victim's family, and again they discuss the history of the lineage:

> He will tell them 'This is the land of my forefathers, and I do not want bloodshed here'. There were no problems between you before. Thus it comes to an agreement.
>
> (Interview September 2005, Gambella, language English)

(iii) Kuor—Paying for the Crime

The next step is Kuor, literally 'paying for the crime'. It is the negotiation phase. The victim's family defines its claim, and then the family of the perpetrator is called. The king will urge them to pay. The 'advance' or guarantee, already

[9] The traditional beads which derive from Ocwudho, who brought them from the river; they are also used as dowry. Nowadays these items are often substituted by money (Ethiopian Birr, the local currency).

paid by the nyieye has to be refunded, too. Another common practice is to use a future bride price for a daughter to pay the debts:

> Even if he is a poor person, we record that he took the demuy from the kwaaro or nyieye, and after his daughter is grown it can be paid back.
>
> (Akwor Ochala, interview October 2005, Gambella, interview language Anywaa, translated into English)[10]

(iv) The Peace Ceremony

After payment, the agreement will be settled and sealed by a major ceremony with both families/clans. During this ceremony the story of the lineage will be explained again, and elders from both sides will talk. A bull—or another animal—will be ritually slaughtered, divided into two parts, one half for each clan. The spear-tips (one from each family) are blunted and bent, and the spears are kept as a witness for the agreement in the inside of the roof of the king's house.

(v) Conflicts with Different Ethnic Groups

Traditionally, these processes were exclusively used for settling conflicts within the Anywaa community. But even though I was told that a tradition of peacemaking with other tribes does not exist, the elders felt that if the need arises, the procedure could be made available also in relationships with outsiders: it all depends on the initiative of the leaders. A peace agreement between the Anywaa and the Majangir, which roughly followed the above format, was reported, but finally broken in 2001. Another peace ceremony was jointly conducted by the Anywaa and the Nuer in Abol in 2006, but reportedly broken after some months by the Nuer, as Anywaa complained (interethnic dialogue conducted in Abol, September 2007).

(vi) Prevention

There are procedures in place to prevent conflicting villages from going to war. People are responsible, elders are advisors and before going to war they have to meet. If there is not enough reason to go to war, they will decide for negotiation. And if they cannot solve it alone, they can always call other kings as mediators.

[10] The Nuer practice of marriage arrangements (Chuol Gew describes this and other practices as assimilation strategies, Chuol Gew, 2003: 9) between the families to guarantee the sustainability of an agreement is not known by the Anywaa.

(d) Conflict Resolution among some of the Highlander Groups

The term 'highlanders' as such is not uniform, and develops its specific meaning only in the context of Gambella. They form a heterogeneous group, and stem from various regions of Ethiopia. 'Highlanders' in the Gambella town mostly come from the relatively more developed areas of the central and northern part of the country. This group of highlanders dominates the commercial sector and the civil service (although affirmative action in favour of the indigenous groups has shown some results). Another group of highlanders lives in the rural areas as cultivators, where they were resettled during the Dergue's resettlement programmes from 'overpopulated' areas into planned modern villages. This influx came from diverse regions and ethnic backgrounds, such as Tigrayans from the very north and Kambatta and Haddiya from the south of the country (Meckelburg, 2008: 176). They might not come from the same original ethnic and cultural background, but share the experience of resettlement, expressed in observations such as 'we have now become the oxen that have been yoked' (Pankhurst, 2002: 133). Moreover, these highlanders have developed a group identity in an alien environment, being targeted by local shifta (robbers).[11] Many 'highlander' interviewees state that their respective conflict resolution systems play a vibrant role in contemporary life, within their communities, as Workene, a highlander from Amhara origin explains:

> We are living here together in our villages in Gambella, and we have to solve our problems properly (sic) among ourselves, before going to the kebele[12] or taking a case to court.
>
> (Interview October 2005, Gambella, language English)

(e) Conflict Resolution among the Kambatta of Gambella

The Kambatta constitute one of the biggest ethnic groups of non-indigenous background in Gambella. They were one of the communities that were resettled to Gambella during the resettlement programmes in the 1980s. Ironically, their history of origin within the Ethiopian central state places them in the periphery as much as the people of Gambella. As settlers in the new environment though, they are connected with the central state in this local context. They were deeply resented by the local Anywaa at the time

[11] More than 60,000 highland farmers from northern and southern Ethiopia were brought to the Gambella region during the 1980s. All of the resettlement villages were established in traditional Anywaa territory, which has not only induced the demographic anxiety of this community, but the incidence of local 'shifta' (robbers).

[12] Local administration.

of arrival who fought them with utmost violence, which has been replied in kind whenever possible.

Nowadays, the Kambatta live as farmers in their own villages within the Anywaa administrative area (Abobo). The villages, or settlements, do not have names, but are referred to as village 11, 12 etc, even by the villagers themselves. In Gambella town they occupy a specific area, called Kambatta safer (village). They speak their language and practise their own customs. Conflict resolution is practised by the elders as part of village life in the rather new environment.

(i) The Initiation of Conflict Resolution

In these villages or settlements a constant institution exists that is perceived by the villagers as a traditional court:

> When there is conflict, even among the families, there are elders, arbitrators (shimagelle) to go to. They try to solve the problem. And there is also a kind of arbitration, it is called in Amharic edir. It exists in every village (as a social security system). Then there is the edir-danya— the judge of the village. Only if all this fails, the case will be presented to the kebele court.
>
> (Elder, interview January 2007, Shebo, interview language Kambatta, translated into English)

The committee, or the court, is a permanent institution; its members are assigned certain positions such as chairman, secretary, etc. The members are well known to the next administrative level, the woreda. The woreda administration is dominated by the Anywaa officials, and the Kambatta villagers feel that they 'need to finish a case, before it can be presented to the court' (interview, September 2008).

(ii) The Process

The Kambatta's court follows what they call 'cultural law'. This is a set of norms and stories that are orally transmitted, not written: 'The knowledge has been passed from father to son. As you said, there are stories, traditional knowledge' (interview, January 2007, Shebo, interview language Kambatta, translated into English).

Here is an excerpt of one of the interviews conducted with a group of elders (January 2007):

> Q: Stories? Which are most meaningful for you?
>
> (he is not sure). For instance, if someone borrows something from me and he does not give it back, they will say, 'this is not our culture. In order to survive as a people you should follow the rules. This is what our forefathers inherited to us. We should live in peace'. They will even threaten the person, telling him that, if

> he does not return the thing, the spirit of his forefather would come upon him as a lightening and split his forehead.

It is interesting to note that the threat of the ancestral spirits seems to play a crucial role here.

(iii) The Ceremony

If there was a specific ceremony in the old times, at the places of origin, they do not seem to be practised any more nowadays in the new environment. The system seems more integrated into the juridical system of the country. People perceive it as a prerequisite before being able to bring a case to court.

(iv) Prevention

The public procedure serves to teach the young and warn the public.

(v) Conflicts with other Groups

As already mentioned, the Kambatta have been in often violent conflict with the Anywaa since their arrival in Gambella. Negotiations or peace talks in modern or traditional ways have never so far been explored. The stage of conflict can be described as cold—the relationship among the groups is controlled by fear and guided by avoidance. 'When we are in the forest and see them collecting firewood, we run—and they run away, too', a Kambatta man reports laughing, seemingly happy that the fear is at least mutual (interview, September 2007, interview language Kambatta, translation by Fr Assefa Erdado).

(f) Conflict Resolution among the Haddiya of Gambella

The Haddiya have their place of origin in southern Ethiopia—like the Kambatta.[13] They thus share a common background as re-settlers, which—combined with similarities in the language—might have brought them together in the new environment of Gambella. They live together and also intermarry (interviews in Shebo, September 2007) while they are caught in protracted violent conflicts in their homeland. According to my Haddiya resource person, they practise a very similar system of conflict resolution, which they still prefer to the court system. The two groups also share

[13] Ulrich Braukämper is one of the authors recommended for further reading on this large ethnic group in the south of Ethiopia.

the history of resettlement (Kurimoto, 2001: 268). Moreover, the term 'Kambatta' is often used as a general term for these settlers.

(i) The Initiation of Conflict Resolution

The information available relates to the procedure in the advent of homicide, as most cases dealt with in this procedure are about killings, rapes or similarly grave or capital offences. Among the Haddiya, the initiation of the process of reconciliation is not formalised. The elders of a community or the parties themselves are able to initiate it. It was reported though, that in most cases the parties themselves look for a mediator:

> They look for people who are old and who know how to do reconciliation. Sometimes they look for people who live far away—for instance they would walk for two days or more to find them. In addition to finding a mediator,[14] the parties will form their own group of elders seven/seven from each side for example. The mediator should come from a different clan, but there are exceptions that the third person comes from one side. Most important is that he is very respected by both sides.
>
> (Interview, September 2005, Gambella, interview language English)

Some cases are referred to the traditional institutions by the courts. In these cases, the court nominates and invests the chairperson and main arbitrator/mediator. Traditionally though both parties have to agree on the final group composition of elders, including the participants from the other party's side.

(ii) The Process

The process itself does not have time constraints. As the aim is to find a consensual solution, everything is discussed in detail: the elders will discuss the relationship of the families or clans, including their ancestors. I was told that already in many cases this will lead to some conclusions or preliminary insights. The mediators' practise 'shuttle diplomacy': meetings with the mediator will take place in different locations, among others at the places of the conflicting parties; or at the place of an important witness. This will depend on the case and the circumstances. Witnesses will be heard as necessary.

Conflicts are settled by payment of compensation. The final decision is taken by the elders, after listening to both parties. The group of elders

[14] The resource person used the term 'mediator'; whether or not the role of the third person should be rather defined as 'arbitrator' or 'judge' in technical terms, does not need to be decided in this context.

decides by majority vote, after the impartial man has given his suggestions. A consensual decision is appreciated.

(iii) The Ceremony

The outcome of the negotiating/truth finding process will be sealed and celebrated in a major ceremony. A cow, sheep or goat will be slaughtered in a ritual way, and the heads of each party drink locally made beer from one cup as a sign for future understanding. The parties walk over the blood of the animal, thus taking an oath for the future.

(iv) Prevention

This ceremony allegedly also serves to prevent further unrest and killings, and to maintain peace. As already mentioned above, there is no formality as to when to initiate the process. Responsible leaders are free to start the procedure when tensions arise. The elders may try to reconcile before killing starts:

> Generally the leaders and elders have to be informed before a case is brought to the court, or before starting to fight. It works very well, much better than even decisions taken by the high-court.
>
> (Interview, September 2005, Gambella, interview language English)

(v) About Conflicts with other Ethnic Groups

In Gambella, the Haddiya live in close neighbourhood with the Kambatta and practise their traditional systems of conflict resolution among themselves. They could not recall having practised any informal or traditional negotiation or mediation strategy with any of their adversary groups, namely not with the Anywaa.

(g) Conflict Resolution among other 'Highlander' Groups of Ethiopia

Available studies on traditional systems of conflict resolution are mushrooming after only scarce material was available for many years. As this contribution is basically founded on field studies, only a very short overview will be given here.

Pankhurst and Getachew suggest in their most comprehensive overview on customary dispute resolution in Ethiopia that traditional practices are ubiquitously found throughout the country. They found comparable customary practices everywhere, but observed that these institutions were generally limited to a particular constituency within one ethnic group (2008: 257).

An earlier publication (Giday Degefu, 2000: 43) concludes that the major ethnic groups of Ethiopia have similar systems in place—understood as opposed to the modern or Western ways of settling conflicts. Giday Degefu collected examples from the three Semitic language groups of the Amhara, Tigray and Gurage, and the Kushitic speaking Oromo.

From the criteria underlying this article, the following conclusions can be drawn. In all groups, the initiation of the conflict resolution system is relatively informal. The Gurage though know stable committees and institutions for the settlement of different kind of conflicts—between neighbours, inter-clan or inter-tribal disputes. The Amhara and Tigray on the other hand proceed like the Haddiya—elders are selected by the disputants 'with the belief that they know the history of a given family better than others' (Giday Degefu, 2000: 43). In Tigray, these are often close relatives or church elders, in more recent times also elected committees of the TPLF[15] (Shimeles Gizaw and Tadesse Gessese, 2008: 220; Giday Degefu, 2000: 116,117)

Some of these traditional processes seem to be more elaborated than reported in the context of Gambella. The Gurage for instance know an appeal system, as the Oromo do. The Oromo have an elaborated system that is embedded in their system of governance. Gadaa councils decide on severe offences, and the penalty can be physical punishment up to the verdict of a death sentence and confiscation of property (Areba Abdella and Berhanu Amenew, 2008: 178; Giday Degefu, 2000: 152).

In all cases, the committees of elders finally decide and find a verdict. Whether or not these decisions are taken by majority vote is not clear, but there is a strong indication that the committees seek unanimity. The Gurage reportedly reach a verdict via majority vote (Giday Degefu, 2000: 24) but in other cases their 'goal is to reach a decision by consensus' (Giday Degefu, 2000: 34).

Settlement is mainly by payment of penalties; the Tigray and Amhara also know the settlement of feuds and homicides by intermarriage (Giday Degefu, 2000: 118). Here in the north of Ethiopia even to ask for forgiveness is a formal way to settle a conflict and for reconciliation. A specific ceremony among the Amhara to resolve a feud ritually is to make the criminal jump over a gun lying on the ground (Giday Degefu, 2000: 47). Amhara living in Gambella report that ad hoc committees of elders will try to solve problems amicably, before reporting a case to the police.

IV. COMMON FEATURES AND DIFFERENCES

The following chart may summarise the characteristics of some of the approaches.

[15] TPLF is the Tigrayan People's Liberation Front, core of the current government.

	Initiation of the Process	*Process*	*How is the Final Decision Taken?*	*Final Ceremony*	*Settlement*	*Prevention*
Nuer	Initiative of the elders/ad hoc committees	Discussing the family/clan relations	Group of elders—impartial mediator decides—spirit curses or blesses	Animal sacrifice and feast; spear blunted and bent	Payment of cows/intermarriage	The process itself is seen as prevention; it serves to educate others. A major concern of the process is the prevention of acts of vengeance.
Anywaa	Initiative of the perpetrator, who seeks asylum from retaliation; ad hoc committee led by the kwaaro, who forms the committee according to the specific needs of the case	Finding the family lineage and the 'truth'—aiming to prevent further killings	Decision taken by the king or headman; consensus tries to be achieved	Animal sacrifice and feast; spear blunted and bent	Payment of demuy or money	The process itself is seen as prevention; it is public and serves to educate others. The active initiation prevents retaliation
Kambatta	Elders (shimagelle) form a permanent committee	Largely informal; orally transmitted law is applied	Consent; process perceived as precondition before a case can be brought to the court	None	Restitution, or penalty in money; acceptance of guilt	The process is public and serves to educate others

(Continued)

	Initiation of the Process	*Process*	*How is the Final Decision Taken?*	*Final Ceremony*	*Settlement*	*Prevention*
Haddiya	Initiation flexible/ committee of elders formed ad hoc	Committee has to be formed in consensus; appeal to a traditional high court	Group of elders, majority vote, but consensus preferred	Ceremonial feast/walking over the blood of the sacrificed animal	Penalty in money	The process is public and serves to educate others
Tigray	Ad hoc committees; chairperson often a church leader	Discussions on the case	Group of elders decides	No specific ceremony	Penalty in money; asking for forgiveness in the name of the Lord; intermarriage; exile	Not known
Amhara	Ad hoc committees, chosen by the disputants; appeal to the woreda court	Local village elders; appeal to the court	Group of elders seeks to compromise; decisions taken by the elders	No specific ceremony	Penalty in money; blood indemnity and ceremony of jumping over a gun in cases of homicide	Not known
Gurage	Stable institutions	Precise procedures, including an instance of appeal	Majority vote	No specific ceremony	Penalty in money	Not known
Oromo	Gadda Council; committees of elders	Discussion, including the political environment of a case	Majority vote	Spear blunted and buried (Borana-Oromo)	Physical punishment (including the death sentence); confisca-tion of property; penalty in money	Not known

General differences seemingly appear in the systems of the north and the southern/western part of Ethiopia. This may be based on the century old traditions of monotheistic belief systems that were dominant in the highlands of Ethiopia, influenced by the Ethiopian Orthodox Church and Islam. Some of the northern approaches to conflict seem more individualised (individual guilt can be overcome by asking for forgiveness) while the local and southern approaches appear more rooted in the collective notion of clan and family ties, and the curse or blessing of the gods and spirits. This borderline though is not sharp. The way of production, the respected lifestyles in general, play an evenly strong role in defining the specific approaches in customary processes. Most obviously pastoralist societies, who migrate seasonally, have developed structures that can cope with this lifestyle. The specific symbols of peace and reconciliation reflect these differences. Cattle play a central role in pastoralist peacemaking processes and ceremonies. With the Nuer, for instance, social status is defined by the cattle in spiritual, not merely material respects. More sedentary farmers or traders from different ethnic history lack this understanding of cattle and see it rather as a simple commodity. And yet, there are still similarities among all customary approaches presented here. These include the possibility of settling feud by blood money, and the strong position of the elders as third party who take decisions and apply penalties. All groups report that the councils of elders try to find solutions unanimously, even though a majority vote is possible.

This finding as such is not amazing, but points to a potential problem in Gambella, where people of great diversity are dwelling. This implies, that finding a common process which serves the needs of all parties to understanding and to reconciling may be difficult to find. As much as the killing of a cow remains a meaningless ritual for an Amhara, the pure asking for forgiveness—even in the ritual way by kissing the victim's knee—might be without any relevance for a Nuer, Anywaa or Oromo. Therefore, in a setting like Gambella, where people of extreme diversity live together without having had the opportunity to develop a shared culture, the answer to the initial question about the relevance of customary approaches needs to be differentiated. This shall be discussed in the following part in more detail.

V. THE CONTRIBUTION OF TRADITIONAL APPROACHES TO SOLVE CONTEMPORARY CONFLICTS

It is difficult to predict to what extent enforcing and strengthening traditional mechanisms of conflict resolution could contribute to sustainable peace in the region. When comparing the different traditions, I have shown that the ways of solving conflicts by traditional means are as different as the people. Most procedures are deeply rooted in the history and social structure of the respective group—a history that lies outside the region in many cases. It is hard to imagine finding one traditional system, or even a merger of some of them, that would be acceptable to all the ethnic groups in the region.

Therefore, the question of the validity of traditional approaches to conflict transformation cannot be answered in a general manner. The situation is complex. There are some other variables and factors not to be forgotten, the political environment being one. As mentioned above, federalism in Ethiopia is based on ethnicity and brings with it a potential for conflict along ethnic lines. Moreover, the belief systems of the groups are different, and the symbols they use are similar only at a superficial level. It is doubtful whether these conflicts—considering the political and material interests at stake—can be solved with reference to traditional conflict resolution and prevention models alone. On reviewing the findings, a differentiated approach seems to be necessary to answer my primary question: are traditional conflict resolution systems able to deal with the complexity of contemporary conflicts?

I argue that customary forms of overcoming conflict have their place in intra-ethnic disputes and dissents within a local community. Seen from the point of view of the local discourse, traditional, or perceived traditional structures, may be referred to in strictly local disputes, or when state structures are neither transparent nor reliable, as is often the case. They also represent a way of achieving material justice in lieu of a judiciary that still faces considerable weaknesses in terms of independence and accessibility. Moreover, courts are often perceived as just another institution of the state. In this context, a certain degree of re-traditionalisation represents an attempt to reorder society, giving recognition to local traditions and values. When viewed as exclusive alternatives though, both modernisation and traditionalisation might create new problems. Given the state of development in the region, the implementation of good government structures—with an independent judiciary and accessible impartial institutions to hear grievances—will not be achieved everywhere and overnight. And even if this were possible, it is doubtful whether the people would accept the ways and procedures of a modern judiciary.

Thus traditional forms of conflict resolution clearly have a role to play in conflicts between families and clans of a single ethnic group—like the ongoing fights between different Nuer clans. Here, people know the practice, and the procedures enjoy credibility among the community. Traditional systems seem to be best suited to addressing the issues at stake. There are obvious limitations even in these cases though, as far as the incompatibility with core beliefs of modern formal law is concerned, especially with core human rights standards (Pankhurst and Getachew Assefa: 263ff in further detail). It may be recalled, for instance, that women simply do not have any active role to play in traditional procedures (see above Fn 5), whereas they are the first to suffer from the results of conflicts. In principle, every system that claims to resolve conflicts should be accessible to all parties concerned. Another concern relates to whether or not the traditional methods lead to deeper understanding and self-determination. It is certainly difficult to find elements of self-determination and a potential for emancipation in procedures which curse and predict immediate death for anyone who breaks the spell imposed on a peace agreement. On the other hand, the traditions are owned by the community and are performed publicly in most cases. They certainly keep community values alive and provide a sense of togetherness that enhances solidarity and self-governance. Moreover, as the procedures are not codified, they are subject to change in the future. The common ground and collective understanding that they are based on, may further transform them in the process of the practice. Without going deep into these arguments, it still can be stated that in the long run the review of traditional systems of conflict resolution has to be done with respect to their inclusiveness and their emancipative potentials.

Another question is how the traditional approaches serve their purpose in protracted inter-ethnic conflicts, such as between Anywaa and Kambatta settlers, to name one. Here, to my observation, traditional and customary approaches reach their limits. Not only are the procedures different, but also the underlying expectations. In fact, inter-ethnic peace accords that were sealed in alleged traditional ways were often reported as failed. There may be different reasons for these failures and any individual case may also be different. In reviewing a failed peace agreement between Anywaa and Nuer, an interviewee from the ethnic group of the Anywaa recalled that, 'the cattle was slaughtered, everyone said that they were sorry, but then the Nuer attacked us again. They are unreliable' (interview, November 2006, Gambella, interview language English). She was disappointed, specifically, about the lack of appreciation for the ceremony that seemed meaningful to her, but not necessarily to the Nuer on the other side. Then she added, 'Before, there was no reconciliation between different tribes. Just fight. Peacemaking in these relationships was unknown of'.

In inter-ethnic conflict, the flexibility of modern mediation strategies might indeed be a real asset. These procedures do not only focus on finding agreements, but on re-linking groups and individuals in the process. They provide ample opportunities to empower the participants in taking their destiny into their own hands, to take decisions on their own, thereby increasing self-determination. The outcome may be peace, but as John Paul Lederach said, 'rather than seeing peace as an end state, (...), peace is a continuously evolving and developing quality of relationship' (Lederach, 2003: 20) This means that the people of Gambella need to decide—with the help of outsiders or without—whom they want to call, and which procedure they need to follow. The process will require patience—it is slow, and a lot of 'palaver' will be needed until a necessary consensus is reached.

The last question to be answered is, what do external mediators need to know about the specific traditions of the different peoples they start working with? In recent years, more and more outsiders come to conflict-ridden zones like Gambella, working for government agencies, international organisations, NGOs or churches. Many are trained in mediation strategies. Would it be recommendable to adapt any of the traditional procedures, and to co-opt them into postmodern mediation strategies?

I would like to approach these questions from a transformative point of view.[16] The stated complexity of conflict—even in situations of crises—opens new space for a development of the people, a space that might not have existed in previous times. To reach this level of interaction, mediators have to develop a real understanding of the parties, of their perceptions, their views of the world and their standpoint in this particular conflict. It is a banality to state here that any mediator in any conflict needs to meet and understand the parties just where they stand: in their different belief systems. If these perceptions can be mediated, a new process of understanding can be set in motion. This will not be done without further conflict. But a mediation—mediators, who are able to facilitate understanding, re-linking[17] lost ties or facilitating new relations among and between the communities—should be able to help the parties go through these processes of change less violently. Mediators need to be able to react flexibly to the communication needs of all parties in the process. Sensitive forms of intermediation have the potential to facilitate understanding between divided groups, and to develop better communication structures; links, which may allow the stakeholders in conflict to handle a variety of problems in a more cooperative manner.

Following this logic, reconciliation and mediation processes should be developed in a creative way, responding to the different needs of the people involved. This in practice may lead to a variety of approaches, depending on the specific context. The overriding characteristic of all methods needs to be their ability to contribute to more self-determination, an improved capacity to cope with future conflicts and an increased potential to solving these conflicts by peaceful means.

Eventually, any mediation and peace building attempt will only be effective if the initiative comes from the grassroots; a bottom-up approach. Mediation and conflict resolution should always be voluntary, not executed by the authority of the state. There is some evidence that peace building attempts taken by successive governments in Ethiopia never succeeded or were

[16] In his recent book *The Moral Imagination*, John Paul Lederach stresses the need for mediators to envision themselves as artists of social change processes—with the full energy of an artist's intuition and imagination (Lederach, 2005: 73).

[17] The relevance of 're-linkage' in conflict transformation is best described by Johan Declerck (2005).

short lived (Falge, 2006, with reference to cases in the SNNP). One reason for this finding might be that with government involvement, the specific voluntary nature of the process, a core feature of any mediation process was often thwarted in the past. As outlined above, a strong element of all traditional systems is the process of finding the appropriate elders—people who are accepted by all stakeholders. It is interesting that at exactly this important point the old wisdom meets modern findings: The mediator/arbitrator and the process need to be chosen and accepted by all parties. This insight was often neglected in previous cases of government involvement. The procedure of finding the elders was skipped. (This may also happen, in other institutions, such as international organisations and NGOs that are eager to produce quick and visible 'success stories'.) As one of my Nuer friends mentioned as an aside: 'If government is involved, the procedure is somewhat different. In these cases the government will organise the programme and also elect the elders. That might not have the same credibility and strength as the voluntary procedure, which is initiated by the elders themselves' (interview, September 2005, Gambella, interview language English).

In the long run, any (voluntary) conflict resolution systems that are rooted in civil society and based in its grass roots will develop best, once the state is able to provide for the basic services in terms of security (police) and justice (judiciary). Traditional—or re-traditionalised conflict resolution systems, developed bottom-up, within the society, can play their role in conflict prevention, transformation and facilitating understanding. They will never be able to replace these basic services of the modern state that are legitimised by the rule of law and which guarantee safety and security for the population through the power monopoly that lies exclusively with the state.

Within this framework of stable statehood though, this creative bottom-up approach will have the potential to further develop the traditional systems of conflict resolution and give them new forms and meaning in the process. It is part of the character of all systems that they emphasise on the process as such and on the interaction between the participants. This alone opens opportunity for further development.

REFERENCES[18]

Areba Abdella and Berhanu Amenew (2008) 'Customary Dispute Resolution Institutions in *Oromia*' in A Pankhurst and Getachew Assefa (eds), *Grass-Roots Justice in Ethiopia, The Contribution of Customary Dispute Resolution* (Addis Ababa, Centre Français d'Études Éthiopiennes).

[18] Ethiopian names are listed in their original order, ie, personal name, followed by the father's name. The personal name is used in private and public life, whereas the father's and grandfather's name indicate the descent of the person.

Avruch, K (2002) 'What do I Need to Know about Culture?' in JP Lederach and JM Jenner (eds), *A Handbook of International Peacebuilding* (San Francisco, Jossey-Bass).

Baechler, G (2002) *Promoting Peace: The Role of Civilian Conflict Resolution* (Bern, Staempfli Publishers).

Braukämper, U (1980) *Geschichte der Hadiya Süd-Äthiopiens. Von den Anfängen bis zur Revolution 1974* (Wiesbaden, Verlag Franz Steiner).

Bush, RAB and Folger, JP (2005) *The Promise of Mediation: The Transformative Approach to Conflict* (San Francisco, Jossey-Bass).

Chan Gatkuoth (2007) 'Gambella Conflicts: The Role of the Government in Preventing and Resolving Conflicts' in WGC Smidt and Kinfe Abraham (eds), *Discussing Conflict in Ethiopia, Conflict Management and Resolution.* Proceedings of the Conference 'Ethiopian and German Contributions to Conflict Management and Resolution', Addis Ababa 11–12 November 2005 (Münster, LIT-Verlag).

Chuol Gew (2003) 'Understanding Root Causes of Conflicts in Gambella with suggested Management and Prevention Methods' (paper, Gambella).

Clapham, C (2002) 'Controlling Space in Ethiopia' in W James, DL Donham, E Kurimoto and A Triuzi (eds), *Remapping Ethiopia* (Oxford, James Currey).

Deklerck, J, 'Re-lier la dé-linq-uance'.Quelques réflexions sur les principes générales et les différences culturelles de la médiation' in J-P Bonafé-Schmitt and M Jacoub (eds), *Médiation et Justice Restauratrice: Actes du 2ème Séminaire International Francophone sur la Justice Restauratrice et la Médiation,* IUKB, Sion, Suisse, 2005.

Dereje Feyissa (2004) 'Events leading to the December Massacre and its Aftermath' (unpublished paper).

—— (2005), *The Experience of Gambella Regional State* (Osaka, Kyoto University Press).

—— (2008) 'Layers of Conflict in the Gambella Region, An Interactive Approach' in EM Bruchhaus and MM Sommer (eds), *Hot Spot Horn of Africa Revisited, Approaches to Make Sense of Conflict* (Münster/Berlin, LIT-Verlag).

—— (2008) 'Customary Dispute Resolution Institutions in Gambella Region: The Case of the Nuer' in A Pankhurst and Getachew Assefa (eds), *Grass-Roots Justice in Ethiopia, The Contribution of Customary Dispute Resolution* (Addis Ababa, Centre Français d'Études Éthiopiennes).

Duss-von Werdt, J (2005) *Homo Mediator, Geschichte und Menschenbild der Mediation* (Stuttgart, Klett-Cotta).

Encyclopaedia of Social and Cultural Anthropology 559.

Evans-Pritchard, EE (1940) *The Political System of the Anuak of the Anglo-Egyptian Sudan* (New York, reprinted 1977).

Evans-Pritchard, E-E (1956) *Nuer Religion* (Oxford, The Clarendon Press).

Falge, C (2006) *The Global Nuer. Transnational Modes of Livelihoods* (Martin-Luther-Universität Halle-Wittenberg, Halle).

Giday Degefu Koraro (2000) *Traditional Mechanisms of Conflict Resolution in Ethiopia* (Addis Ababa, EIIPD).

Huyse, L (1998) *Young Democracies and the Choice between Amnesty, Truth Commissions and Prosecutions* (Leuven, Leuven University Press).

Kurimoto, E (1992) 'Natives and Outsiders: The Historical Experience of the Anywaa of Western Ethiopia' 43 *Journal for Asian and African Studies.*
—— (2001) 'Capturing Modernity among the Anywaa of Western Ethiopia' in E Kurimoto (ed), *Rewriting Africa: Towards Renaissance or Collapse?* (Osaka, JCAS).
Lederach, JP (2003) *The Little Book of Conflict Transformation* (San Francisco, PA).
—— (2005) *The Moral Imagination: The Art and Soul of Building Peace* (Oxford, Oxford University Press).
Meckelburg, A (2008) 'Some Preliminary Considerations on Collective Violence, Identity and Conflict and their Coherence: The Case of Gambella, Western Ethiopia' in EM Bruchhaus and MM Sommer (eds), *Hot Spot Horn of Africa Revisited, Approaches to Make Sense of Conflict* (Münster/Berlin, LIT-Verlag).
Pankhurst, A (2002) 'Surviving Resettlement in Wellega' in W James, DL Donham, E Kurimoto and A Triuzi (eds), *Remapping Ethiopia* (Oxford, James Currey).
Pankhurst, A and Getachew Assefa (eds) (2008) *Grass-Roots Justice in Ethiopia, The Contribution of Customary Dispute Resolution* (Addis Ababa, Centre Français d'Études Éthiopiennes).
Pfaffenholz, T (2001) 'Designing Intervention Processes' in *Berghof Handbook for Conflict Transformation* (Berlin, Berghof).
Perner, C (1994) *Living on Earth in the Sky. An Analytic Account of the History and the Culture of a Nilotic People* vol 1 (Basel, Helbing & Lichtenhahn).
Population Census Commission, Federal Republic of Ethiopia (2008) *Summary and Statistical report of the 2007 Population and Housing Census* (Addis Ababa, central Statistical Agency).
Saner, R (2005), *The Negotiation Expert* (The Hague, Martinus Nijhoff Publishers).
Shimelis Gizaw and Tadesse Gessese (2008) 'Customary Dispute Resolution in Tigray Region: Case Studies from Three Districts' in A Pankhurst and Getachew Assefa (eds), *Grass-Roots Justice in Ethiopia, The Contribution of Customary Dispute Resolution* (Addis Ababa, Centre Français d'Études Éthiopiennes).
Sommer, M (2008) 'Perceptions of Fairness Expressed in Contemporary Narratives of the Nuer living in the Ethiopian Region of Gambella: their Relevance to Conflict Transformation' in EM Bruchhaus and MM Sommer (eds), *Hot Spot Horn of Africa Revisited, Approaches to Make Sense of Conflict* (Münster/Berlin, LIT-Verlag).
—— (2010) 'Ethiopian Federalism seen from the Perspective of the Regional State of Gambella: Cause of Conflict and Fierce Competition or Access to Resources and Democratic Participation?' in E Grawert (ed), *After the Comprehensive Peace Agreement Signs of Change?*' (Oxford, James Currey).
Strecker, I and Pankhurst, A (2003) *Bury the Spear* Video (Göttingen, IWF).
Zewde, Bahru (1991), *A History of Modern Ethiopia, Eastern African Studies* (Oxford, James Currey).

10

Conclusion

THE VARIOUS AND rich contributions selected in the present volume reveal the difficulties met by specialists in constructing a still young discipline. The first reason is that mediation takes place in a variety of countries with different cultural, political, economic and social environments making a delicate methodological extrapolation. Secondly, mediation is conducted in many different ways—modern or traditional, more or less respectful of ethical principles—in conflict resolution and consolidation of peace. The third reason, which highlights the complexity of the diagnosis, is related to the diversity of the players involved—individuals, social groups with various degrees of professionalisation and training, official institutions more or less ideologically and financially dependent on states and mandatory.

Even though it seems hardly possible to draw any general conclusion from the case studies analysed in this volume, the critical examination of these very differences brings to light a certain number of common elements and criteria which are essential to successful mediation. Beyond the singularity of each case, most chapters propose fruitful reflections on the wider question of the mediator's position and on the necessary requirements of independence, impartiality and absence of decision-making power, formulated by the mainstream doctrine. Indeed, such principles do not only clearly differentiate mediation from negotiation and conciliation; they also open an exciting reflection about the legitimacy of the role and action of the mediator in the eyes of the populations directly concerned.

In more specific terms, three key ideas emerge from this corpus of research. First, mediation efforts must be adapted to the cultural environment and tap local resources and competences in order to guarantee that these initiatives, often managed from the outside, will be legitimate. Secondly, mediation must also further politics of recognition, in the sense given to it by Axel Honneth (Honneth, 1995), ie, taking into account the symbolical rather than material dimension of the conflict as well as the needs in terms of security and identity, as developed by John Burton (Burton, 1972). Mediation cannot thus be envisaged without the acceptance and acknowledgement of the 'Other', without an attitude of 'mutual respect' which forbids any temptation of imposing one's values, without the respectful recognition of the physical and mental integrity of the opponent, of his or her 'identity specificities', beliefs, religion, culture, standards and historical traumas. These are the prerequisites for effective mediation which may reconcile the pursuit of peace and the defence of human rights. Mediation enables the populations concerned to express their feelings and frustrations, to articulate their claims and to initiate a process of symbolical compensation for the victims. Thirdly, mediation cannot be initiated independently of political considerations—in terms of power play and social relations—of the various other initiatives in peacekeeping and peace building undertaken locally and of the intricate and often overlapping *loci* of negotiations. Following John Paul Lederach's famous pyramid (Lederach, 1997), any mediation initiative must take into account and interrelate three levels of influence: top leadership (military, political, religious leaders), middle range leadership (ethnic, religious, academics, humanitarian leaders) and grass-roots leadership (local, indigenous, NGO, community development).

The selection of contributions in this volume offers some tentative answers to the two hypotheses presented in the introduction. The first hypothesis, according to which mediation initiatives and state strategies complement each other, is confirmed in the case of the Community of Sant'Egidio, the so-called 'velvet glove of the Vatican's diplomacy', through its active involvement in networks regrouping governments and international institutions. Peace initiatives such as those conducted by Viola Boelsher, Aurélien Colson and Alain Pekar Lempereur and financed by some major international organisations, may also be seen as bringing added value to traditional diplomacy and regarded as a more or less conscious de-politicisation strategy eclipsing or bypassing state intervention. However, the development of a specific and relevant pacification model in Northern Ireland and Ethiopia does not easily fall into the above-mentioned category, considering the fact that such initiatives clearly follow a bottom-up logic. It is also difficult to speak of a complementary process in the case of Chiapas and the Basque country where mediation initiatives tend to be more personal, sectorial or local, than institutional.

The second hypothesis is that initiatives 'from below', initiated by 'peacemakers' fostered by 'beliefs' and interests which are not only political, may eventually lead to blurring the frontiers between state and non-state actors and favour the emergence of an increasingly influential epistemic community developing an 'industry' of democratic promotion (Santiso, 1998). The present state of research does not offer any definite answer on this specific issue. Increasing empowerment and furthering the respect of the 'Other' among local populations is probably an ethical rupture in political conflict resolution. However, it would be risky to think that this new philosophy has spread among political spheres, for lack of interrelation between the different levels and modes of action. If we admit the potential feasibility of such an osmosis process, it would then be difficult to determine precisely the specific role of mediation among all the political, social, cultural and economic initiatives taken by the various players involved. In actual fact, we may say that international action in peacemaking is subjected to tensions, not to say fraught with contradictions. It is indeed torn between its old paternalistic and authoritarian demons and the acknowledged fact that legitimacy cannot be built on the sheer use of force. The majority of the authors in the present volume converge on the key question of legitimacy as a necessary condition for the effective implementation of mediation. Their analyses of the strategies adopted by the local players are quite revealing. International action is caught in between an ethno-centrist and often unconscious desire to spread 'the good political model' and make 'just peace', and the paradoxical pursuit of more autonomy and self-determination for local populations.

It is obviously difficult to assess precisely the nature and effectiveness of political mediation. Contrary to the quantitative approach adopted by some American researchers—an approach which may be regarded as inappropriate since it does not differentiate between mediation and negotiation processes and mixes up different political, cultural and social conflicts—only qualitative analyses can offer the necessary tools to fully apprehend the potentialities of mediation to change the rules of the political game.

In my view, it is essential to take into consideration two variables which have not been much studied to date—the independence of the mediators and the methodology of the mediation process. The first variable makes it possible to assess the degree of political, economic and cultural autonomy of the mediators, not only from traditional state diplomacy, international organisations and institutionalised NGOs, but from the various peacemaking arenas. The second variable offers the possibility of placing political mediation in a continuum ranging from the most directive model—the main objective is here to find a formal agreement—to the least directive one—the main objective, in a logic of communication, being to change the representation of the 'Other', and lead individuals and groups to control their own destiny through empowerment. To take up a commonly-used image in the world of mediation, the question is to know whether mediators attend to what is most urgent first, ie, put an end to hostilities, without opening the 'black box' of the conflict, whether they just half-open the black box so that needs may be addressed within a reasonable time limit, or if their ambition is to keep it open so that all emotions and feelings may be fully expressed and new relations durably established. The neotenic potentialities of mediation—in the sense of a metamorphosis of political conflict regulation—are all the stronger if mediators are independent from the powers that be and if they adopt a non-directive and transformative methodology. Conversely, a high degree of dependence coupled with a directive method does not necessarily mean breaking away from the traditional modes of regulation. With these two indicators, we can thus have a better approach to mediation and determine whether it is a mere disguise for old traditional diplomacy or a new, effective and dynamic movement initiated by small players working for the promotion of a just and positive peace.

REFERENCES

Burton, J (1972) *World Society* (Cambridge, Cambridge University Press).

Honneth, A (1995) *Struggle for Recognition: The Moral Grammar of Social Conflicts* (Cambridge, Polity Press).

Lederach, JP (1997) *Building Peace. Sustainable Reconciliation in Divided Societies* (Washington DC, United State Institute for Peace).

Santiso, J (1998) 'Circulation des idées et relations internationales' in MC Smouts (ed), *Les nouvelles relations internationales* (Paris, Presses de Science Po) 227–51.

Index

www.ingramcontent.com/pod-product-compliance
Lightning Source LLC
LaVergne TN
LVHW052316200926
848481LV00002B/581